Emperor Charles V

Publication of this book was generously assisted by a grant towards the costs of translation made by the Prins Bernhard Cultuurfonds

To Helli Koenigsberger, a great authority and a good friend

Emperor Charles V 1500–1558

WIM BLOCKMANS
Professor of History, University of Leiden, The Netherlands

Translated by Isola van den Hoven-Vardon

A member of the Hodder Headline Group
LONDON
Co-published in the USA by Oxford University Press Inc., New York

First published in Great Britain in 2002 by
Arnold, a member of the Hodder Headline Group,
338 Euston Road, London NW1 3BH

http://www.arnoldpublishers.com

Co-published in the United States of America by
Oxford University Press Inc.,
198 Madison Avenue, New York, NY10016

© 2002 Wim Blockmans
English translation © 2002 Arnold Publishers

All rights reserved. No part of this publication may be reproduced or transmitted in any form or by any means, electronically or mechanically, including photocopying, recording or any information storage or retrieval system, without either prior permission in writing from the publisher or a licence permitting restricted copying. In the United Kingdom such licences are issued by the Copyright Licensing Agency: 90 Tottenham Court Road, London W1T 4LP.

The advice and information in this book are believed to be true and accurate at the date of going to press, neither the author[s] nor the publisher can accept any legal responsibility or liability for any errors or omissions.

British Library Cataloguing in Publication Data
A catalogue record for this book is available from the British Library

Library of Congress Cataloging-in-Publication Data
A catalog record for this book is available from the Library of Congress

ISBN 0 340 72038 7 (hb)
ISBN 0 340 73110 9 (pb)

1 2 3 4 5 6 7 8 9 10

Production Editor: Jasmine Brown
Production Controller: Bryan Eccleshall
Cover Design: Terry Griffiths

Typeset in 10 on 13 pt Plantin by Cambrian Typesetters, Frimley, Surrey

What do you think about this book? Or any other Arnold title?
Please send your comments to feedback.arnold@hodder.co.uk

Contents

Maps	vii
Chronology	ix
Genealogies	xii
Justification	1

1 An *imperium* of forty years   3

Magnificent mourning	3
A difficult departure	8
The Habsburgs: a dynasty for Europe	13
The education of a Christian prince	19
Mission impossible?	22

2 A grand strategy?   25

Territories and dynasty	25
The Holy Roman Empire	30
Strategic options	34
Unforeseen circumstances	40

3 Honour, rights and land   47

A foreign king	47
The XVII Provinces	51
Italy: the key to world hegemony	57
France – again and again	64
1536–1537	68
1542–1544	72
1551–1553	74
Right, ambition and necessity	76

4 Protector of the Catholic Church — 80

The great misunderstanding — 80
Give and take — 86
Authoritarian Reformation — 92
The fiasco — 97
Persecuting heretics — 99
The soul of the Indian — 106
Christendom divided — 108

5 Charles' political system — 116

The absent prince — 117
The emperor's family — 120
Servants of the emperor — 125
The network — 133

6 The cost of the Empire — 139

Objectives — 139
The tragedy of a viceroy — 140
Strategy, resources, choices — 147
Money, money and money again — 154
Discussion and repression — 160

7 The image in balance — 169

The creation of a classical hero — 169
Personality and fate — 176

Selective bibliography — 185
Index of proper names — 188

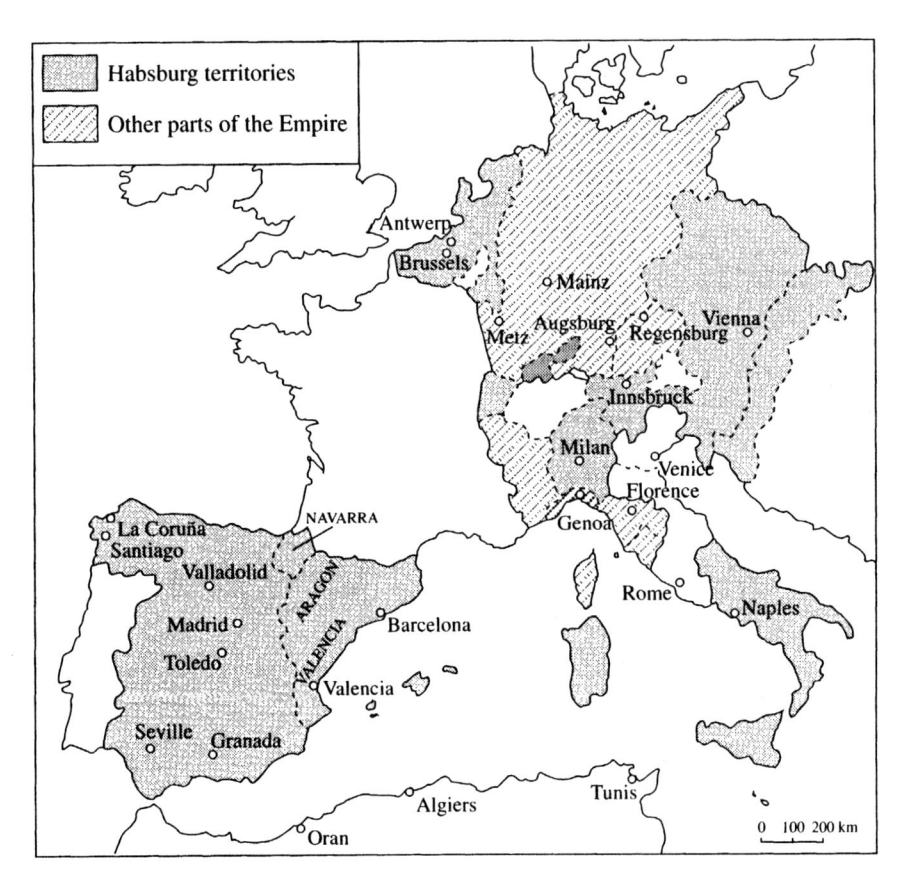

Map 1: Habsburg lands in Europe

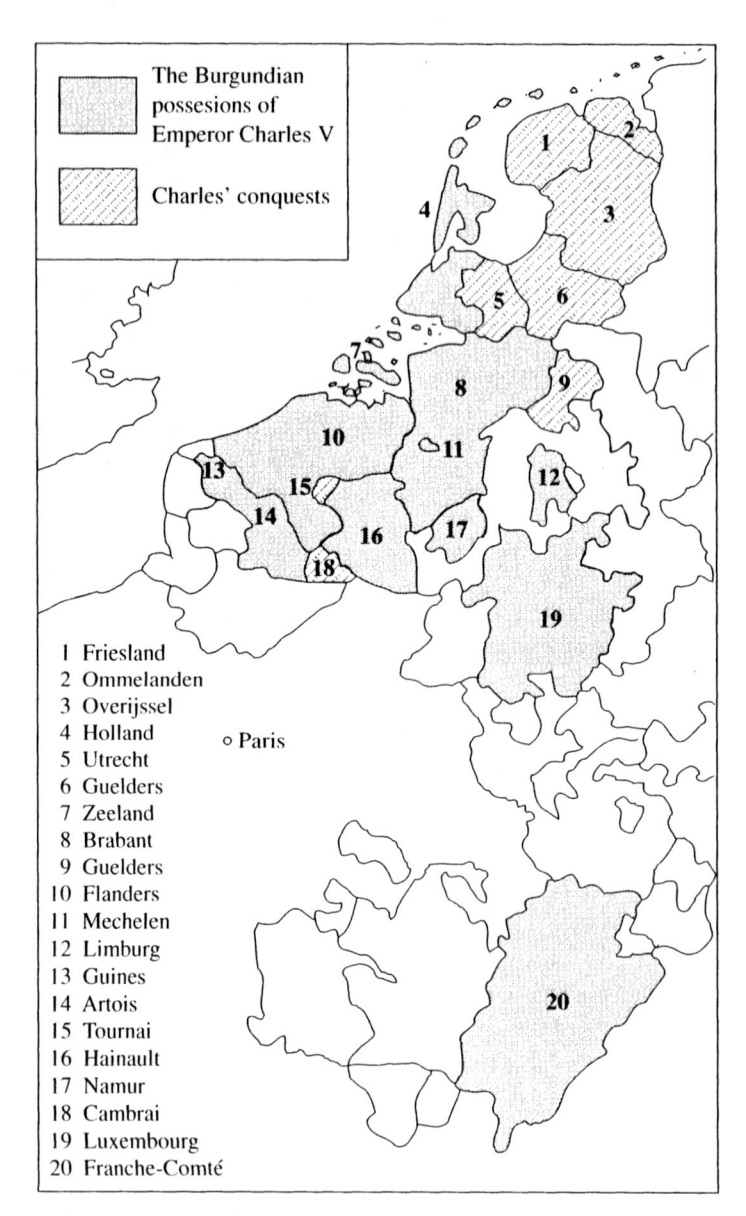

	The Burgundian possesions of Emperor Charles V
	Charles' conquests

1 Friesland
2 Ommelanden
3 Overijssel
4 Holland
5 Utrecht
6 Guelders
7 Zeeland
8 Brabant
9 Guelders
10 Flanders
11 Mechelen
12 Limburg
13 Guines
14 Artois
15 Tournai
16 Hainault
17 Namur
18 Cambrai
19 Luxembourg
20 Franche-Comté

Map 2: Habsburg Low Countries (1543)

Chronology

1496	20 October	Marriage of Philip (the Handsome) of Habsburg to Joanna of Castile; his sister, Margaret, marries Crown Prince John of Castile in the spring of 1497.
1500	24 February	Charles is born at Ghent.
1515	5 January	Prince of the Low Countries.
1516	23 January	Death of King Ferdinand of Aragon, at which Charles claims the title of King of Spain.
1517	September	Arrival in Spain.
1518	February	*Cortes* of Castile at Valladolid.
1519	28 June	Elected as Roman King.
1520	23 October	Crowned at Aachen as 'elected emperor'.
1520–22		Revolts of the *communeros* and *hermandades* in Spain.
1520	May	*Cortes* of Castile at Santiago de Compostela; journey to England, the Low Countries and Germany.
1521	April/May	Luther sentenced at the Diet of Worms.
1521–29		First war with France.
1521	November	Conquest of Lombardy.
1522	9 January	Adrian IV elected pope, dies on 14 September 1523.
1522	27 April	French defeated by imperial army at La Bicocca.
1522	July	Charles returns to Spain (until July 1529).
1523	July	*Connétable* Charles de Bourbon enters Charles' service.
1523	November	French defeat in Lombardy.
1524–26		Peasants' War in Germany.
1524	26 October	Francis I takes Milan.
1525	24 February	Francis I taken prisoner at Battle of Pavia.

Chronology

1526	16 January	Treaty of Madrid; Francis I is released on 17 March.
1526	10 March	Charles marries Isabella of Portugal.
1526	22 May	League of Cognac between Francis I, Clement VII, Sforza, Florence and Venice.
1527		Resumption of war; imperial troops plunder Rome from 6 May.
1528		French invasion of Naples; siege of Naples lifted in August; Genoa, with Andrea Doria, chooses Charles; French autumn offensive against Milan and Genoa is a failure.
1528	October	Charles gains control over the bishopric of Utrecht and Groningen.
1529	29 June	Treaty of Barcelona between Charles and Clement VII.
1529	July	Charles travels to Italy.
1529	3 August	Ladies' Peace of Cambrai.
1529	Sept–Oct	Turks lay siege to Vienna.
1529	Sept–Aug 1530	Siege of Florence.
1530	24 February	Pope crowns Charles emperor at Bologna.
1530	June–Nov	Diet of Augsburg.
1530	Nov-Dec	Negotiations with Clement VII at Bologna.
1531	5 January	Ferdinand is elected Roman King.
1531		Mary is regent in Low Countries. Charles stays there a year and introduces government reforms.
1531	27 February	Formation of League of Schmalkalden.
1532		Diet of Regensburg.
1532	September	Turkish invasion of Lower Austria; Charles in Vienna.
1532	October–1533	Discussions with Clement VII at Bologna.
1533	April	Return to Spain.
1535	June–August	Expedition to Tunis.
1535–36		Triumphal journey through Italy.
1536–37		Second war with France; French occupy Savoy; Charles invades Provence.
1538	17 June	Truce between Paul III, Charles and Francis I.
1538	14 July	Meeting between Charles and Francis I at Aigues-Mortes.
1539	1 May	Death of Empress Isabella.
1539	Nov–Dec	Festive journey through France.

1540		Suppression of revolt in Ghent.
1541	April–September	Diet of Regensburg.
1541	September	Negotiations with Paul III at Lucca.
1541	Oct–Nov	Unsuccessful expedition against Algiers.
1542–44		Third war with France.
1542	20 November	New Laws for the West Indies.
1543	May	Charles leaves Spain until spring 1556.
1543	4 September	Subjection of Guelders; Cambrai taken on 10 November.
1544	July–August	Invasion of Champagne; siege of Saint-Dizier.
1544	18 September	Peace of Crépy.
1545	December	Opening of the Council of Trent.
1546	April–August	Diet of Regensburg.
1546	July	Philip II made duke of Milan.
1546	Aug–Dec	Danube expedition against Protestant princes.
1547	24 April	Battle of Mühlberg.
1547	September	'Militant' Diet of Augsburg.
1548		Diet of Augsburg; Interim of Augsburg published 15 May; reorganisation of Burgundian Circle.
1549		Inauguration of Crown Prince Philip in the Low Countries.
1550–51		Negotiations between Charles and Ferdinand with Mary over the Habsburg succession.
1551–59		Fourth war with France.
1552	15 January	Henry II makes pact with German Protestants.
1552	April–July	Revolt of Protestant princes; Treaty of Passau signed 31 July.
1552	Oct–Dec	Siege of Metz.
1553	September	Campaign in Artois.
1554		Philip made king of Naples; 25 July, Philip marries Mary Tudor.
1555	Feb–August	Diet of Augsburg led by Ferdinand; Religious Peace.
1555	25 October	Charles abdicates in the Low Countries.
1556	16 January	Charles abdicates in Spain.
1556	3 August	Charles abdicates as emperor.
1556	September	Departure for Spain.
1558	21 September	Charles dies at Yuste.

Genealogies

Burgundy–Habsburg (1)

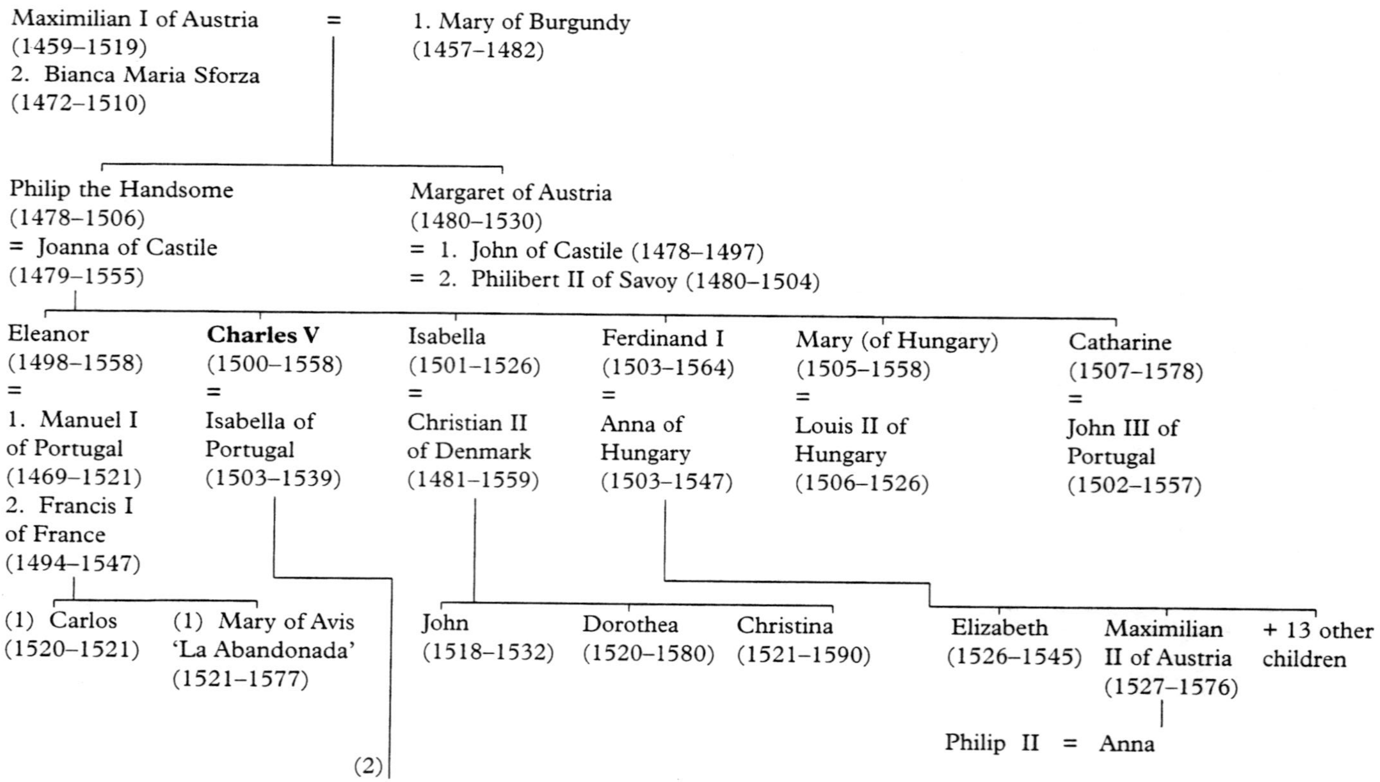

Maximilian I of Austria (1459–1519) = 1. Mary of Burgundy (1457–1482)
2. Bianca Maria Sforza (1472–1510)

Philip the Handsome (1478–1506) = Joanna of Castile (1479–1555)

Margaret of Austria (1480–1530)
= 1. John of Castile (1478–1497)
= 2. Philibert II of Savoy (1480–1504)

Eleanor (1498–1558) =
1. Manuel I of Portugal (1469–1521)
2. Francis I of France (1494–1547)

Charles V (1500–1558) = Isabella of Portugal (1503–1539)

Isabella (1501–1526) = Christian II of Denmark (1481–1559)

Ferdinand I (1503–1564) = Anna of Hungary (1503–1547)

Mary (of Hungary) (1505–1558) = Louis II of Hungary (1506–1526)

Catharine (1507–1578) = John III of Portugal (1502–1557)

(1) Carlos (1520–1521)
(1) Mary of Avis 'La Abandonada' (1521–1577)

John (1518–1532)   Dorothea (1520–1580)   Christina (1521–1590)

Elizabeth (1526–1545)   Maximilian II of Austria (1527–1576)   + 13 other children

Philip II = Anna

(2)

Burgundy–Habsburg (2)

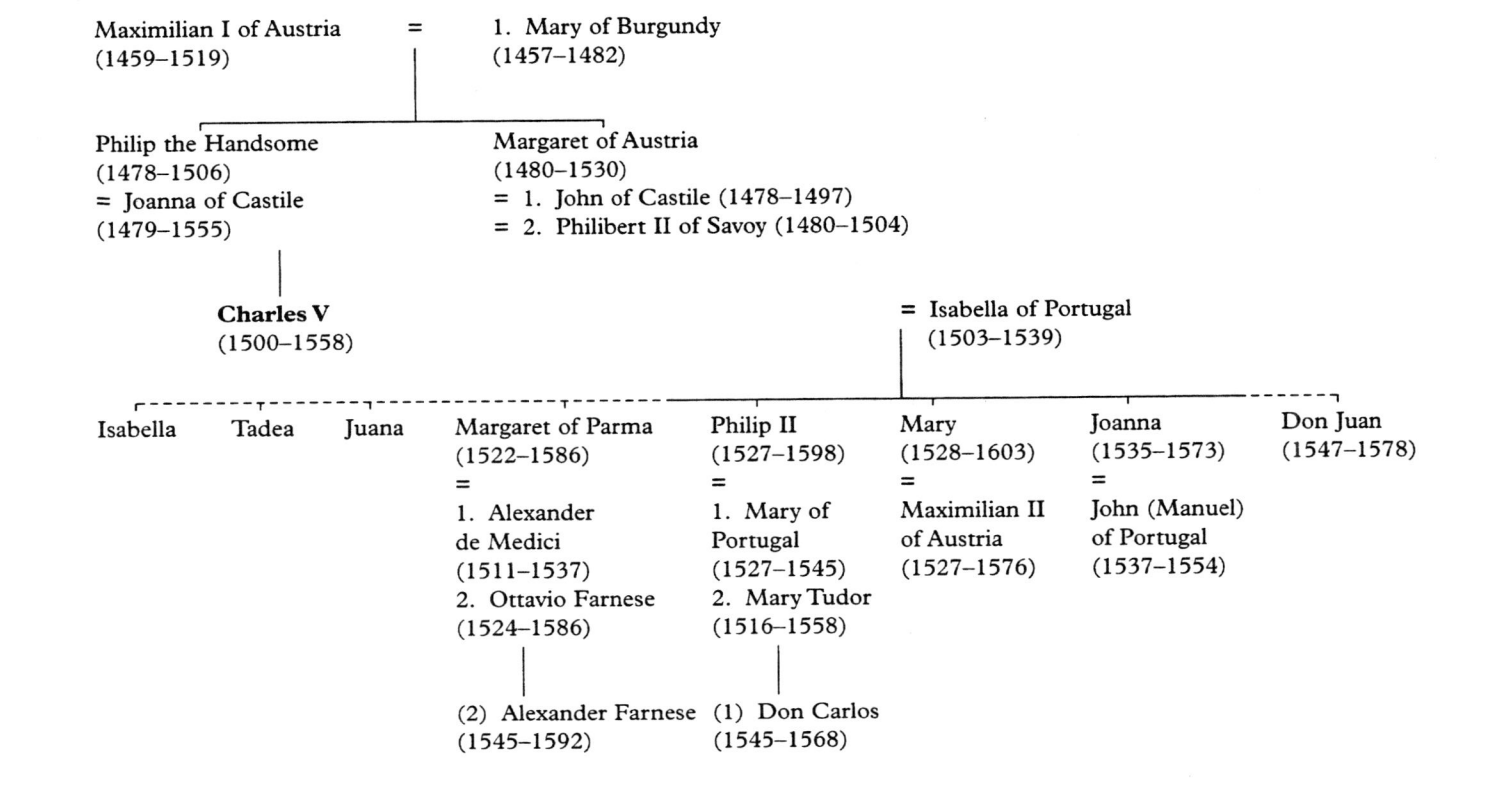

Maximilian I of Austria (1459–1519) = 1. Mary of Burgundy (1457–1482)

Philip the Handsome (1478–1506)
= Joanna of Castile (1479–1555)

Margaret of Austria (1480–1530)
= 1. John of Castile (1478–1497)
= 2. Philibert II of Savoy (1480–1504)

Charles V (1500–1558) = Isabella of Portugal (1503–1539)

Isabella | Tadea | Juana | Margaret of Parma (1522–1586) | Philip II (1527–1598) | Mary (1528–1603) | Joanna (1535–1573) | Don Juan (1547–1578)

Margaret of Parma =
1. Alexander de Medici (1511–1537)
2. Ottavio Farnese (1524–1586)

Philip II =
1. Mary of Portugal (1527–1545)
2. Mary Tudor (1516–1558)

Mary = Maximilian II of Austria (1527–1576)

Joanna = John (Manuel) of Portugal (1537–1554)

(2) Alexander Farnese (1545–1592) (1) Don Carlos (1545–1568)

Aragon–Castile

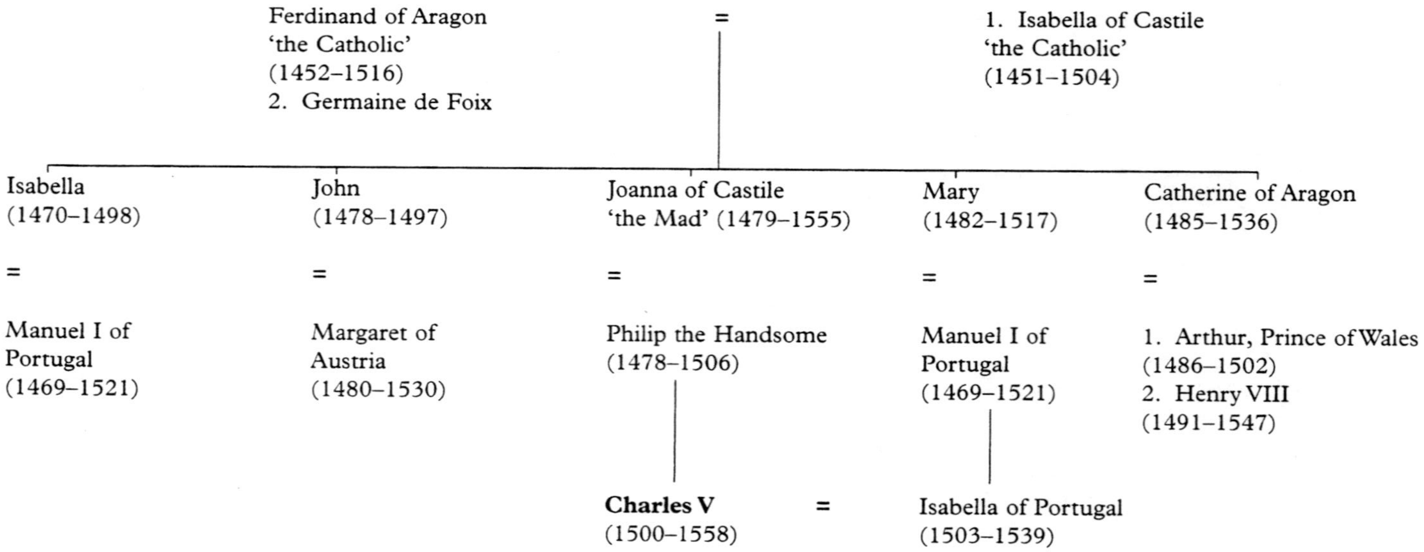

Ferdinand of Aragon
'the Catholic'
(1452–1516)
2. Germaine de Foix

=

1. Isabella of Castile
'the Catholic'
(1451–1504)

Isabella
(1470–1498)

=

Manuel I of
Portugal
(1469–1521)

John
(1478–1497)

=

Margaret of
Austria
(1480–1530)

Joanna of Castile
'the Mad' (1479–1555)

=

Philip the Handsome
(1478–1506)

Charles V
(1500–1558)

=

Isabella of Portugal
(1503–1539)

Mary
(1482–1517)

=

Manuel I of
Portugal
(1469–1521)

Catherine of Aragon
(1485–1536)

=

1. Arthur, Prince of Wales
   (1486–1502)
2. Henry VIII
   (1491–1547)

Portugal–Avis

Manuel I of Portugal (1469–1521)
1. Isabella of Aragon (1470–1498)
2. Eleanor of Austria (1498–1558)

= 2. Mary of Aragon (1482–1517)

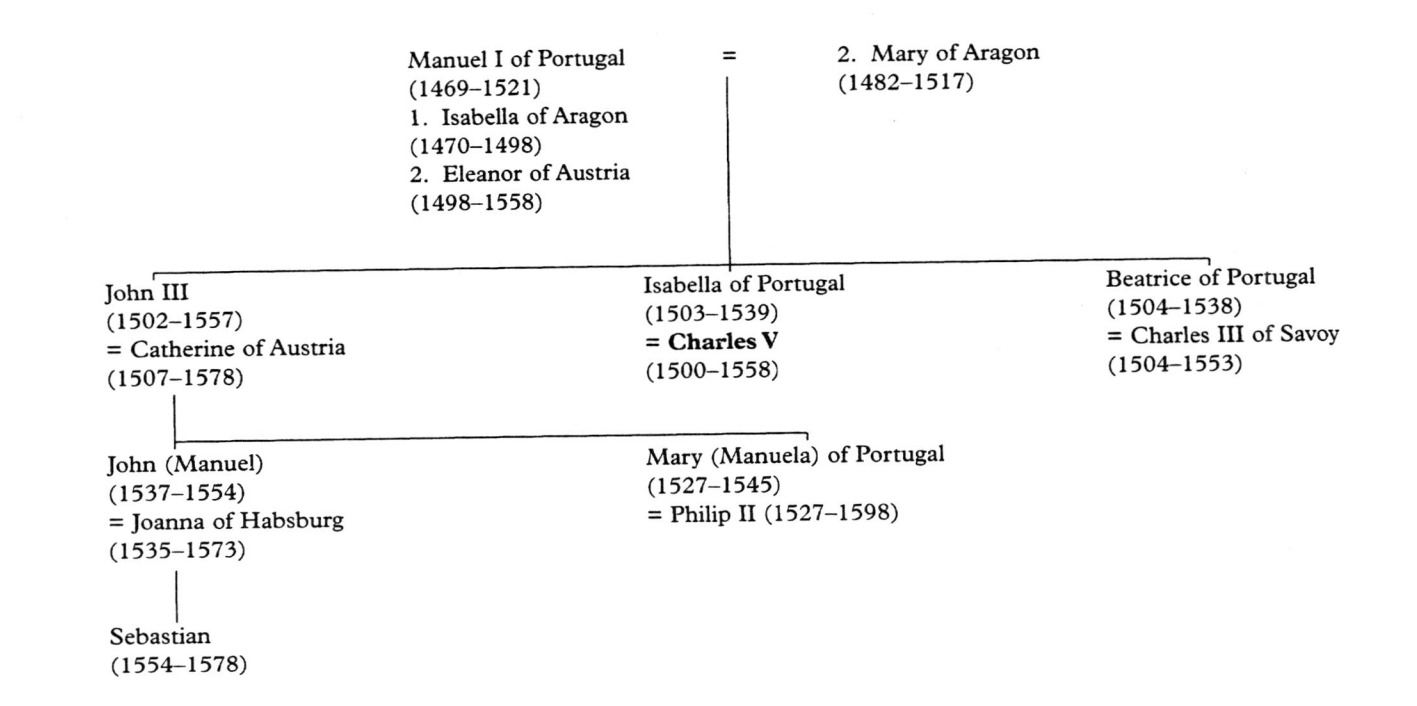

- Isabella of Portugal (1503–1539) = **Charles V** (1500–1558)
  - Mary (Manuela) of Portugal (1527–1545) = Philip II (1527–1598)
- Beatrice of Portugal (1504–1538) = Charles III of Savoy (1504–1553)

John III (1502–1557) = Catherine of Austria (1507–1578)
- John (Manuel) (1537–1554) = Joanna of Habsburg (1535–1573)
  - Sebastian (1554–1578)

Hungary

Vladislav II
(1456–1516)
= Anna de Foix († 1506)

├─ Anna of Hungary
│ (1503–1547)
│ = Ferdinand I of Austria
│ (1503–1564)
│
└─ Louis II of Hungary
   (1506–1526)
   = Mary of Hungary
   (1505–1558)

The families of Chalon and Nassau

John IV of Nassau (1410–1475)
- Engelbrecht II (1451–1504)
- John V (1455–1516)
  - Henry III (1483–1538) = Claudia of Chalon
    - René of Chalon (1518–1544)
  - William the Rich (1487–1559)
    - William the Silent, Prince of Orange (1533–1584)

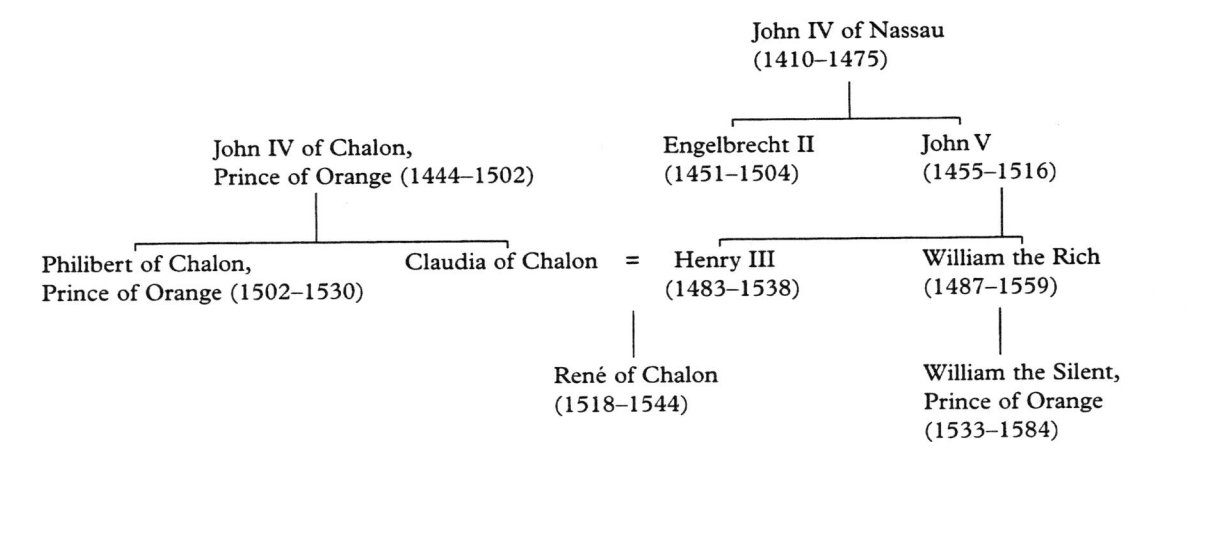

John IV of Chalon, Prince of Orange (1444–1502)
- Philibert of Chalon, Prince of Orange (1502–1530)
- Claudia of Chalon

Justification

In many countries the commemoration, in 2000, of the five hundredth anniversary of the birth of Emperor Charles V has received a great deal of attention from politicians and the general public, in the shape of exhibitions, lectures, symposia, concerts and festivals. A large number of books have also been published, in various languages, most of them simply with the title *Charles V*. The title has a certain appeal. Some of the books were written by specialists who have spent their entire career researching the subject; others are the work of enthusiastic amateurs. This book belongs to neither of these categories. It aims to present the most recent research synthetically and comprehensively.

Was yet another contribution to this plethora of books necessary? Charles' European empire embraced many countries and it is remarkable how differently he has been treated, from a historical viewpoint, in each of them.[1] I have tried not to confine myself to just one regional or ideological perspective, but to put myself on the level of the interaction between the emperor, his opponents inside and outside his *imperium*, and his subjects. There are, of course, various traditions concerning the man and his context: a Spanish historiographic tradition, a Catholic–German–Austrian, a Lutheran–German, a Belgian, an Anglo-Saxon and a Mediterranean one.[2] Apart from national and other ideological perspectives, there are two other difficulties. First, the subject is all-enveloping: it covers half of Europe, the Mediterranean world and the colonies for more than fifty years. Because the body of source material is so massive it is impossible to survey the whole of it on the basis of just one original study. The progress of efforts made since the middle of the nineteenth century, especially in Germany and Austria, to publish the most important correspondence and acts of state leaves a lot to be desired. Secondly, few scholars are able to study the sources and publications in all the relevant languages, including Italian and Dutch. This has resulted in an underexposure of two strategic parts of the *imperium* in most international literature.

This study, which has resolutely striven to be succinct, cannot claim to have dealt with the Spanish and Italian literature to the same depth as with the literature in other languages, but it is supported by current research in these linguistic areas. For this reason it hopes to offer a more balanced view of all parts of Charles' European *imperium* than even the most recent works in major languages. The focus on Europe, without proportional attention being given to the colonies, has been chosen because there is a coherency in it, while colonisation did not yet then have any real meaning for Europe, in so far as it did not have any fundamental influence on internal power relations.

The book is not a biography in the strict sense. It was not without reason that Karl Brandi, Charles' biographer, began his classic book with the arresting sentences: 'There are historical personalities with a superhuman creative power, who build on their own elemental energy and can thereby prescribe the laws of thought and action for centuries. Charles V was not such a person.' Brandi did, however, look for 'the great' in the emperor, and found it in his linking of out-of-date views with new entities. To me, it no longer seems desirable to go in search of a great personality. The question I found intriguing was this: what can one person, whom a quirk of fate has given an inordinate amount of power, achieve? How much freedom of action did he in fact have? Did it help him to reach his objectives? What unwanted results ensued from his actions?

The first half of the sixteenth century offered an exceptionally dynamic background: voyages of discovery made the world larger, science and technology passed through revolutions, Christian thought underwent a powerful renewal, the population and economy of Europe grew. The tension between the will of an individual and the power of structures reached a dramatic climax under Charles. The aim of this book is to make available the most recent findings of modern scholarship.

Notes:

1. Interesting aspects, not dealt with here, include the creation of the image of the emperor in later popular literature, and its ideological use in the iconography of nation states in the nineteenth century. For this see: H. Lox, *Van stropdragers en de pot van Olen. Verhalen over Keizer Karel* (Leuven, 1999); *Mise-en-scène. Keizer Karel en de verbeelding van de negentiende eeuw*, exh. cat. (Ghent, 1999).
2. See the remarks in A. Kohler, *Karl V. Eine Biographie* (Munich, 1999), 19–23; M. Fernandez Alvarez, *Carlos V, el César y el hombre* (Madrid and Yuste, 1999), 27–43.

1
An *imperium* of forty years

Magnificent mourning

At two o'clock in the afternoon of 29 December 1558 a funeral procession of a splendour never before seen passed through Brussels. It left the palace on the Coudenberg and made its way down Berg Street to St Gudula's, the main church of the city, to celebrate the solemn requiem mass. There, a funeral chapel, a *chapelle ardente*, had been erected where, above the catafalque, an enormous iron construction, resting on 20-foot-high pillars, carried 3,000 candles, each one weighing a pound. Three king's crowns, one emperor's crown and a number of crosses towered another 40 feet above the real crown, chain, sceptre and orb of the late emperor, Charles the Fifth. The following day, another solemn requiem mass was sung in the same church. Ranged along the walls of the church were the banners of all the principalities of the dead emperor that had been carried in the procession. Six monumental stained-glass windows, from models by Bernard van Orley and Michiel Coxcie, which had been fitted in the church between 1537 and 1547, illuminated the whole Habsburg dynasty.

The gateway to the palace on the Coudenberg was draped for the occasion with a 6-metre-long velvet cloth bearing the imperial coat of arms. The great hall of the palace was completely hung with black cloth, as were the stout, wooden barriers on either side of the processional route, intended to keep the thousands of spectators at a distance. Between the barriers a width of 20 feet was kept open for the funeral cortège. Behind them stood some 2, 000 members of the city's guilds in mourning garb, each carrying a burning torch adorned with the emperor's coat of arms. The procession itself was strictly hierarchic and under the command of the first king-of-arms of the Order of the Golden Fleece. In front were the local clergy from the parishes, convents and chapters. After them came the singers of the chapel royal and the court chaplains, then many prelates, abbots and bishops from the Low Countries, Spain, Italy and other of the king's lands. The official report, which was published soon afterwards by Christophe Plantin in Antwerp, was unable to give any details about the last of these. The court chronicles, of course, contained extensive accounts of the ceremony, as did the letter that an amazed English spectator, Richard Clough, wrote a few days later to his business associate Sir Thomas Gresham, the renowned agent for the English crown in Antwerp.[1]

After the clergy came the civic officials and members of Brussels' council, followed by representatives of the towns and Provincial States of 'the lands of hither', the traditional designation of the Low Countries, contrasting with 'the lands of thither' – Burgundy, Franche-Comté and their dependencies. Next was the turn of the officials of the administrative institutions of the duchy of Brabant: Chamber of Accounts, sheriff, chancellor, the Council. When the various echelons and organs of the city had passed by it was the turn of the court. It was flanked on either side by two hundred poor people, dressed for the occasion in mourning apparel, and each carrying a flaming torch with miniature coats of arms. They personified the Christian charity of the court, which was exhibited especially on high days and at solemn ceremonies. Members of the court were followed by the Spanish and German halberdiers of the royal guard. Between this double row walked the servants of the court, two by two and in ascending rank, from stable lads to various *gentilshommes*, 'all in large numbers'.

The symbols of Charles' power, heralded by trumpets and drums, formed the climax of the procession. High nobles carried the banner of the emperor, adorned with his device *'Plus Oultre'*, the Pillars of Hercules and the cross of St Andrew. His riderless horse, swathed in a cloth decorated with its master's emblems, was led in front of his great standard picturing St James – the patron saint of Spain – felling an unbeliever. Heralds, a riderless horse with its saddlecloth covered in heraldic symbols and a nobleman carrying the banner came from each of the more than sixty principalities and lordships. The bright colours of the flags and scutcheons and the flickering torches formed a sharp contrast to the uniform black of the clothing. Next came the insignia of Charles himself, his pennant, banner, standard and flag, scutcheons, the chain of the Golden Fleece and the four imperial insignia: sceptre, sword, orb and crown. Behind this walked king Philip II in a long mourning gown and cap; he was followed by knights of the Golden Fleece, members of the administrative councils of Italy and Aragon, and the viceroys of Naples, Milan, Aragon, Sicily and Catalonia. Then came the members of the three governing councils of the Low Countries, the Council of State, the Privy Council and the Council of Finances. Last in the cortège were the king's archers.

This sort of procession formed an excellent means of mass communication between monarch and subjects. On the one hand, the town formed the backdrop to an event in which both the local community and other representatives of the people could reveal themselves in their corporate ranks, and at the same time show their devotion to the dead monarch and his successor. On the other hand, the court seized such opportunities to show itself in all its splendour to the people and to the European public, which received its information from printed and oral accounts. The hierarchy of the procession reflected the hierarchy of the state. The vast authority of the dead emperor was in this way clearly visible to all the spectators. The symbolism of the emperor's victories added lustre to the honour of the dynasty, and its political aims and achievements. The funeral obsequies provided the dynasty and its subjects with an opportunity to confirm their bonds of loyalty in an emotional way.

The printed report of this *Magnifique et sumptueuse pompe funèbre* contains 33 coloured copperplates of the chapel of mourning, the insignia and the standards in this part of the procession. They were designed by Hiëronymus Cock and identify all the important figures and flags. The highlight of the procession was a float, which entirely hid from view the men underneath who propelled it forward. The float depicted an enormous galleon drawn over the ocean by two sea horses. It sailed between islands where Turkish flags had been torn down and the imperial flag raised. Behind the ship two elephant seals pulled the Pillars of Hercules, upon which the following words were legible: '*You have rightly assumed the sign of the Pillars of Hercules, conqueror of the monsters of your time*'. The rear pillar carried a full explanation in Latin, which was also carried in the printed accounts. It calls the ship *Victoria*, to illustrate the triumphs of the illustrious and most Christian emperor. Twelve triumphs were described – an allusion to the Twelve Labours of Hercules – and apparently also depicted on the vessel's hull. The engraving shows five on the port side, among them the discovery and conversion to Christianity of the New World and the conquests of Genoa, Coron and Patras in the Peloponnese, and Tunis. The idea for a series of Charles' Twelve Conquests had already been seen in Maarten van Heemskerck's series of engravings of the same name that Hiëronymus Cock published in Antwerp in 1556. Iconographically, and in the choice of themes, however, the two series are independent.[2] An eagle's head adorned the galleon's bowsprit. It was further adorned with coats of arms, standards and pennants: the flag on the tallest mast pictured Christ crucified above the Pillars of Hercules, a very direct association of the dead emperor with God. The symbolic Ship of State was steered by the three theological virtues: Hope on the forecastle with her anchor, Faith midships, and Charity on the poop deck at the helm. In the front of the poop deck stood an empty throne decorated with the imperial eagle and the emperor's crown.

The splendour of this funeral procession had never before been seen. Not long before, however, Brussels had witnessed a similar, though more sober, ceremony in memory of Mary Tudor, queen of England and consort of Philip II, who had died in London on 17 November. The ceremony was in the style of the English royal house, whereas that in Charles' memory was clearly fixed in the Burgundian tradition. The symbolism of the ship was linked to a triumphal carriage that had been seen in Brussels on 13 March 1516, in the mourning procession for Ferdinand of Aragon, Charles' grandfather. No less a person than Jan Gossaert was responsible for the design, which, as in 1558, displayed an empty throne ornamented with a globe and the royal device. Here, too, the struggle against the Moors had formed the principal motif. The galleon *Victoria* remained in the possession of the city of Brussels and would be used on several other occasions, including the Joyous Entry of Albert and Isabella in 1596, and more processions.[3]

What lent particular lustre to the ceremony in Brussels was the presence of Philip II, who had already succeeded his father in Italy in 1554, in the Low Countries in 1555 and in Spain in 1556. The account, which was probably written by herald Pierre de Vernois, was published by Plantin with versions in Dutch, French, German, Spanish and Italian; at least 180 copies were sold between 1560 and 1565; various translations from the Italian of a Milanese account appeared in Paris and Lyons. All this indicates not only decidedly propagandist objectives on the part of the court, but also commercial profitability and, therefore, international public interest in the memorial service. For forty years the emperor, who had abdicated his various thrones in 1554, 1555 and 1556, had reigned over a vast number of lands. Those forty years had seen far-reaching developments that had a profound effect on his contemporaries.

It was a wise move for Philip to make political capital out of the funeral obsequies. The death the previous month of his consort, Mary Tudor, had deprived him of his influence in England. It did not seem likely that he would ever inherit Charles' imperial title as it had been bestowed on his uncle Ferdinand earlier in the year. In Charles' almost permanent absence Ferdinand had acted as his representative since 1522 and, from 1531, with the title of Roman king, he had in fact governed the German Empire. The German princes recognised him as their superior, while Philip was a complete stranger to them. In addition, Ferdinand had a large number of children and his eldest son, Maximilian, cherished his own ambitions. To balance these two drawbacks, however, Philip could boast of his recent victory over the French. In 1557 his troops had triumphed at Saint Quentin and in the summer of 1558 at Gravelines. The French had agreed to a truce, which on 3 April 1559 was to become the Treaty of Cateau-Cambrésis. It brought an advantageous end to the forty-year struggle between the Habsburgs and Valois that had occupied most of Charles' reign. The wars between them had almost ruined both sides, but Philip could now establish Spain's superiority in western Europe. It was to last for nearly a century. A Spanish negotiator remarked, 'In truth, God Himself must have guided these peace negotiations for, although everything has been settled to our advantage, the French are also content with them'.[4]

The display of Charles' glorious victories, his numerous princely titles and the insignia of the highest secular authority in Christendom, together with Philip's appearance as the new sovereign of the prestigious Order of the Golden Fleece, affirmed to the entire world the unrivalled power and splendour of the new ruler, although he was neither emperor nor king consort of England. At the end of the requiem mass in St Gudula's, William of Orange symbolically expressed this ambition. As sovereign prince of Orange he was the highest-ranking knight of the Golden Fleece and the Order's spokesman. Moreover, in August 1556 Charles had entrusted him, as German prince of the House of Nassau, with the discussions over his abdication in the Diet, and it was he who would take the orb, which he had carried in the funeral procession, back to the Empire.[5] According to Richard Clough, he stood in front of the funeral chapel, struck his breast and said in a loud voice, pausing between the sentences, 'He is dead. He is dead forever. He is dead, and his place has been taken by another who is greater than ever he was.'[6]

Then Philip removed his cap of mourning. Through the rituals he was able to assume the full worth and renown of his father and, strengthened thereby, to pursue his own reign. The triple variation on the French ritual for the transfer of royal power with its proclamation, 'The king is dead. Long live the king', emphasises the continuity of the position in spite of death. In 1516 during the funeral service for Ferdinand of Aragon the herald of the Order of the Golden Fleece had called out the king's name three times, followed by the words, 'He is dead', and the lowering of the royal standard of Aragon. Then the herald called 'Long live doña Joanna and don Carlos, the Catholic kings', and Charles set aside his mourning robe and raised a consecrated sword from the altar to the acclamation of the masses.[7] Thus, on two occasions, St.Gudula's church in Brussels formed the background to the succession of the power of Spain, with Charles as the central figure on both occasions.

In many cities throughout his empire requiem masses were held for the emperor, who died at his residence near the monastery of St Jerome at Yuste in Estremadura on 21 September 1558. The first of them took place in the Escorial. A mourning tumulus was built in Valladolid. In 1559, on 24 February, Charles' birthday, a funeral procession went to the Dominican church in Augsburg on the initiative of Charles' brother, the emperor Ferdinand. He commissioned a famous local armourer to make funerary armour portraying the dead emperor with his symbols. Some pieces of this armour have been preserved: a jousting helmet embellished with an imperial crown, a sword, a round shield with the heraldic emblems of the emperor, a horse's headpiece and a saddle. In four pages of written text and 37 drawings a manuscript describes the coats of arms of the two emperors and the patricians of Augsburg and the procession itself, in which – in addition to the remaining pieces already referred to – three badges, a coat of mail and twelve banners can be seen. In its form and participants the procession in Augsburg was linked to the German chivalric tradition and the local elite, but it did not reflect the European dimensions of Charles' empire such as had been demonstrated in Brussels. Ferdinand was intent upon presenting himself as the newly elected emperor and, in that capacity, his brother's successor. A week later there was a funeral procession in Rome, and one in Mexico on 30 November. Our information about this comes from the 27-folio printed report, which includes an illustration of the *túmulo imperial*, the bier adorned with the symbols of power: crown, sword, helmet, coat of mail and standard. The account shows quite clearly that in Mexico, too, all levels of society, including high Indian officials, took part in the procession from the cathedral to the church of St. Francis.[8]

A difficult departure

Charles had left Brussels on 6 August 1556 for good, in order to join his sisters Eleanor, the former queen of France, and Mary, the sometime queen of Hungary and for twenty-five years regent of the Low Countries, and settle in a small palace built for him near the monastery of St Jerome at Yuste in Estremadura. He had chosen Yuste for its mild climate and the gently rolling countryside. He was accompanied by a household comprising some fifty persons.[9] From 1554 onwards he had systematically relinquished the heavy responsibilities resting on his shoulders. On the occasion of the marriage of his only son, Philip, to Mary Tudor, the queen of England, on 25 July 1554, Charles had given him the kingdom of Naples so that he would be equal in rank to his wife. The marriage contract set a seal on the good relations that Charles had fostered with England during most of his reign, but it excluded Philip from the power and the succession. Charles insisted that Philip leave England in the first week of 1555 to attend to the government of his hereditary lands. He then summoned the

Order of the Golden Fleece in chapter to ensure that it would accept the transfer of sovereignty over this prestigious order of chivalry to his son.

On 25 October the emperor appeared with Philip and Mary before the States General of the Low Countries, which he had summoned to the great hall of the palace on the Coudenberg. There are several eyewitness accounts of this meeting, all of which underline the emotional tension of the solemn occasion. The emperor appeared before them, a physically broken man, leaning on his stick and supported by the young courtier and commander, William of Orange. He had a statement read explaining that he was relinquishing his rule over the Low Countries in favour of his son, because his health suffered in those chill lands, the Spanish air was better for him. He implored his subjects to continue to serve God and His holy faith and to observe justice and unity, and he begged them to show the same loyalty and devotion to Philip as they had shown to him. Then, with great difficulty, the emperor rose and started to speak in French. In a fatherly tone he took stock of his life, as he had once done in the summer of 1550 during a long boat trip on the Rhine. He reminded the assembly of the ceremony that had taken place in that same hall forty years earlier when, on the feast of the Epiphany, almost fifteen years old, he had been declared of age, and had been entrusted by his grandfather, the Emperor Maximilian, with the government of the Low Countries. The death the following year of his other grandfather, Ferdinand of Aragon, had made it necessary for him to depart for Spain. When Maximilian died in 1519 and he strove to be elected emperor, he 'did not do so ambitious for more dominions, but for the good of a number of his kingdoms and lands, particularly those of hither'. Then he looked back over his travels: he had made nine journeys to Germany, six to Spain, seven to Italy, ten to the Low Countries, four to France and two to Africa; he had sailed on the Atlantic Ocean three times, the Mediterranean eight. Now he was preparing for his final journey. He thanked Mary for her wise and able government. He regretted that he was not leaving his lands in peace and stressed that, if he had often gone to war, it was always against his will, for his enemies had always forced him to take up arms to defend his lands. All this had been a great strain upon him, as was now obvious from the state of his health. He had felt for a long time that he no longer had the strength to carry his heavy burden. He recalled his unsuccessful attempt to retake Metz from the French in 1552; later he managed to defeat the king's attack on Artois. In a voice full of emotion and with tears in his eyes, the emperor ended his speech with the humble request that his faults be forgiven, for it had never been his desire to cause hurt or injustice to any one of his subjects.

The entire assembly was moved to tears by so much humility on the part of such a mighty ruler. Speaking on behalf of the States General the first *pensionaris* (chief official) of Antwerp, Jacob Maes, affirmed the loyalty and affection of the subjects towards Charles and his son, after which Charles passed the authority over the Low Countries on to his son, Philip, who knelt before him. Philip let Cardinal Granvelle speak for him because he did not consider his own French good enough to respond. This at once cast a shadow on the ceremony. He promised to return to the Low Countries should this be necessary, but he failed to keep the promise; he did not really have much interest in the region. Finally, Mary rose to announce her own departure and declared that her concern and affection for her fatherland would remain intact. The following day Philip and the States General swore oaths of loyalty to each other; the king promised to protect and uphold the law, the people pledged their faithful service. The States General would hold him to his oath until 1581 when they declared that his dominion over them had lapsed.

The transfer of the other principalities was of a far less personal nature. On 16 January 1556, in Brussels, Charles signed the documents relating to the Spanish, Italian and American realms. The free imperial county of Burgundy, Franche-Comté, which was part of the German Empire, passed into Philip's hands by proxy during an assembly of the States General on 10 June 1556. The question of the imperial dignity was rather more complicated because election to it lay in the hands of the electors. In 1531, after Charles had been crowned emperor by the pope, they had chosen Ferdinand, his three-year-younger brother, to be Roman king. In that capacity he was the permanent representative of the emperor who was, after all, usually outside the Empire. Even during the 1520s Ferdinand had represented Charles, who was then Roman king, in the Empire, but only on a personal footing, with the archduchy of Austria as his *Hausmacht*, the patrimony of the Habsburg dynasty that was the real power base in their role as German kings.

Charles had wanted to arrange the succession to the Empire in 1555, but the political situation at the time was not suitable. Ferdinand was anxious about a Turkish offensive in Hungary, and about pressure from Henry II of France with whom the Habsburgs were still at war, and in the Empire itself the recently agreed Religious Peace needed stabilising. He worked carefully at this and was content enough with the authority that Charles had effectively mandated to him in August 1556, shortly before his departure for Spain. In February 1558 the electors eventually assembled at their traditional venue, Frankfurt-am-Main, and had no difficulty in designating Ferdinand as 'elected Roman emperor'. Charles, too, had been given this title in 1519; then it was the general intention that it would be ratified by a formal coronation by the pope, which did indeed take place in 1530. This would be the last coronation of a Roman emperor by a pope. In 1558 the College of Electors consisted of just six members because the seventh, the king of Bohemia, was the Roman king, Ferdinand himself. Of these six, three temporal princes – the duke of Saxony, the margrave of Brandenburg and the count palatine – had just chosen for the Reformation and would assuredly have taken offence at a coronation by the pope. The enthronement at Aachen, which took place a few weeks later, confirmed the new political reality in the Empire and in its relations with Rome. Between 1519 and 1558 a permanent change of direction had taken place.

In yet another respect the end of Charles' reign heralded a new era: the unity of an extensive Christian empire in western Europe, that he had personified for nearly half a century, disintegrated. When Ferdinand had been recognised as Roman king in 1531, Charles should have realised that it would be impossible to prevent his eventual succession as emperor, after decades of loyal service and *de facto* government of the German lands. At the time Charles already had a four-year-old son, Philip, but it would be unreasonable to burden him with the government of Germany – a task which, moreover, Ferdinand had already fulfilled for ten years. From the time of the Emperor Otto I in the tenth century the reigning emperors had tried to curb the election rights of the German princes by having their sons recognised as Roman king while they still lived, and thus trying to force the hereditary succession. In every case the Roman king elected during the father's lifetime did indeed become his successor. Maximilian was crowned king of the Romans in 1486 in order to ensure the Habsburg continuity during his father's lifetime. He in turn opened negotiations in 1518 to achieve the same for his grandson Charles, but died before he could gain his objective. When Ferdinand had served his brother with unswerving loyalty for more than thirty years there was surely no way that he would not be the new emperor. Although Ferdinand had grown up in Spain he had with strategic care manoeuvred himself into a position where he could not be ignored, even by Charles himself.

The next question, therefore, was who was to succeed Ferdinand: his eldest son, Maximilian, or Charles' son, Philip? Charles made every effort to restore the unity that was so precious to him as soon as possible, by persuading Ferdinand to recommend Philip as Roman king, and thus his chosen successor as emperor. This matter was the subject of bitter negotiations between the two brothers in Augsburg in 1550–51, sometimes in the presence of their sons Philip and Maximilian. It was the first time that Ferdinand was not prepared to lay aside the interests of his own family – he had fifteen children – in favour of his brother's. At first Charles tried to reserve the imperial crown directly for Philip. When Ferdinand rejected this suggestion outright, Charles attempted to make Ferdinand accept Philip as his successor and to support his candidature before the electors. During the long months of talks Mary had to be called twice from Brussels to clear the air and work out a compromise. Charles could not see that Philip was considered a complete stranger in the German Empire, and even less that his radical Catholicism made him unacceptable to half of the electors and members of the estates. In response to the first objection he said that Ferdinand himself had come as a Spaniard to the German Empire and settled there well, completely ignoring the fact that Ferdinand had never fulfilled any responsibilities outside the Empire and Hungary. On the second point, Charles found it particularly difficult to acknowledge the defeat of Catholicism in large parts of the Empire, because he had looked upon the defence of the Church as his most important mission. It was Mary who finally suggested a complicated compromise in which Ferdinand would become emperor and would make every effort to have Philip elected Roman king, and Philip would then in turn plead for Maximilian. The ties between them would be affirmed by marriage with their cousins. This particular part of the agreement was a typically Habsburg solution: Maximilian had already married Charles' daughter Mary in 1548, and in 1570 Philip eventually married Anna of Austria, who bore him an heir. Developments in the German Empire, however, made it impossible to realise the agreement straight away. The electors and the estates in the Diet rejected any sort of interference from Philip. In 1558 the division into a Spanish and an Austrian branch of the house of Habsburg became a fact. In Charles' eyes the split put the seal on a double failure: that of political unity and that of unity in the Catholic Church. Philip would never fulfil a function in the Empire. After Ferdinand's death in 1564 Maximilian was to become emperor, and after him other scions of the Austrian branch of the Habsburgs.

The fact that in 1555 Charles – who after 1548 suffered increasingly from frequent and serious attacks of gout – took the highly unusual step of abdicating, is most certainly connected with his growing awareness of the impracticability of his fundamental political objectives. He no longer felt able to make the superhuman physical effort demanded by the unremitting journeys and campaigns. He appeared to have lost the battle for the unity of the faith precisely in the German – the 'Holy Roman' – Empire, while the wars against France, the Turks and Italy seemed utterly hopeless at that time. His subjects paid a fortune in taxes, and yet he was to leave an almost bankrupt state. Although he was unwilling to admit it, it all seemed too much for one man; a man who, like his mother, Queen Joanna of Castile, who died barely six months before his abdication, suffered from bouts of depression.

The Habsburgs: a dynasty for Europe

Charles' birth at Ghent on 24 February 1500 was welcomed with frenzied joy. He was the second child and first son of Philip of Habsburg, known as 'the Handsome', and Joanna of Castile. For the baptism, between 9 and 10 o'clock in the evening of 7 March, the people of Ghent had constructed a wooden gangway 1 metre high, 2 metres wide and 700 metres long, along which the procession could make its way from the Prinsenhof to St John's Church, visible to and unhindered by the people. The gangway was decorated with three times thirteen gates, some of which were larger than the others and had allegorical names: the Gates of Wisdom, Justice and Peace. All the gates were decorated with coats of arms and torches, 10,000 of them altogether, according to the candlemakers' guild involved. On the Lys the clarions sounded from a brilliantly lit ship and the dragon on the belfry spewed fireworks. A walkway had been stretched between the spires of the belfry and the church of St Nicholas. The designer of the spectacle walked on planks above his construction to place a cartwheel with torches on top of the spire of St Nicholas' church. Never before at the birth or reception of a ruler had Ghent witnessed such a spectacular show of light, recorded the chronicler, Jean Molinet.[10] As was customary, some three or four hundred dignitaries took part in the procession. First, the masters and administrators of the craft guilds, the town magistrates, knights and squires of the court, members of the Council of Flanders, knights in the Order of the Golden Fleece and, lastly, the close relatives of the young prince. Of special interest was Margaret of Austria, the widow of John of Castile, who had recently returned from Spain. Margaret of York, the dowager duchess of Burgundy, carried the child to the font. The two Margarets stood as godmothers. The godfathers were Charles of Croy, prince of Chimay and John Glymes, lord of Bergen op Zoom and first lord-in-waiting and grand chamberlain to Archduke Philip. The baptismal name, Charles, was chosen for Charles the Bold, duke of Burgundy and consort of Margaret of York, who had perished in 1477.

Charles' parents had been married in Lier in October 1496, part of the double marriage of the Spanish and Burgundian heirs with the other's sister, Margaret of Austria and Joanna of Castile. Negotiations for these marriages had begun in 1494 as a diplomatic response to the French invasion of Naples.[11] King Ferdinand of Aragon aimed to secure his rights to

Naples by an alliance with the Habsburgs. The Roman king, Maximilian, recognised Ludovico il Moro as duke of Milan in exchange for a large sum of money and marriage to his daughter, Bianca Sforza; he hoped for a coalition of all France's enemies and an eventual division of Italy between the houses of Habsburg and Aragon. He thus laid down the lines of the entire policy of his grandson Charles, although it was impossible then to foresee that Charles would become the universal successor to four dynasties – Trastamara, Aragon, Burgundy and Habsburg.

The marriage of John of Castile and Margaret took place in Burgos in 1497. John's other sister, Isabella, was married to King Manuel of Portugal, with the express purpose of uniting all the kingdoms of the Iberian peninsula under one crown. Fate ensured, however, that this union of crowns was not to be, but it created another, which had been excluded as far as possible by the clauses of the 1495 marriage treaty. One after the other, John and his premature child died in 1497, his sister Isabella in 1498, and in 1500 her young son, the Iberian heir apparent. Joanna and her husband Philip thus became first in line to the throne of Castile. In 1502 and 1503 they travelled through Spain to have their claims recognized. The *cortes* of Castile did this at Toledo on 22 May 1502. After the death of her mother, Isabella the Catholic, in November 1504, and the birth of their daughter, Mary, on 15 September 1505, Joanna and Philip embarked for Spain in January 1506 to be recognized as monarchs of Castile. Philip, however, died at Burgos on 26 September and Joanna began to suffer from severe mental illness, symptoms of which had appeared earlier. Although she would remain queen in name until her death in January 1555, her father, Ferdinand of Aragon, took over the government of the two Iberian kingdoms. A son was born out of his second marriage (to Germaine de Foix) in 1506 but when the boy died in 1509 and Ferdinand remained childless, he agreed that his eldest grandson, Charles, should succeed to both Castile and Aragon. He insisted on having some say in the matter of Charles' education, who thus had a Spanish, German and English tutor in addition to William of Croy. His second grandson, born in Spain and named after him, grew up there and enjoyed his utmost affection, but had to move to the hereditary Austrian lands when Charles succeeded in Spain in 1517. Their youngest sister, Catherine, born in 1507 after her father had died, lived in Tordesillas with her mother and would eventually marry King John III of Portugal.

The four other orphan children of Philip and Joanna were educated at the court of their aunt, Margaret of Austria. After her third marriage and second widowhood (from Duke Philibert of Savoy), she rejected every attempt by her father and brother to be used again as a pawn on the royal marriage market. In 1507 she agreed to undertake the guardianship of her four young nephews and nieces and the government of the Burgundian Low Countries, while the counties of Artois, Franche-Comté and Charolais and the lordship of Mechelen belonged to her widow's portion. The court at Mechelen had a lot to offer the children. The city was flourishing during a period of general prosperity and the court was a magnet to artists and scholars from miles around. Musical performances in the court chapel were under the direction of Hendrik Bredemers. Dutch composers enjoyed an international reputation and received offers from courts in other lands. Peter Alamire copied music in exquisite manuscripts that were often used as gifts for royal connections. They could be found at the court of Archduke Philip the Handsome, his sister Margaret, John III of Portugal, Henry VIII, Pope Leo X, Elector Frederick the Wise of Saxony and Duke William IV of Bavaria. Many of the manuscripts were decorated with the portraits and coats of arms of the recipients: they were obviously exclusive gifts in diplomatic relationships. This was evidently true in the case of the elector, who possessed no fewer than 11 manuscripts; he was given them not only because of his passionate love of music but also because Margaret was anxious to secure his vote in the imperial election of 1519.[12]

Margaret herself possessed a substantial library; a catalogue dating from 1523–24 records 335 manuscripts and 44 printed books, but in fact she owned even more. She made a point of collecting beautiful manuscripts from various collections of Burgundian rulers and their confidants, personally commissioned some 40 manuscripts, and inherited or bought others. In 1511 she made her best deal, buying '78 parchment manuscripts bound in velvet of diverse colours' and an unspecified number of unbound books on parchment and paper. For this she paid Charles of Croy, prince of Chimay and one of Charles' godfathers and tutors, the sum of 5000 pounds. Her collection included practically everything that one would expect to find in the library of a west European prince in about 1500: romances of chivalry, histories, moralising works, books of hours as well as Boccaccio's *Decameron*.[13]

The three oldest royal children in Mechelen, Eleanor, Charles and Isabella, at first had lessons together from Dutch and Spanish teachers, but their mother tongue was French. This was the language in which they would continue to correspond with each other. When he was nine Charles was put into the care of a new tutor, William of Croy, to learn the arts of horse riding and combat sports, together with pages of the court. The girls, too, received instruction in hunting and other forms of physical exercise. The Croy family had a long record of service to the dukes of Burgundy. Its members had included knights of the Golden Fleece and governors of the southern border provinces, where most of their estates lay. They were known for their inclination to plead for good relations with France. This was true, too, of William of Croy, whom Charles' father appointed governor-general of the Low Countries when he left for Spain in 1506. From 1509 he had an increasing say in the education of the young prince, who was generally described as rather slow and sometimes quick-tempered.

The court at Mechelen was still wholly Burgundian in style. Charles himself was strongly imbued with chivalric ideals such as had enjoyed a revival in tournaments, feasts and stories at the time of his great great-grandfather, Philip the Good. The emperor practised his knowledge of Castilian by making a translation of his favourite work, *Le chevalier délibéré*, an allegorical poem telling the story of the chivalric quest of the dukes Philip the Good, Charles the Bold and Mary of Burgundy. Olivier de la Marche, chronicler and ceremony master at the court of Burgundy, had completed the work in 1483, and very soon it went to a number of prints in both French and Dutch. At Charles' request, a version in verse was produced by the courtier Hernando de Alcuna, in more correct Castilian than the emperor could command, and was published by Jan Steels in Antwerp in 1553 and 1555.[14] The chivalric atmosphere at the court flourished once again during the week of festivities that Mary of Hungary organised at her castle at Binche in August 1549 in honour of the Joyous Entry of Prince Philip into each of the provinces of the Low Countries. The emperor and many members of the Order of the Golden Fleece were present. The chivalric romance, *Amadis de Gaulle*, was the source of inspiration for a game in which the knights had to disguise themselves and brave a series of dangers in order to set free Mary's courtiers, imprisoned in the *Château Ténébreux*, after pulling a sword, inlaid with pearls, from a stone. The last participant, and only winner, turned out to be none other than Philip who, having removed his disguise, was rewarded by Mary with the imperial laurels. She praised his moral strength that had broken the dark spell and freed the captives. The allegory provided a stage on which the high nobility showed by ritual means that they approved of the place of honour that Philip would in future occupy among them.[15]

The court at Mechelen was open to humanistic currents, which were embodied in the personal contacts with scholars, lawyers from the High Court – the highest court of the Low Countries had its seat in Mechelen – and professors from the University at Leuven. Among these professors was Adriaan Floriszoon Boeyens of Utrecht, who in 1512 was given special responsibility for Charles' education. He remained his spiritual advisor during the early years in Spain and was elected pope in 1522 through Charles' agency. Henry of Bergen, bishop of Cambrai, in whose see

Mechelen fell, was a brother of Charles' other godfather, John, lord of Bergen op Zoom. Working closely with the dowager Margaret of York the bishop made strenuous efforts to reform the monasteries and ensure their strict observance of the Rule. His secretary was Erasmus of Rotterdam, whose studies in Paris he paid for and whom he introduced at court. From the time of Charles' majority in 1515 Erasmus enjoyed the title of councillor, a stipend of 200 guilders and a canon's benefice. He remained in Leuven and close to the court in Brussels until October 1521. He was admitted to the University as professor of theology in 1517 and founded the College of Three Languages with the help of a legacy from the Mechelen lawyer, humanist and art-lover, Jerome van Busleyden. During the six years that Erasmus served as advisor to the young Charles, he wrote a number of political treatises, which I shall look at later. Although the young prince's artistic sensitivity was not so highly developed as that of his aunt Margaret, and he had fewer intellectual interests than his sister Mary, during his boyhood years he was imbued with a sincere ideal of inner devotion and convinced of the necessity of reforming the Catholic Church in that direction from within.

Roman King Maximilian used his six grandchildren as pawns in his political alliances, and Charles and the Habsburgs in general followed his lead in this. In 1513 Charles was betrothed to the sister of Henry VIII, Mary Tudor. A year later, however, she married the elderly king of France, Louis XII, who died within a few months. In 1521, during negotiations at Calais with Gattinara, Charles' grand chancellor, Cardinal Wolsey promised Henry's five-year-old daughter, the other Mary Tudor, as a possible bride for Charles. The uncertainty over this lasted for five years until Charles finally chose Isabella of Portugal for his bride. Eleanor was married to King Manuel I of Portugal, who had earlier been married to her aunt Isabella, a daughter of Ferdinand of Aragon. Charles' younger sister Isabella married Christian II of Denmark by proxy in 1514. One of Maximilian's ambitions was to strengthen his dynasty's grip on the kingdoms of Bohemia and Hungary. Bohemia had been the homeland of the German kings in the second half of the fourteenth century, which had resulted in its king being made elector. Together with Hungary, it was now ruled by Vladislav Jagiello, whose younger brother Sigismund was king of Poland. In a treaty in 1491 Maximilian had ensured that he would succeed Vladislav, should the latter die childless. However, Vladislav remarried and, as an old man, fathered a daughter in 1500 and a son in 1506. Even before the birth of the son, Maximilian had arranged a new treaty and a double marriage of the two Hungarian children with two of his Habsburg grandchildren. He was, of course, afraid of the claims of Sigismund who, through his marriage to a sister of the influential magnate, Johan Zápolya, could count on the strongly nationalistic and anti-Habsburg sentiments of the Hungarian nobility. By bringing military pressure to bear from the territory of the Teutonic Order in the north of Poland, as well as in Hungary itself, Maximilian was able to neutralise these rival claims. In July 1515 he received both kings in Vienna amidst great splendour, and the planned double wedding was so specified by treaty that Crown Prince Louis would marry Mary and Anna of Hungary would marry one of Maximilian's grandsons. He had Ferdinand in mind, but dared not mention him formally by name as he was under the guardianship of his other grandfather, the king of Aragon, after whom he was named. He preferred to reserve Charles for a more important bride from France or England, when the right moment arose.

After the death of Ferdinand of Aragon in January 1516, during the funeral ceremonies in Brussels on 13 March Charles had himself and his mother proclaimed as 'Catholic kings'.[16] On 22 April Charles informed his brother that he and their grandfather Maximilian had decided to marry him to Anna of Hungary.[17] To be on the safe side the marriage took place by proxy immediately, in Brussels. Maximilian had ordered Mary to leave Mechelen in May 1514 to learn German in Vienna and Innsbruck, and to get to know the traditions and history of the Habsburg dynasty. Most Hungarian nobles considered the Habsburg intrusion as an encroachment on their national independence, but balanced it against the substantial protection it should afford against Turkish attacks. Vladislav's death in 1516 intensified the confusion in Hungary because Louis, his successor, was barely ten years old. Maximilian's death in January 1519 led to delay on the side of the Habsburgs, too. It was only during the Diet of Worms in 1521 that a definitive agreement was reached with Charles as the new head of the Habsburg dynasty. In order to conciliate Hungarian concerns about a sufficiently large power base for the defence against the Turks, Charles abdicated his share of the hereditary Habsburg lands in favour of Ferdinand. Ferdinand, in turn, had to pledge his total commitment to the cause of the Habsburg dynasty.

In May 1521 Anna and Ferdinand were able to marry in Linz while the peasants of the Tirol were in revolt. The anarchy that was prevalent in Hungary and was further fanned by the Turkish advance and capture of Belgrade on 28 August delayed the marriage of 15-year-old Louis and the 16-year-old Mary. It eventually took place and was consummated in January 1522. Next year there were investitures for them in Bohemia, Moravia and Silesia and after laborious negotiations they managed to obtain a certain amount of support there against the Turks. All the agreements specifically stipulated that in the event of the young king dying without issue then his sister Anna and her consort would succeed to his rights.[18] After the disastrous Hungarian defeat at the battle of Mohács in 1526, where Louis was killed, the defence of the remains of the Hungarian kingdom fell to Anna and, on her behalf, Ferdinand. Despite all the obstacles, the Habsburgs had established themselves as a dynasty on a truly European scale.

The education of a Christian prince

At the suggestion of the chancellor of Brabant, Jean le Sauvage, in 1515 Erasmus composed a 'king's mirror' for the prince, who had just been declared of age; this was a traditional genre aimed at the personal, moral and political education of a young monarch. It included elementary rules for the control of bodily functions and table manners, as well as instruction in politics and policies. One wonders whether Charles had enough Latin fully to understand the implications of the text. He certainly had to learn Latin and used it for some of his correspondence, notably with the Hungarian court, although this was evidently a secretary's work. The work gives some idea of the sort of advice that Erasmus and the other advisors would have given to their young pupil.

Like so many humanistic scholars Erasmus had a deep-rooted belief in the influence and importance of education. For that reason 'children should be placed at the earliest age under the supervision of the most highly valued and honourable teachers so that they may acquire knowledge about Christ and enlightened scholarship that is in the best interests of the State. For, according to Plato, such is the effect of education, that if it is good it can make man an almost godly being, but in the opposite case, man will degenerate into a savage animal'. But 'nobody profits more from the study of Christ than a prince'. He should be freed from his physical impulses because 'not all parts of the spirit are of equal worth, for some command and others obey, and the body has only to obey. Thus the ruler who is the head of the State should be the wisest and the furthest removed from all impure feelings. Just as all forms of slavery are contemptible and shameful, so there is no worse thing than servility to one's own deficiencies and passions. A slave should not hold sway over free people.'

Of all the forms of government imaginable Erasmus considered the monarchy the most preferable because 'if a sovereign is in God's image then all things are equally under one head'. Nevertheless, the monarch holds an office of service, with a power granted and controlled by the people:

> Even if there were not a monarch there would always be a State. But a monarch cannot exist without a State. In short, the monarch presupposes the

State, but not vice versa. . . . If there were a monarch who possessed every virtue, then a pure, unrestricted monarchy would be desirable; if that will ever happen I do not know. Judging by the state of all human affairs it would be good and desirable if a ruler possessed average qualities. In such a case the monarchy can best be complemented, moderated and restrained by aristocracy and democracy so that it will not degenerate into tyranny but will keep the various elements in balance. If the monarch is well-intentioned towards the State he will see that this does not diminish his power but actually increases it; otherwise, it is good that there is something that will curb and break the power of the potentate. . . . The law over people is not the same as that over cattle. A large part of authority depends on the consent of the people, where the origins of kingship can be found.

In the Adagium, *War is Sweet for Him Who Does Not Know It*, that Erasmus dedicated to his patron, Antoine of Bergen, in 1514, he formulated the same idea even more succinctly: 'The same law does not apply to people, who are by nature free, as to cattle. The rights that you sovereigns possess are granted by the will of the people. But, if I am not mistaken, the giver can also take back, especially when his interests are not being served.'

The form of government that Erasmus envisaged was based on one where the citizens had some understanding of institutions and laws, 'for even the most humble people have common sense', an essential condition for officials to act wisely and honourably. 'In a free state the tongues must also be free.' Justice should be directed at counterbalancing Fortune, 'for it is the fate of the lowly to be exposed to wrong-doing'. The monarch should also strive 'to avoid exceptional inequality of wealth'. Like his friend Sir Thomas More, who was writing his famous *Utopia* at the same time, Erasmus pleaded for public establishments to care for the elderly and infirm, and for state education. 'Incomes can best be increased by putting an end to useless expenditure, dispensing with unnecessary services and avoiding wars . . ., holding the greed of public servants in check, aiming at adequate government rather than extending the state.'

His most fervent plea, often repeated, was for peace:

> Let the ruler consider how desirable, beautiful and salutory peace is, how disastrous and cursed war; what a flood of suffering is brought by even the most just war – if, indeed, any war can be called just. . . . Why do rulers not call mediators in if a quarrel arises between them? There are many bishops, abbots, scholars and magistrates who could provide better solutions than slaughter, pillage and universal tribulation. No ruler can punish his enemy without first attacking his own subjects. . . . Often the suffering that you inflict on your own people is crueller than that inflicted on the enemy. . . . Even against the Turks we should not take up arms without reflection, I believe. We should first consider that the kingdom of Christ was formed and enlarged entirely by other means. It is possible that it should not be enlarged by any means other than those through which it could originally grow and

expand. . . . Judging by the normal character of those now waging these wars, it is more likely that we shall degenerate to the level of the Turks than that the Turks will convert to Christianity.[19]

After the death of Julius II Erasmus had ridiculed the hawkish pope in an anonymous satirical pamphlet. Under the title *Julius Shut Out of Heaven* he makes the protagonist plead with Peter:

> I have reorganised financial policies, increased our revenues, conquered Venice, attacked Florence, driven the French out, and I would have driven the Spanish out too, if I had not come up here. I killed a few thousand French, broke treaties, celebrated great triumphs, put up expensive buildings, and left half a million ducats in the treasury. And I did none of this through my birth, for I do not know who my father was, nor through my scholarship, for that I do not have, nor through my popularity, for people hate me, nor through my kindness, for I was cruel. In Rome I was looked upon more as a god than a man.[20]

In 1517, at the instance of the Brabantine chancellor, Erasmus dedicated a distinctly pacifist work, his *Lament for Peace that is Scorned and Rejected by People Everywhere*, to the young Charles. Boldly, the humanist confronted rulers with their responsibilities, though without naming names:

> Let us look at the wars of the last twelve years. If we consider their causes then it must be obvious that they all started for the rulers' sake but were waged to the detriment of the people, for the people had not the slightest interest in them. . . . Now, the mere fact that a neighbouring state is more prosperous is almost seen as a legitimate reason for starting a war. Let us be honest: what other reason was there, and can there still be, for attacking France, except that it is by far the most flourishing of all lands?[21]

Some years later, in 1520, Erasmus accompanied Charles, by now Roman king and emperor elect, to a meeting at Gravelines with Henry VIII, who had just signed a pact of friendship with Francis I. His familiarity with the English aristocracy made him particularly suitable for such a diplomatic mission. It was the last occasion on which the ardent pacifist would act as an advisor in royal circles. In 1517 he had declined to follow Charles to Spain. He dedicated his Latin translation of the gospels to the four most prominent Christian princes of his day. He chose the Gospel of St Mark for Francis I, with the following dedication:

> From the depths of my heart I wish that every Christian monarch would truly consider, on the basis of real evidence, how much it would be to his advantage to choose an unjust peace in preference to the most just war.[22]

By the time that war broke out between Charles and Francis, Erasmus had already left court and moved to Basle.

Mission impossible?

Erasmian thought is assumed to have been strongly represented among the Dutch advisors surrounding Charles in Spain. In that context there springs immediately to mind the part played by Adrian of Utrecht, by now a cardinal and bishop of Tortosa, who was regent in Spain during Charles' absences. He died, however, in 1523, and others gained influence with the young king. In 1527 a Spanish translation of Erasmus' *Enchiridion militis christiani*, the 'Handbook of a Christian Soldier', appeared; this had first been published in 1503, enjoyed widespread popularity after 1515, and ten years later had been translated into five vernacular languages. The Spanish version was dedicated to no less a person than the grand inquisitor and archbishop of Seville, Alonso Manrique, one of the emperor's first Spanish confidants. The archbishop of Toledo, Alonso de Fonseca, who had baptised the young Prince Philip, the grand chancellor Mercurino di Gattinara and his secretaries, Alonso and Juan Valdés, were also among Erasmus' admirers. Through them, an interest in reading the gospels, the desire to conciliate and an endeavour to mediate between different religious persuasions, as well as the link between theology and humanism, became widespread through diverse sectors and layers of Spanish society, and had the support of the highest court circles. The *Enchiridion*, a theory about the divine seed that indicates spiritual reformation, contained criticism of monasticism and the institutional Church and was later put on the Index of proscribed books.[23]

Most polemic pieces, some of which have been mentioned above, did not really belong to the Erasmian tradition in Spain, which rather consisted of law-abiding works aimed at assimilation.[24] In any case, the courtiers took little notice of Erasmus' caution to 'check the greed of public servants'. It was in fact Erasmus' patron, Jean le Sauvage, who, with others, immediately made himself extremely unpopular by using royal privilege to appropriate the revenue taxes on the export of fruit from the kingdom of Granada, and then leasing them out for nine years for 168,000 ducats.[25] Whether Charles actually paid much heed to the wise admonition that aristocracy and democracy could correct the monarch's human frailties remains to be seen. He certainly retained the message of peace as an ideal in his mind, yet he was almost constantly thinking about the wars that he believed he had to fight, and he hastened to take up arms without first taking recourse to any form of mediation. Unhampered by any feelings of remorse, he sowed death and destruction in diverse lands for very obscure purposes. Could he have acted differently, more along the lines advised by his scholarly counsellor?

What opportunities did this Charles have to influence the course of history? He lived in a time full of discoveries, surprises and expectations. The world seemed larger, and yet more accessible, than had been thought for centuries. Thanks to the calculations of his forefathers and the whim of the dynasty's fate, he came to stand at the head of more, vaster territories than any ruler in Europe between 400 and 1800. For nearly forty years 40 per cent of all Europeans were his subjects. His lands contained the most productive silver mines and the greatest trading centres of Europe, and the treasures of the Indians too. Seldom in Europe was so much power concentrated for so many decades in the hands of one man. If he had such a passionate desire for peace, as he repeatedly declared, could he not then have brought about a more enduring one? Were, as he claimed, only his enemies responsible for the almost continual wars, which in the long run brought him so little? His personal qualities made little impression on contemporary observers. Would a more astute mind, perhaps, have been better able to achieve those objectives? Or were they beyond the reach of even the best-equipped ruler in the first half of the sixteenth century? Did the structures of the states encourage oppression and the almost inevitable wars, while individuals played but a marginal role? And yet, at the same time, did not Charles' era see some individuals pit their religious conscience against the authority of the universal Church and gain a great following in a very short time?

The times and world of Charles V formed a tight web of frictions and ambitions. To realise the ideals of a Christian monarch was a unique challenge. Were those ideals too sublime, or were they perhaps outdated? Was it simply that the exceptional concentration of material resources in the hands of the emperor made it impossible to achieve such lofty objectives? Or was it just the implementation that failed? Finding an answer to these questions seems to be an exercise in what really decides the course of history: individuals, structures or material resources?

Notes:

1. L. Voet and J. Voet-Grisolle, *The Plantin Press*, 6 vols (Amsterdam, 1980–83), no. 939A, 605–8; J. Jacquot, 'Panorama des fêtes et cérémonies du règne', in J. Jacquot, ed., *Fêtes et cérémonies au temps de Charles Quint* (Paris, 1960), 467–72, 490–1; S. Schrader, ' "Greater than Ever He Was". Ritual and Power in Charles V's 1558 Funeral Procession', *Netherlands Yearbook for History of Art*, 49 (1998), 69–93.
2. F. W. H. Hollstein, *Dutch and Flemish Etchings, Engravings and Woodcuts, c. 1450–1700* (Amsterdam, 1949–) vol. 4, 231, vol. 8, 24; I. M. Veldman and G. Luijten, eds, *The New Hollstein*, 'Maarten van Heemskerk' (Amsterdam, 1994),

Vol. 2, 200–11; B. van den Boogert and J. Kerkhoff, *Maria van Hongarije: Koningin tussen keizers en kustenaars 1505–1558* (Zwolle, 1993), 260–2.
3. R. W. Scheller, 'Jan Gossaerts Triomfwagen', in A. M. Logan, ed., *Essays in Northern European Art presented to Egbert Haverkamp-Begeman* (Doornspijk, 1983), 228–36; L. Duerloo and W. Thomas, *Albrecht en Isabella, 1598–1621* (Brussels, 1998), cat. no. 287. The ship is pictured here in the Brussels Procession of 1615, together with other floats from the time of Charles V.
4. G. Parker, *Philip II* (Boston and Toronto, 1978), 63.
5. Kohler, *Karl V.*, 354.
6. Schrader, ' "Greater Than Ever He Was" ', 86.
7. K. Brandi, *Kaiser Karl V. Werden und Schicksal einer Persönlichkeit und eines Weltreiches. Quellen und Erörterungen*, Vol. 1 (Munich, 1937), 52.
8. *Welt im Umbruch: Augsburg zwischen Renaissance und Barock*, Vol. 1: *Zeughaus* (Augsburg, 1980), 538–83.
9. Fernandez Alvarez, *Carlos V*, 811–24.
10. Jean Molinet, *Chroniques (1474–1506)*, vol. 3 (Brussels 1937), 468–70.
11. H. Wiesflecker, *Kaiser Maximilian I.*, vol. 2 (Munich, 1975), 32–43.
12. E. Schreurs, ed., *De schatkamer van Alamire. Muziek en miniaturen uit keizer Karels tijd,1500–1535*, exh. cat. (Leuven, 1999), 88–110; H. Kellman, ed., *The Treasury of Petrus Alamire. Music and Art in Flemish Court Manuscripts, 1500–1535*, exh. cat.(Ghent and Amsterdam, 1999), 66–165.
13. M. Debae, *La Librairie de Marguerite d'Autriche* (Brussels, 1987), xvi–xxiii.
14. P. Cockshaw, C. Lemaire *et al.*, *Charles le Téméraire, 1433–1477* (Brussels, 1977), 120–3.
15. E. Peters, '1549 Knight's Game at Binche: Constructing Philip II's Ideal Identity in a Ritual of Honor', *Netherlands Yearbook for History of Art*, 49 (1998), 11–35.
16. Brandi, *Kaiser Karl V.*, 52.
17. M. Fernandez Alvarez, *Corpus documental de Carlos V*, vol. I: *1516–1539* (Salamanca, 1973), 74 n.26.
18. L. V. G. Gorter-van Royen, *Maria van Hongarije regentes der Nederlanden* (Hilversum, 1995) 53–76; Wiesflecker, *Maximilian I.*, vol. 4 (Vienna, 1981), 181–204, 569.
19. Erasmus, *Institutio Principis Christiani* in *Opera Omnia*, IV, 1 (Amsterdam, 1974), 194–204; translation P. E. Corbett (London, 1922), 25–62; Adagium: *Dulce Bellum Inexpertis* in *Opera Omnia*, IV, 1, 146–8.
20. R. H. Bainton, *Erasmus of Christendom* (London, 1965), 134.
21. *Querela Pacis*, in *Opera Omnia*, IV, 2 (Amsterdam, 1977), 1–100.
22. J.-C. Margolin, *Guerre et paix dans la pensée d'Erasme* (Paris, 1973), 268.
23. Brandi, *Kaiser Karl V.*, 223–4; C. Augustijn, *Erasmus* (Baarn, 1986), 40–51.
24. M. Bataillon, *Erasme et l'Espagne* (Paris, 1937; republished in 3 vols, Geneva 1991); S. Seidel Menchi, 'Do we need the 'Ism'? Some Mediterranean Perspectives', M. E. H. N. Mout *et al.*, eds, *Erasmianism: Idea and Reality* (Amsterdam, 1997), 57.
25. S. Haliczer, *The Comuneros of Castile: The Forging of a Revolution, 1475–1526* (Madison, 1981), 138.

2
A grand strategy?

Territories and dynasty

In 1525 Emperor Charles V had 72 official titles, including 27 kingdoms (20 of them in Spain alone), 13 duchies, 22 counties and nine seigniories. A few more in the Low Countries would be added later. As he himself said, more crowns than his poor head could bear. Some of the titles had only a symbolic significance, such as that of duke of Athens and king of Jerusalem, which dated from the time of the crusades. He still held the title of duke of Burgundy, although Burgundy had been under French rule since 1477. In the agreements of 1521 and 1522 he had transferred all the hereditary Austrian lands to his brother Ferdinand. Nevertheless, the relative titles appeared at the beginning of his documents.[1] The abundance of titles reflected above all the variety of legal foundations for the exercise of power that had been created in the course of centuries of hereditary successions, unions and divisions.

Some of these territories had a long history of internal political unity, such as the kingdoms of Naples and Sicily, or of alliance through proximity, such as the kingdoms of León and Castile. In other cases, the dynastic union was of more recent date: that of Castile and Aragon, for example, which had been governed jointly since the marriage of their 'Catholic kings', Isabella and Ferdinand, in 1474, but which were ruled by one and the same king only on the accession of Charles. Ferdinand united the crowns of Aragon and Naples in 1504. From 1384 to 1543 the principalities of the Low Countries were ruled by the dukes of Burgundy; the fates of a number of them, such as Artois and Guelders, were changeable, and during Charles' reign another six 'provinces' would be acquired in the region. Above all, in 1500 the union of the Habsburg Burgundian lands with those of the Spanish crown could be expected, although it did not take place until 1516 and 1519, with the successive deaths of Charles' grandfathers, Ferdinand and Maximilian. Charles' empire as a whole was new, and most of its component parts enjoyed a longer tradition of autonomy than of unity. With the concept of an imperial state in view, he tried to remodel the old principalities into a more centrally governed empire, but in reality it proved to be very hard to manage.

These traditions of autonomy were expressed in written and unwritten law, in rights and customs that were granted, imposed and took shape in the collective consciousness of a political community over the centuries. At his investiture every new ruler had to swear to respect and uphold the laws and customs of the land. This he did in the presence of the representatives of the people who could come together, in whatever chosen construction, to demand that their privileges be maintained. The assemblies, which were known as parliaments in Naples, Sicily and Sardinia, *cortes* in the Spanish kingdoms, *Ständetage* in the German territories, and *standen*, *états* or states in the Low Countries, met no more than once a year. They formed the institutions established through centuries-old tradition that gave voice to the political and statutory identity of the people.

The fragmented pattern of political units reflected the stormy history of their creation; it set into an institutional frame a vast number of events and structural facts which led to political formations, in some cases extensive and in others minuscule. Geographical conditions played an extremely important part in this, of course; they influenced the establishment of spiritual and secular centres of power, opportunities for communication, and the interaction with other entities. It all helped to shape regional cultures, languages, legal traditions and historical awareness. In the eleventh century the Norman conquerors had brought relatively centralised government apparatus to the very varied cultural substrata of Sicily and Naples. This unity was absent in the alpine lands of Austria, which never underwent that sort of foreign invasion.

It was, therefore, utterly inconceivable for Charles to strive for unity of government across such a plurality of territories. The enormous variety of political and legal traditions was a hindrance, the barriers of language were too high, and sixteenth-century means of communication made it impossible. Ultimately, the unity of Charles' empire was vested in his person, who, under various titles, was ruler in every land. By extension, the Habsburg dynasty can be seen as the critical factor in the creation of unity. All medieval monarchs had marriage policies and Charles' grandfather, Maximilian, was no exception. The simple fact was that the German Empire was very extensive and situated in central Europe, so that it had many neighbours. Royal weddings were useful to stabilise relationships, to make good relationships permanent, and to restrict conflicts. Negotiations over possible marriages were a continuous part of planning an alliance or speculating about the transfer of territory. Conditions for the dowry and the succession of any possible male or female issue were a fixed ingredient.

Women in particular were the vulnerable pawns in this man's game. The fate of Charles' aunt, Catherine of Aragon, whom Henry VIII divorced, was miserable; for years it was the cause of great tension in international relationships and in relationships between Church and State. The fate of Charles' second sister, Isabella, was also painful; she was publicly insulted by the adultery of her 22-year-older consort, Christian II of Denmark. When he was removed from his throne in 1523, he sought help in the Low Countries from his brother-in-law, Charles, for his war against the Hanseatic towns. Charles supported him, even though it was not in the commercial interests of the Low Countries. After ten years of marriage, Isabella died at the age of twenty-five; her children remained at Mechelen in the care of the regent Margaret, in exchange for the discharge of Christian's debts. Christian remained a thorn in the Habsburg flesh until well into the 1530s. Personally and dynastically, the affair was a fiasco.

Charles' eldest sister, Eleanor, the widow since 1521 of Manuel I of Portugal, was also in a delicate position. In the context of the Spanish–Portuguese weddings she was married in 1519 to Manuel, who had previously been married to her aunts, Isabella and Mary, daughters of Ferdinand of Aragon. Manuel died in 1521 after Eleanor had borne him two children, of whom only Mary, the youngest, born in that year, survived. The Habsburg marriage politics now required Eleanor's disposability in other areas. She had to leave her small daughter in Portugal and would not see her again until she returned to Spain near the end of her life. Mary, known as *La Abandonada*, the abandoned one, could only be persuaded to meet her with the greatest difficulty. Under the Treaty of Madrid of January 1526 Eleanor was to marry Francis I, whom she met during the last weeks of his captivity in Spain. Once safely back in his kingdom Francis dissociated himself from the treaty, and once again war broke out between her brother and her betrothed. In the spring of 1528 Eleanor retired in desperation to a convent. On 7 July 1530, however, she did marry Francis I, but was unable to bear him children. She had to put up with the king's open visits to his various mistresses and the honour he paid them in public. This was especially true of Anne d'Heilly who, as duchess of Etampes, enjoyed a particularly influential position at court for the rest of Francis' life.[2] Eleanor was unable to stop Francis from fighting a number of wars against her brother Charles, which made her own position extremely stressful. A letter written by the queen in her own hand to her brother on 1 September 1544 is particularly characteristic: she expressed her unutterable delight that he and Francis had entered into peace talks after confronting each other with enormous armies for months on end, and Henry VIII had invaded in the north. She expressed the hope that this would be the beginning of a long, certain peace.[3] This emotional note was played at the most sensitive moment. After Francis' death in 1547, she joined her sister Mary in Brussels, and would finally die with her and Charles in Spain, all three in 1558.

Charles also made use of his dynasty to exercise his authority in the form of temporary regencies during his travels abroad and lengthy governorships in distant regions. He demanded not only total loyalty to the dynasty from members of his house, but also their subordination to him as its head. He stipulated this when he appointed his brother Ferdinand governor in the German Empire in 1521; this loyal relationship lasted for thirty years. When he left for Spain in 1517 he appointed his aunt Margaret to be regent again in the Low Countries, on the warm recommendation of Maximilian. Subject to various conditions, she had fulfilled this function during the years of his minority from 1507 to 5 January 1515 – Epiphany, and the day that Maximilian had chosen to proclaim his grandson's majority. Her princely position was further recognised when she was granted Franche-Comté, the free imperial county of Burgundy. This experienced woman was subtle enough to safeguard her own freedom of action even while formally recognising the full authority of her nephew. Mary, her successor, managed this even better, because as his five-year-younger sister she had no problem in recognising Charles as her sovereign; within the affectionate intimacy of their relationship, she used her superior intellect to let her own views prevail. Empress Isabella was naturally Charles' regent in Spain during his long absences; later, their son Philip and daughter Mary and her consort Maximilian would fulfil these functions.

The difficulty encountered by Charles' regents was in balancing his ambitions and orders, dictated by his overall strategy, with the realities of the regions. For his subjects, it was not the overall dynastic solidarity that counted, only their loyalty to the ruler of their territory. The sense of identity extended only very faintly beyond the local and territorial level.

A common demand of the representatives of the people was that they did not wish to be governed by foreign officials. A foreigner was anyone coming from outside the boundaries of the territory, a Castilian in Valencia, for example, or someone from Hainault in Flanders. Provision for this had been incorporated in the constitution of Brabant since the fourteenth century, sworn by the duke at his Joyous Entry and named after it. The parliament in Naples frequently pressed for a similar agreement but could do nothing to alter the fact that the viceroys were always foreigners: from 1522 to 1528, Charles of Lannoy, from 1528 to1530, Philibert of Chalon and, from 1532 to 1553, Pedro de Toledo. The regents in the Low Countries, Margaret and Mary, were accepted as indigenous. Ferdinand had spent his childhood in Spain and had to make an effort to assimilate in the Low Countries in 1518 and to the German Empire after 1521. But assimilate he did, stayed in the territory, identified with it, and was gradually accepted as 'German'. The people were willing to accept that their ruler, or his highest deputy, was a foreigner, as long as he did not bring foreign officials with him. Charles did that in Spain in 1517; his officials took the most important and lucrative positions so shamelessly for themselves that the wrath it kindled in the Spaniards was one of the causes of the revolt of the *comuneros*. For years the *cortes* opposed the foreigners, always from the Low Countries, but Charles got round the objections to some extent by giving them papers of naturalisation. As king in a foreign country he naturally needed advisors whom he could trust completely and who would ensure that his 'higher' interests took priority over regional ones.

The tension between Charles' imperial and dynastic vision and that of his subjects could be seen in their general unwillingness to pay for wars in what they considered foreign countries. In 1536, when the Franco-Habsburg war flared up again on all fronts, the representatives from Holland to the States General of the Low Countries declared that they were not prepared to win Italy for the emperor, nor Denmark for the count palatine Frederick (who was married to one of the daughters of Christian II and Isabella of Habsburg). The States of Flanders had their own point of view: they said that the Low Countries were not rich enough to help the emperor conquer France and Italy.[4] There could be a wide chasm between dynastic interests, as defined by Charles, and the interests of the individual lands; this was quite evident in the tense relationship with Denmark, purely dynastic in origin, which caused serious damage to the commercial interests of the Low Countries.

The Dutch provinces nevertheless loyally authorised the exceptionally high taxes asked, albeit under protest. Similarly, Naples and Sicily carried a large part of the financial burden of the wars in Lombardy and Piedmont, and the lion's share of all the efforts fell on the Castilian treasury. The parliaments and *cortes* protested consistently against the massive outflow of their capital for wars in other lands: each time, the government was obliged to make concessions that in turn strengthened the position of the local leaders. In Naples, in 1536, they received compensation for 55 of their complaints, *capitoli*, in exchange for the heaviest taxation ever imposed in that kingdom.[5] In order to pursue its dynastic objectives the central government continually had to concede some power, which meant that its attempts at centralising administration were constantly thwarted.

Charles' *imperium* consisted of many, extensive, mostly prosperous, regions, but there was continual friction between his ambitions and those of prominent subjects. In order to persuade them to satisfy his ever-increasing requests for military, and especially financial, support for his dynastic objectives, Charles had to tolerate the weakening of his authority in every part of the empire in favour of local and regional elites.

The Holy Roman Empire

This paradox was felt most keenly in the German Empire. When the seven electors unanimously elected Charles emperor in Frankfurt-am-Main on 28 June 1519, they bestowed on him the highest position of secular power in the West. The German king – whom they actually elected – was the only person whom the pope would consider crowning as Roman emperor. The Empire included – in addition to the German lands, together with Holstein and Prussia stretching with Riga to the Gulf of Finland – Bohemia, Moravia and Silesia, and bordered with Krajina on the Adriatic; in the west, the free county of Burgundy (Franche-Comté) and Savoy belonged to it, and in Italy, Genoa, Lombardy and Tuscany. The greater part of the Low Countries, with the exception of Artois and Flanders to the west of the Scheldt, formed part of it. It took a whole month to travel through the Empire from north to south or from east to west.

In all the peripheral areas of the Empire there had been a tendency towards independence for many centuries. The Italian republics and territories had already fought the emperors of the house of Hohenstaufen for autonomy. The dukes and counts of the Low Countries took little notice of the emperor. He had been unable to put an end to Burgundy's expansion in the first half of the fifteenth century. The land of the Teutonic Knights in Prussia had been under the suzerainty of the kings of Poland since 1466, although its grandmasters, such as Albrecht of Brandenburg-Ansbach, who took office in 1511, tried to withdraw from it with the support of the emperor and the Empire. When it was secularised and became a temporal duchy in 1525 Prussian ties with the Empire were cut. The Swiss Confederation had come into being at the end of the thirteenth century, as a defence system against the growing power of the Habsburgs in the region. The differences were sharpened by the fact that, from 1438, the Habsburgs were German kings. Maximilian's attempt to join forces with the Swabian League against the Swiss ended in a crushing defeat in 1499. The ties were not formally broken, but the members of the Confederation had their ancient liberties confirmed and were indemnified against further interference from the Empire; after 1531 they never again appeared at a

Diet. In the north, the duchy of Holstein was allowed to form an indissoluble alliance with Danish Schleswig.

In the light of this territorial disintegration it is easy to understand why Maximilian, and Charles and Ferdinand after him, made the utmost effort to acquire and retain Bohemia and Hungary, and were so anxious to keep France out of Savoy, Piedmont and Milan. In reality, it was more a matter of dynastic interests than of state policy, but the difference was becoming increasingly blurred.

The elite of the German Empire often used the term 'German nation', which was grafted on to the emperorship (although those roots were in fact Italian) and a certain communality of language. During the 1520s some political commentators emphasised the dire situation in which the nation found itself, either as a result of the suppression of religious freedom or the threat from the Turks. Time and again the political reality showed that it was exceptionally difficult to achieve any extraterritorial solidarity, or even co-operation.[6]

The German king, or Roman king, was elected, but the imperial honour was only fully secured with his coronation by the pope, in principle in Rome. Despite intensive efforts, Maximilian never succeeded in making the journey to Rome and achieving the desired results. This was partly because his relationship with the pope did not offer any prospect of a favourable outcome. Julius II, the martial pope whom Erasmus shut out of Heaven, did not care to endanger his own position in Italy by strengthening the authority of the Roman king. Finally, in 1508, Maximilian had himself proclaimed 'elected Roman emperor' in the cathedral at Trent. Charles was given this title straight away at his coronation at Aachen in 1520, because the electors were not keen to place the imperial dignity entirely in the hands of popes whose impartiality was no longer generally recognised.

The Roman king, whether named emperor or not, did not have much power on account of his position. On the contrary, the electors took such care to attach so many conditions to the choice that they gradually became de facto co-regents of the Empire. The *Wahlkapitulationen*, the chapters for the election, had already been printed and circulated before Charles' coronation and formed a frame of reference to which the emperor could be kept.[7] As the highest liege lord in the Empire he could demand the fealty of his vassals and settle disputes following feudal law: this was an extremely archaic instrument of power. The emperor exercised his authority over dozens of towns that were directly dependent on the Empire. The German Empire was barely acquainted with the beginnings of a central administration that was still in the hands of one of the electors, the archbishop of Mainz, who was also traditionally arch-chancellor. There was no regular taxation, and certainly no standing army. In all such institutional developments the German Empire lagged far behind England, France, Castile and the Burgundian Low Countries, for example.

It was not until 1495 that the Diet began to function on a regular basis as the highest organ in the German Empire for legislation and political decision-making. The arch-chancellor, the elector-archbishop of Mainz, was responsible for the organisation and administration of the Diet. Unlike other principalities, where the ruler's chancellor was an official dependent on his king or prince, this elector fulfilled a triple function that made him almost unassailable. He was able to perform his administrative tasks in the light of his role as elector and prince of the Church. At a time of religious differences the consequences of this were clearly evident. Whereas Henry VIII could liquidate the cardinal–chancellor Wolsey, such a fate was inconceivable for the elector-archbishop–arch-chancellor.

The constitutional structure of the Empire was extremely complicated. At the level of both the Empire and the individual principalities there was a duality between the monarch and the representation of the estates; in addition, diverse relationships were directly dependent on the Empire. At the level of the Diet most of the representatives were themselves territorial princes. Its three branches functioned alongside each other, but making decisions required the agreement of at least the first two estates. The first College of the Diet consisted of the six electors (when Ferdinand became king of Bohemia he could no longer represent that electorate before the Empire and the emperor). The second was made up of the bishops, counts and lords. To the third group belonged the towns, which had an advisory voice, but which provided a substantial contribution to the approved financial expenses of the Empire.

During Charles' reign the Diet assembled almost every year. In his absences the emperor and the Diet of Worms in 1521 provided for the institution of the *Reichsregiment* (Regency Council), consisting of Ferdinand as imperial governor and 22 members representing the estates. Until 1530 this was the most important governing body in the Empire. Because the princes sent their advisors as representatives it was increasingly composed of the lower nobility and lawyers from the bourgeoisie. In that circle this led to the beginnings of a rationalised administrative machinery at the level of the Empire which could free itself from the estates. In the light of the complex and often technical questions raised, after 1521 the emperor insisted on the formation of committees with a limited number of members from each of the six branches of which the Diet, within the Colleges, was composed: the six electors, the 70 spiritual and secular rulers, the 70 prelates, some 120 counts and lords, and about 65 imperial towns. In this way the emperor clearly hoped to achieve a more effective, centralising, decision-making process, more open to his influence than was possible in the plenary sessions. The defence against the Turks, for example, required adequate financial and military organisation. It was therefore decided in principle that an imperial tax, *der gemeine Pfennig*, would be levied on all the estates, following a fixed proportional system, in order to finance the imperial army. With regard to public order, under Maximilian, steps were taken, such as the guarantee of national peace, whereby private wars or feuds between princes and institutions directly subordinate to the Empire were in principle declared illegal. An imperial court of justice, the *Reichskammergericht*, was established to punish breaches of the law in the name of the Diet. In practice, the estates in the various territories showed little inclination to allow their financial prerogatives to be thwarted by those of the Empire. The finances for the army were transformed into quotas of horsemen and lansquenets, the execution of judgements of the *Reichskammergericht* ran into serious opposition from the large principalities in the north and east. At the Diet of 1512 efforts were made to introduce regional alliances on the basis of the older leagues, to be responsible for the enforcement of public order and the execution of the verdicts of the *Reichskammergericht*. These 'Imperial Circles' grouped various territories together, with the exception of the hereditary Habsburg lands and Bohemia, and were expected to raise the money required to carry out the policies of the Empire. In the course of time they would come to acquire some political significance, although the great principalities in the east, Saxony and Bavaria in particular, remained unassailable. The great political crises faced by the Empire in the 1520s (almost entirely without the involvement of the emperor who was occupied in Spain with the Italian and French questions), including the revolt of the Imperial Knights in 1524, the Peasants' War in 1525–26 and the Reformation, put an end to the attempts to centralise the power of government at the imperial level.[8]

The prestigious title of Roman emperor could only be given substance by the application of the imperial dynasty's own resources, its *Hausmacht*, and through tedious negotiations with the Diet. In both the first and second Colleges Catholic prelates had the greatest influence: this gave the emperor some support in religious issues. On the other hand, the strong autonomy of the territorial princes meant that they would only make minimum funds available at the central level, and then only in return for compliance with their demands. Even the powerful Catholic dukes of Bavaria never gave their full support to the religious policies of the emperor, because they considered their main role should be to oppose the Habsburgs, their territorial neighbours. These relationships of power explain why the emperor was able to achieve so little in the immense region to which he owed his highest title.

Strategic options

Charles' lands were very extensive and situated far from each other: this caused immense problems in the protection of their borders and in communications. Normally, it took three weeks for a letter from Valladolid to reach the cities of north Italy, four weeks to Brussels and six to Vienna. In 1504, in response to the Castilian succession, the Taxis family had started a direct courier service between Spain and the Low Countries: 106 stages with at least two horses ensured the connection straight across France. In 1516 Charles reached an agreement with the Taxis company for guaranteed delivery times for his correspondence to Spain, Germany and Italy. Two years later, an agreement was reached with Francis I to allow their couriers diplomatic immunity and unhindered passage in times of peace.[9] Control of the free county of Burgundy and the alliance with the adjacent duchy of Savoy were of particular importance to the Habsburgs, because this gave them an assured line of communication when they were at war with France. France, on the other hand, was surrounded by Habsburg lands and must have felt threatened by the union of so many neighbouring lands under one hand which held, moreover, the formal right of the Empire to intervene in northern and central Italy. Conversely, the French lands posed a constant obstacle to Charles, hindering communications between his territories. France enjoyed the advantages of a compact territory and relatively centralised administrative institutions.

Charles experienced more than just the disadvantages of the slowness of communications between his diverse territories; he also found it necessary to move as often as possible to those regions where his presence could least be spared. It has been estimated that between 1517 and 1555 Charles spent one day out of every four travelling.[10] The king's absence was felt almost everywhere as a loss because, as he wanted to make all decisions himself, it resulted in enormous delays in the decision process. The appointment of regents, viceroys and governors resolved the problem only to a limited extent, witness the busy, extensive and detailed correspondence between the emperor and his representatives. Charles only spent time in Naples and Sicily in 1535–36. In 1516–17 Spain had to press for a long time to see the new king, who left again in May 1520 for his coronation in Aachen: this created bad feeling in Valencia where he had not yet appeared before the *cortes*. From July 1522 he remained in Spain, the very heart of his possessions, for a full seven years, but then long absences followed. He did not set foot there from 1543 until his abdication in 1556. Before 1543 he had only made three visits, each of a few months, to the Empire. Only Brussels was host to Charles for longer than 1100 days, or three years, in the course of his entire life. He resided for more than 365 days in Valladolid, Madrid, Toledo, Monzón and Barcelona and in Augsburg and Regensburg. His main travelling routes went from there to the seas and through Lombardy along the Rhine and the Danube.[11] Further, his itinerary shows a strong concentration in north, south and central Castile. Charles was increasingly confronted with all the problems of government by remote control and the heavy burden that the journeys placed on him personally, on his marriage and on his household. It is no coincidence that the only palace he had built, in the Alhambra in Granada, remained unfinished and unoccupied.

Because France was closed in by Habsburg possessions, and Charles literally found it difficult to avoid France, for more than 30 years the two most powerful sovereigns of the western world were involved in a fateful confrontation. This geopolitical fact had an extra dimension in that the two adversaries had at their disposal resources of people, capital and military strength in concentrations never before seen. Their personalities could not be ignored either. They belonged to the same generation, and not only did they know each other well but, in a sense, they also respected each other. The five-and-a-half-year-older Francis was physically superior and more charismatic than Charles, who was pallid and slow, with a lower jaw that was too large, a mouth that hung open, and indistinct speech. During some periods, certainly until their rivalry to be elected Roman king in 1519, and during their joint visit to the castles of the Loire and through Paris in 1539, when Francis was married to Charles' eldest sister Eleanor, they enjoyed very cordial relations. Geopolitically, France and the Habsburg lands were the two European super powers that could not ignore each other. The Habsburgs had the advantage of a larger population and more land, but the disadvantage of these lands being scattered.

The period in which Charles V lived was characterised by a general increase in population. In about 1550, according to a cautious estimate, circa 70 million people lived in western and central Europe, eight and a half million more than in 1500, and an increase of 14 per cent. At 23 per cent the Low Countries showed the strongest increase, Italy and Spain with 8½ per cent and 9 per cent respectively were obviously below average, while Austria and Bohemia with 3 per cent barely kept up with the trend. Measured in terms of population France, with 19 million inhabitants, was the largest country in Europe, followed by the German Empire and Italy with 14 and 11.4 million respectively. Politically speaking these last two powers were not so significant because they were divided into several, almost autonomous, units. Some three million people must have lived in the XVII Provinces of the Low Countries, seven and a half million in Spain. The censuses of the kingdom of Naples show that its population almost doubled between 1505 and 1561, when it was just under two million. Sicily reached one million in 1570, Milan and its duchy had 800,000 inhabitants in 1542. The Iberian kingdoms, south Italy and the state of Venice achieved a marked growth in population throughout the whole of the sixteenth century, but growth was weak in north and central Italy, continually devastated by wars and economic crises. If all those who could call themselves Charles' subjects were to be counted they would total more than 28 million, or 40 per cent of the population of west and central Europe. The Habsburgs' other great rival, Sultan Sulaimān, counted 13 million subjects in about 1530, a number that increased sharply during the following decades. Henry VIII could call himself king of four million English, Welsh and Irish.[12]

The size and population of a country does not say very much about its wealth, and certainly nothing about the state's ability to appropriate a substantial part of that wealth for itself. Throughout the entire sixteenth century state revenue from taxes grew far more strongly than population and price inflation, which is undeniable evidence of an increased creaming off of wealth from the people. The fiscal capacity of a region had a considerable influence on its military position. Above all, the rapid availability of a lot of ready cash in the theatre of war decided the generals' ability to pay their troops, retain them and be assured of their loyalty. Charles was exceptionally fortunate in that all the great financial centres in the west were situated in his empire. To Antwerp, Seville and Augsburg were added Milan, Genoa and Florence in 1525, 1528 and 1530 respectively. These towns were home to the great trading and banking houses, which could rapidly arrange monetary transactions all over Europe. Their credit had been a powerful support for Charles during the imperial election. He continued to appeal to them, and to the financial markets in general, right up to the end of his reign, enabling him to mobilise more money, more quickly, than his rivals. In the beginning, the great merchants and financiers saw many advantages in the protection of such a great empire that could help them to improve their relations with the centres of growth at the time. In the first half of the sixteenth century the economic core regions were in north Italy, south Germany, Catalonia, Castile and her colonies, and the Low Countries. The dynastic union made commercial dealings between all those centres of growth much easier. Such strong commercialisation brought a double advantage: the availability of large amounts of credit and strong fiscal capacity in those areas.

Over a half-century the average tax revenues of most western European states roughly doubled, but during war years expenditure suddenly increased to two or even three times the normal level. Although expenditure later fell as the troops were disbanded and their pay stopped, the loans that had been taken out still had to be repaid at a high rate of interest, so that the war continued to influence the budget for many years. In spite of all these fluctuations, and although the data is not always conveniently available, it is none the less worthwhile to compare the fiscal might of the most important states at the beginning of the sixteenth century. The accounting unit used is the number of tonnes (1000 kg.,) of pure silver represented by total state expenditure.[13]

Individually, France clearly had the most resources, followed by Castile, England and Venice. Dynastic unions, however, caused the balance to swing in favour of the Habsburgs (to which could be added revenues from Aragon, Sicily and possibly the German lands). The modest budgets of the German principalities form a glaring contrast to those below. This was true, too, of the hereditary Habsburg lands, although they benefited from the exploitation of silver and copper mines; the county of Württemberg, a temporary Habsburg possession, had three tonnes, and the margravate of Hesse one tonne. In the German Empire as a whole regular taxation had been introduced only briefly before 1500; by then it produced about five tonnes. On the other hand the Swiss Confederation represented five tonnes, and the imperial city of Nuremberg two tonnes.

The figures show clearly the strategic options available to those in power at the beginning of the sixteenth century. Had France managed to take Naples and Lombardy and keep Genoa, Piedmont and Savoy as allies, then she could have won the hegemony over Europe, with a fiscal capacity of about 155 tonnes of silver. In contrast, the Habsburg lands would have had no more than 135 tonnes. But in this hypothesis too, the bipolar system of power, whereby alliances with smaller, strategically placed partners could upset the balance, would play a part. The states in question were England and Venice which, in the face of a Franco-Italian hegemony, would,

Table 2.1 Expenditure by the largest states c.1500, in tonnes of silver

HABSBURG		OTHERS	
Castile	12–76	France	42–91
Low Countries	27	England	17–44
Naples	22	Venice	37
Austria	6.6	Lombardy	22

together with the pope, doubtless have joined forces with the Habsburgs to throw no less than 226 tonnes into the ring.

Agreed: as historians, in many ways we have a better picture of the sixteenth-century monarchs' financial resources than they did themselves. In practice, their exchequers, representative assemblies and possible revolts let them know where the limits of the fiscal strength of their subjects lay. Even if they did not have access to such exact figures as we do, they still had an overall understanding of the possibilities – or rather lack of them – of being in control of the different regions. Everybody knew emperor Maximilian had financial problems all through his life: in 1513, for example, he simply did not have the resources to fulfil his promise to undertake a joint action with Henry VIII against France. In his earlier campaigns, against the Swiss in 1499 or the Venetians in 1509, he suffered humiliating defeats for want of well-paid troops. The final test comes on the field of battle, and money is the sinews of war – as everybody had known since Cicero.

Logistic and tactical factors also play an important part in military operations. In 1494 the French king Charles VIII was able to capture Naples, but he could not hold it because of the length of the supply line from his base. From a purely military-technical point of view, his chances of success would have been far greater if he had first annexed the neighbouring areas, Franche-Comté, Savoy, Piedmont or Milan, for example. However, he had no justification for attacking them. In every military action there was a certain respect for legitimate claims, however distorted and disputed they might be. Milan only became an option for his successor, Louis XII, on the basis of the hereditary claims of his Visconti consort. In the meantime, an anti-French coalition had been formed and Aragonese government in Naples strengthened, which made it more difficult to consolidate already won positions.

In spite of their personal ambitions and feelings, Francis I and Charles V acted within a framework of rationality which prepared them, so to speak, for their life-long rivalry. Inevitably they formed the nucleus of two opposing power blocs that stood in each other's way but could not be eliminated. For this reason, when Francis was captured at Pavia in 1525, Charles' decision – made contrary to his earlier agreement with Henry VIII and against his express wishes – not to invade France but in fact to return it to him whole, was all the more remarkable.[14] Their predecessors had already prepared the main theatre of war in Italy. This was not just a matter of distant dynastic claims; it concerned the wealth and imperial lustre of the whole region. Louis XII gladly had himself portrayed as conqueror of Milan, between his imperial forefathers, in typical Renaissance style. This touched a sore spot with poor Maximilian – who was unable to get himself crowned emperor – because he himself, as highest liege lord, had enfieffed Ludovico Sforza as duke of Milan and married his daughter. Every emperor had to consider it his duty to reverse the usurpation. The final humiliation for the emperor was that in 1512–13 it was the Swiss, who had defeated him in 1499, who chased the French out of Milan, occupied parts of the duchy and, on their own authority, replaced Sforza on his throne. This would not be for long, however. In the first year of his reign, Francis I marched over the Alps with a sizeable army and, with the help of the Venetians, defeated the Swiss at Marignano, while the Spanish and papal forces were encamped near Piacenza. Milan capitulated on 16 September 1515.[15]

Once again there was a real challenge to the imperial authority. For the time being, however, Maximilian and Charles were occupied with the Spanish inheritance, which made them choose a safe rear cover because of France. In successive treaties (Noyon 1516 and Cambrai 1517), negotiated for the 'Burgundians' by William of Croy, the Habsburgs declared their friendship towards Francis. Charles would marry one of his still very young daughters and her dowry would include the rights to Naples. In the meantime, Charles would pay a heavy tribute for it. Recognition of these French rights of course damaged the position that Ferdinand of Aragon had held in Naples since 1504. His conquests in Navarre also became a matter for discussion. The good relations were sealed by the exchange of the chains of the Orders of the Golden Fleece and of Saint Michael. In 1517 Maximilian was signatory to a treaty of mutual support: its hidden agenda was the division of Italy. Later that year Francis forged a new alliance with Venice, which stabilised his position in Italy for the time being.[16]

Just as Venice generally supported the French, so England usually took the side of the Habsburgs. Warm relations between the two monarchs were to be expected after Henry's marriage to Charles' aunt, Catherine of Aragon. Indeed, it was important for Charles to maintain good relations with Henry. Both had remained allies over the years in spite of some short-lived alliances between France and England and despite Henry's marital adventures and his separation from the Catholic Church. The alliance was of such importance to Charles that he ignored family and Church objections in order to obviate an Anglo-French coalition. Any such coalition would have been a serious hindrance to communications between his territories, by either land or sea, and would force him to defend many fronts at the same time. Charles' subjects in the Low Countries continually urged him to maintain good relations with England for commercial reasons, while Henry was repeatedly bothered by the Franco-Scottish alliance. He played out the old claims of the English kings to the French crown and repeatedly attempted, with combined Anglo-Habsburg attacks, to force France into a war on several fronts, hoping thus to win some towns and land in the northwest. This succeeded in Tournai in 1513, but later attempts brought surprisingly few results and hardly seemed worth the effort.

When Charles assumed power in Spain the balance of power in Europe was in a state of equilibrium: France, with Lombardy and its allies Venice, Genoa and the pope, represented a fiscal potential of 170 tonnes, precisely the same as the Habsburgs with Spain, the Low Countries, Naples and Sicily. England could make the difference, if sound agreements were reached, if the protagonists were willing to go to the extreme, and if there was some good co-ordination on the ground. All these factors were missing. The election of Charles as Roman king on 28 June 1519 was more than just a personal defeat for Francis I. In his eyes it altered the balance of power to the Habsburgs' advantage, not so much in real terms as in respect of the prestige that was associated with the imperial crown. He considered Charles' sovereignty over north Italy and Tuscany as a threat to his own claims in the area. That was why Francis started a war of aggression, bringing an era of cordial relations between the two great powers to an end.

Unforeseen circumstances

All these courses of action were among those that policy-makers could have foreseen and assessed years before. The alliances of 1517 followed precisely the same patterns as those of 1508. After 1520, a number of external and internal factors would play havoc with the calculations. In 1520 Suleimān II, the Magnificent, became sultan of the Ottoman Empire. In 1516 his predecessor, Selim, had managed to incorporate Syria and Egypt into his already vast empire. Throughout his long reign Sulaimān would form a constant threat to Habsburg and neighbouring lands in central Europe and to Venice's commercial empire in the Adriatic and eastern Mediterranean. Serbia and Bosnia had been conquered in 1459 and 1463 respectively, but in 1521 the conquest of Belgrade, strategically situated on the Danube, left the road to Hungary open for him. A large part of Hungary came into his hands with the battle of Mohács in 1526. In 1396 the West had organised a crusade to counteract Turkish expansion in Bulgaria, but the undertaking ended in disaster. After that the popes lacked the authority and the princes lacked the interest, so that the well-organised Turks could systematically subdue their weakened and divided enemies.

This development was a cause of constant anxiety to Charles. As emperor, he above all had the task of defending the Christian faith, especially the Catholic Church. He took his mission most seriously and throughout his life tried to convince the pope, Francis and other western princes of their sacred duty to join forces and fight back the Turks. He kept on putting the crusades on the agendas of his negotiations. Secondly, the Turks were a direct threat to Habsburg territories: at the battle of Mohács Charles' brother-in-law, Louis, lost his life and his sister Mary her Hungarian crown. In 1529 the Turks laid siege to Vienna. Later the Italian coast was threatened and pirates from north Africa plagued seafarers from southern Spain. Kheir-ed-Din Barbarossa, the ruler of Algiers, placed himself under Sulaimān's command. As the sultan's admiral, his activities made the western Mediterranean unsafe too.

Charles did not succeed in leading a joint Christian force against the Turks: the rivalry between the monarchs in the West was too great to allow that. On the contrary, in order to defend the German Empire he had to buy the support of the German princes with concessions on other policy aspects, considerably weakening his internal position. His great rival, Francis, even went so far as to enter into a pact with the 'infidels' in the hope of being able to break the Habsburg hegemony. In his weaker position he had nothing to lose from the threat from the East. He was in no direct danger and his adversary had his hands full and an uneasy conscience, to boot. Francis explained to the Venetian ambassador:

> I cannot deny that I am glad to see the Turk is strong and ready to go to war, not for himself, for he is an unbeliever and we are Christians, but to weaken the power of the emperor, to force him to incur great expense and to reassure all other governments against such a mighty enemy.[17]

Turkish expansion, then, forced Charles to make concessions at home, and incur heavy expenditure on defence and campaigns. This was the price he had to pay for such an extensive empire: its long borders and coastlines made it very vulnerable.

If the Turkish expansion exerted a negative pressure, another external factor increasingly strengthened Charles' position: the conquests of the Spanish colonists in America. This completely new situation, the consequences of which could not be predicted, brought enormous prestige to the crown of Castile. During his visit to London in June 1522 Charles could show off the rare treasures that Hernando Cortés had sent him from Mexico. Over the following decades the importance of the colonies to the treasury took on such proportions that the exploitation and robbery of the Indians made it possible to finance some crusades. Neither Francis nor Henry had access to a similar source of extra income.

From about 1520 the Reformation developed as a force within the European system of states: for a long time its political consequences were underestimated by contemporaries. The imperial court took insufficient account of it, even when, after the formal condemnation of Martin Luther at the Diet of Worms in 1521, the reformers' ideas continued to circulate widely in spite of Charles' formal prohibition of the dissemination of their doctrine and books. This underestimation is understandable because the effects of the new mass medium of the printing press on public opinion had never been seen on such a scale. In 1515 Pope Leo X had already drawn attention to the publication of heresies through printed works, and for that reason had required that bishops and inquisitors give their permission before anything was printed. Yet these sanctions could not put a halt to public curiosity about them. In the five years following 1517 the number of editions in the German Empire increased nearly sixfold. By 1530 a total of 10,000 different pamphlets had been produced: if 1,000 copies per title were printed this would mean a total production of 10 million pamphlets.[18]

Neither pope nor prince had a grip on the massive response represented by the unprecedented demand to buy this cultural commodity. Leo X, and especially Clement VII, had no idea of the depth of religious feeling that caused support for the Reformation to grow so strongly in German- and Dutch-speaking lands. They interpreted Charles' repeated requests for a general council to reform the Church from within in purely political terms, as an attempt to reinforce the emperor's position at the expense of that of other European monarchs. For this reason – and because the wars against the French and the Turks kept Charles' hands tied – it was many years before any notice was taken of the needs of the masses for a fervent religious revival. In such a vacuum the Reformation was able to grow into a mass movement that even large military action could not subdue. To think purely in terms of power politics was an obstacle to anticipating the reformers' ideals effectively: on the other hand, the breakthrough of the Reformation introduced new relationships in power politics. The division between the French and Habsburg power blocs prevented them from dealing firmly with Henry VIII's break with Rome. From the 1540s onward, the schism between Protestants and Catholics in the German Empire provided Francis and his son Henry II with an opportunity to form coalitions with Protestant rulers against the emperor. When the decision was left to the emperor, religious matters took second place to political matters. In his dealings with both Henry VIII and the German Protestants, Charles could deal pragmatically with his religious principles. In the German Empire, and later in the Low Countries, the Reformation caused an erosion of Charles' power which would not be without consequences in international relations.

Yet another general development, of a completely different nature, would also have a profound influence on the relations between nations and between rulers and their subjects. Far-reaching changes in military techniques took place in the fifteenth century that would have their effect in the sixteenth. In the first place, the introduction and refinement of cannon meant that medieval fortifications could be blown up, putting the assailants of strongholds and towns at an advantage. Generally speaking, only great rulers could afford the expensive artillery and specialised troops needed to operate it, so the new technique usually worked to the advantage of the richer contestants in the struggle for power. The defensive answer to the cannon was developed in northern Italy in the 1520s, in the form of thicker, lower ramparts, filled with earth, and with many-sided bastions at the corners. After 1536 Francis I engaged some of the most renowned Italian engineers to build modern forts along the northern borders of his kingdom. In a short space of time fifteen forts were built on the border with the Low Countries and furnished with more than one thousand pieces of artillery. Venice built new fortifications to protect her colonies in Dalmatia and on Corfu and Crete and the eastern border at Friuli. Along the coast of south Italy a whole chain of towers and fortifications was constructed to resist attacks from the Turkish and Barbary fleets. In the Low Countries the regent Mary had Marienburg built in 1546 and Philippeville in 1553, and citadels were constructed in the major towns of Utrecht, Ghent and Antwerp.

The cost of artillery and fortifications was huge, even for the great monarchies. The cost of waging war was even higher, because of the numerical strength of the armies. In 1494 Charles VIII had taken Naples with 18,000 men. In the 1540s and 1550s, the great rulers led armies of some 45,000 men. In 1552 Charles mobilised a record army of 55,000 for his (unsuccessful) siege of Metz. One reason for the increase in numbers was that, in order to force the modern, fortified towns to surrender, they had to be entirely surrounded. More manpower was needed. There was, moreover, a veritable arms race in the rivalry between the power blocs: one side forced the other at least to equal its efforts. All these military innovations made war an extremely expensive and complicated undertaking. From the 1540s it was seen to be advisable to avoid great pitched battles because of the enormous risks involved. One general result was that taxation shot straight up and, in spite of economic and demographic growth, there was a very real threat that it would cause people to rebel.

All these internal and external factors loomed as immediate, practical problems for policy-makers. One rare document, which contains advice from Charles' most trusted advisors, provides a glimpse of the concrete dilemmas facing them. Charles himself, now nearly twenty-four, does not say much: that may be because of the nature of the papers, which were intended for him. It is impossible to avoid the impression of looking in on a master class of international relations and public administration, where the pupil must be alert and pay attention. We are with the court at Pamplona in the winter of 1523. The Spanish troops are laid up in Fuenterrabia, the fortified town at the mouth of the Bidassoa, the border river in the Pyrenees, the 'key to Spain', which the French had captured in 1521. In that year Charles had arranged with Henry VIII to attack France jointly before May 1523, but Charles had not kept his word and Henry's troops did not invade in the north-west until September. In the summer, an understanding had been reached with the *connétable* of France, Charles de Bourbon, the king's commander-in-chief: with the support of the English and the Habsburgs he would lead a campaign to avenge himself on the king who had robbed him of his very extensive estates. He was to marry one of Charles' sisters, who would bring him a substantial dowry. According to the agreement Charles' troops should have invaded Languedoc, but they never got that far.[19] A French winter campaign in Lombardy has ended in humiliating defeat. Pope Adrian, who had been a staunch supporter of the Habsburg position in Italy, has died. Imperial agents in Rome are working hard to get a Medici to succeed him.

Now the grand chancellor, Gattinara, takes the floor. Under the title 'The monarch's reputation' his speech pleads for maintaining friendships and strictly adhering to alliances that have been entered into, things that had not been done in the previous year. Considering the difficulty of Charles' position, he believes that an honourable truce should be made with France, before even greater costs are incurred. It had been suggested that the duchy of Milan be given to the French in exchange for Burgundy and Bourbon lands. If this happened the French would have vacated Italy, but Lombardy – to which Genoa and Milan were the keys – would still be in danger. Once the French left the contributions of the allies would cease, while the army there would still have to be paid. An envoy would have to travel to the new pope first to obtain his investiture for the kingdom of Naples and then to persuade him to honour the commitments that Adrian had made in connection with the alliance, viz. to pay the soldiers for a further three months. The envoy would then be able to make the vow of obedience. Now it was a matter of urgency to return Milan to its duke so that the people should know for whom they were defending the land, and the neighbouring states would not fear that the emperor wanted to keep Milan for himself. To avoid any rivalry between the generals, archduke Ferdinand or Bourbon should be appointed commander-in-chief. In the matter of administration, Gattinara stressed the need for a clear statement of ordinary and extraordinary revenues and expenditure and debts, especially those growing day-by-day with interest. The advisors also discussed concrete arrangements for government. It later became apparent that the new pope, Clement VII, would immediately stop paying the Habsburg troops.[20] At the end of February 1524 Fuenterrabia capitulated to Charles' troops. Bourbon was appointed his regent in Italy. In April a French army of invasion would once again have to retreat from Italy with large losses. In the light of what we now know about the events of 1525 when Milan, and even Francis I, fell into imperial hands, it is interesting to see how uncertain Charles' advisors were about his position barely a year before. The options for strategic policy were now wide open. Only after the unexpected and unforeseen victory at Pavia in 1525 did the pacification of Italy become the principal aim of Charles' foreign policy at Gattinara's urging, with Lombardy as the queen piece.

The Ottoman expansion, American silver, Reformation, and military technology, each in its own way, threw the strategic plans of the beginning of Charles' reign into total confusion. All the changes occurred at the same time and were a continual hindrance to his plans. In the Treaty of Madrid (1525) the return of the duchy of Burgundy, the dynasty's ancestral homeland, was a firm demand. Later there was never really much discussion about it. Objectives such as governmental centralisation and suppression of the Reformation had to make way for other priorities that were beyond his control. Charles thought that he must pull all the strings himself, and caused all sorts of decision processes to be delayed because of the slowness of communications in his empire and at his own court, which was of necessity becoming increasingly complex. He was faced with choices that did not always suit his regents and subjects. The game was on one board, one emperor against three or four other players.

Notes:

1. Brandi, *Kaiser Karl V.*, 119; Fernandez Alvarez, *Corpus documental*, I, 103.
2. R. J. Knecht, *Renaissance Warrior and Patron: The Reign of Francis I* (Cambridge, 1994, 286-90).
3. Brandi, *Kaiser Kare V.*, 446.
4. H. G. Koenigsberger, *Estates and Revolutions* (Ithaca and London, 1971), 138; W. P. Blockmans and J. van Herwaarden, 'De Nederlanden van 1493 tot 1555', *Algemene Geschiedenis der Nederlanden*, 5 (Haarlem, 1980), 469.
5. G. d'Agostino, *Parlamento e società nel regno di Napoli, secoli XV-XVII* (Naples, 1979), 246-8, 259.
6. G. Vogler, 'Reichsvorstellungen im Umkreis des Bauernkrieges', V. Press and D. Stieverman, eds, *Alternativen zur Reichsverfassung in der frühen Neuzeit?* (Munich, 1995), 23-41.
7. G. Kleinheyer, *Die kaiserlichen Wahlkapitulationen. Geschichte, Wesen und*

Funktion (Karlsruhe, 1968), 45–50, 101–3, 127–8; *Deutsche Reichstagsakten, Jüngere Reihe*, I (Göttingen, 1962), 821.
8. C. Roll, *Das zweite Reichsregiment, 1521–1530* (Cologne, Weimar, Vienna, 1996), 20–1, 329–37.
9. G. Parker, *The Grand Strategy of Philip II* (New Haven and London, 1998), 48.
10. H. Lapeyre, *Charles Quint* (Paris, 1971), 13.
11. H. Stratenwerth and H. Rabe, 'Politische Kommunikation und Diplomatie', in *Kaiser Karl V. (1500-1558): Macht und Ohnmacht Europas* (Bonn and Vienna, 2000), 28.
12. J. De Vries, *European Urbanization, 1500–1800* (Cambridge, 1984), 30; F. Braudel, *The Mediterranean and the Mediterranean World in the Age of Philip II* (London, 1975), 408–10; G. Felloni, 'Economie, finances et monnaie dans les possessions italiennes de Charles V', *L'escarcelle de Charles V: Monnaies et finances au XVIe siècle* (Brussels, 2000), 237. Felloni offers slightly different figures, recognising that a margin of error of 10 to 20 per cent must be taken into account; he concludes that Italy as a whole had 10.8 million inhabitants c.1550.
13. M.Körner, 'Expenditure', in R. Bonney, ed., *Economic Systems and State Finance* (Oxford, 1995), 399–400; W. Schultze, 'The Emergence and Consolidation of the "Tax State". The Sixteenth Century', *ibid.*, 269–70.
14. Knecht, *Renaissance Warrior*, 229.
15. *Ibid.*, 71–7.
16. *Ibid.*, 84–6.
17. *Ibid.*, 295–6.
18. P. Blickle, 'Das Reich zu Beginn des 16. Jahrhunderts', in H. Buszello, P. Blickle, R. Endres, eds, *Der deutsche Bauernkrieg* (Paderborn, 1995), 53–4.
19. Knecht, *Renaissance Warrior*, 200–15.
20. Brandi, *Kaiser Karl V.*, 184–8.

3
Honour, rights and land

A foreign king

Charles may have been designated by both his grandfathers as the only successor to the crowns of Spain, but before their plans could come to fruition certain rites essential to the transition had to be completed. The most important of these was that the *cortes* in the diverse kingdoms recognise him and, not unnaturally, Charles had to be in the country for this. It was not until 8 September 1517, however, that, accompanied by his eldest sister Eleanor, he embarked from Flushing for Spain. After a safe voyage they landed near Villaviciosa on the Cantabrian coast. The two royal children went first to Tordesillas to see their mentally disturbed mother and their ten-year-old sister, Catherine. They felt it necessary to make better arrangements for the young girl than the virtual captivity that had been her fate until then. In January 1520 Charles issued strict instructions that nobody speak with his mother, apart from her attendants, because it would only cause harm.[1] After Tordesillas, Charles and Eleanor met their brother Ferdinand, who knelt respectfully before the king and head of the house of Habsburg before embracing him. He was given the chain of the Order of the Golden Fleece in recognition.

Ferdinand had been born and bred in Spain, and for this reason a number of Spanish grandees considered him a more suitable successor than Charles, who had spent his entire youth in the Low Countries and spoke only a few words of Castilian. On the day that he embarked for Spain Charles had written from Middelburg to his brother accusing some members of Ferdinand's household of conspiring against him.[2] Now the two brothers were reconciled and, together with Eleanor, they made a triumphal entry into Valladolid, the administrative capital of Castile.

All the Spanish kingdoms had undergone institutional developments over many centuries: each one believed that its administrative and judicial autonomy was guaranteed by its own representative institutions, the *cortes* and their permanent delegations. During the many crises of power in the fifteenth century the towns had repeatedly signed treaties to safeguard their territory and rights against the threats of the aristocracy. The towns had jurisdiction over large parts of the surrounding countryside and these treaties, known as *hermandades* (brotherhoods), therefore included a large proportion of the peasant population. If the monarchy failed to guarantee public order then the cathedral chapters, which were large landowners, and the *hidalgos* (urban nobility) also joined these alliances. Between the town magistrates and the deputies in the *cortes* a political ideology had come into being, based on a contractual monarchy: a ruler was expected to govern well, to guarantee that the law would be administered fairly and to work constantly for the interests, possessions and safety of his subjects. If he failed in this then the ties of loyalty binding him to his subjects were threatened. These views were expressed in speeches like those made during the assembly of the *cortes* at Valladolid, the first that Charles attended.[3]

A year after Ferdinand's death, the *cortes* of Castile and Leon had demanded that Charles appear before them in person in October 1517 to swear his oath to their privileges and to receive their homage. This did happen, just in time, but in a highly charged atmosphere, because Charles' advisors had shown remarkably little tact in appointing chancellor Le Sauvage to preside over the assembly. The response was immediate, hard and clear: the *cortes* did not want foreign officials. The delegate from Burgos made a speech making clear the constitutional nature of the Spanish monarchy. There is an unwritten, but none the less clear and binding, contract between crown and people that requires the king to be just; but how can he be just if his servants are greedy? This was an obvious reference to the greed displayed by Charles' close counsellors in appropriating the most lucrative revenues and positions for themselves as soon as they arrived in Spain. 'In essence the king has the same responsibilities as a soldier of fortune, the first of which is to safeguard the proper dispensation of justice. That is why his subjects give up a part of their income and render him service when it is demanded of them.'[4]

Following the traditional pattern, when the new king was recognised a substantial taxation was agreed and a list of 88 complaints was presented. These were political demands put forward by the delegates and included the reparation of breaches of their laws and customs. The fulfilment of these demands was in fact a *sine qua non* for both the recognition of the ruler and the agreement to taxation. The *cortes* asked Charles to stay in the country until he had an heir: this would take some time as he was not yet married and the potential wives were still very young. The *cortes* asked that Ferdinand be allowed to remain in the country as Charles' heir apparent in the meantime. Charles readily agreed to their final request that he learn

Castilian, but as soon as possible he had Ferdinand escorted to Santander and put on a ship to the Low Countries.

In March 1518 Charles negotiated along the same lines with the *cortes* of the kingdom of Aragon in Zaragoza, and in January 1519 with the Catalonian *cortes* in Barcelona. Everywhere he heard the same severe criticism of the government in the preceding years, and the uncertain future. In Barcelona he arranged a meeting of the Order of the Golden Fleece at which a number of important Spanish noblemen were appointed to the Order, a symbolic token of honour. Charles finally arranged the marriage contract for his sister, Eleanor, with the 50-year-old Manuel I of Portugal, with substantial financial concessions on the part of the Portuguese. Manuel had previously been married to their two aunts, Isabella and Mary of Aragon.

Charles received the news of Maximilian's death in February 1519. He deemed it advisable to make haste in his bid for election as Roman king, putting it before all other matters, and left Spain without appearing before the *cortes* of Valencia, which was one of the causes of the revolt of the *Germanias*. During the first two years of Charles' reign in Spain, the Burgundians, or Flemings, as Charles' confidants from the Low Countries were called, were the object of extreme dislike. The succession of a very young, far from brilliant, ill prepared and badly advised king was difficult, especially when his brother enjoyed the sympathy of the people and his mother was formally queen.

Throughout 1518 Maximilian had worked hard to have Charles elected as Roman king and his successor, just as in 1486 he had been elected while his own father, Emperor Frederick III, had been alive. During his last Diet in Augsburg he managed to secure the support of five of the seven electors. The archbishop of Trier was sensitive to the overtures of Francis I, who considered himself to be the obvious candidate, especially since he now ruled Milan. The pope opposed Charles' candidacy, fearing that an emperor who was also king of Naples would have a stranglehold on the Papal States – a fear resulting from the experience with Frederick II in the thirteenth century. When it became clear that Francis I had little chance, Leo X made a fruitless, last-ditch attempt to persuade elector Frederick the Wise of Saxony to stand as candidate.

The candidates campaigned intensively for months. Charles had pamphlets printed appealing to Germany's nationalistic feelings by recalling that he was of 'most noble German blood'. This was a rather exaggerated claim for a French-speaking king of Spain who had been brought up in the Low Countries and never yet set foot in the German Empire. Nevertheless it did give him some advantage over his adversary, of whom it was impossible to say that he was of German origin and whose ambitions of supremacy in Italy were blatantly obvious. The balance of power between the German king and the imperial estates was an important consideration for the electors. Including the Low Countries, most of which belonged to the Empire, the Habsburgs had undoubtedly strong patrimonial territories within the Empire, a *Hausmacht*. In addition, Charles was king of Castile, Aragon, Naples and Sicily, which made him far superior to the other powers in the Empire. He was young and not at all familiar with relationships in the Empire. It seemed likely that his activities would be centred elsewhere and that he would therefore spend much of his time outside the Empire, but that, if necessary, he would be in a position to raise a force of a strength never before seen against the rulers and towns in the territory. Full of doubts, the electors demanded guarantees and, because of the competition, their wishes were fully complied with.

On 1 September 1518 Maximilian and Charles had made all sorts of electoral promises in joint documents. They declared that immediately after the election the privileges of the electors would be confirmed, especially their right to elect freely. Although Charles would be the fourth consecutive Habsburg king since Albrecht II was elected in 1438, he and Maximilian rejected all claims to a right of inheritance to the German crown. They also agreed that all state and court positions would be filled only by Germans, that German and Latin would be the only languages used on imperial business, that Charles would stay in the Empire as often as possible, and that every effort would be made to recover regions of the Empire that had become alienated. Although Maximilian died before Charles was actually elected these terms were included in various articles of the *Wahlkapitulation*, which his representatives negotiated from 28 June to 3 July 1519 with six electors (the king of Bohemia was not present). Charles issued them as decrees shortly after taking his oath and being crowned king. The number of unofficial printings of these terms appearing in the meantime show how much importance was attached to the contract. It grew into a constitutional document that would establish the relationship between king and estates in the Empire for a long time to come. It laid down the occasions on which the Emperor could expect the support of the estates or of just the electors, and attempted to limit the influence of non-German interests on the Empire.[5]

German public opinion, which political pamphlets had made sensitive to the election of the emperor, certainly influenced the choice, to the detriment of Francis I. The Habsburgs had gained in prestige with their decisive military intervention in connection with the Swabian League's efforts against the duke of Württemberg, who had broken the peace of the Empire. Under the leadership of Franz von Sickingen their troops assembled round

Frankfurt to 'protect' the electors from a possible desperate move by the French. On 28 June the unanimous decision was made. King Vladislav of Bohemia cast his vote by proxy.

The objections to Charles could equally well apply to Francis. Francis, however, could not produce any Habsburg forebears, nor vast sums of money, *'grant argent'*, as Maximilian wrote in a letter to Charles on 18 May 1518.[6] The electors certainly heard the chink of Francis' money, and most of them accepted it eagerly, but Charles could always offer more, thanks to the decision of one man, Jacob Fugger the Rich, the great merchant and financier from Augsburg. He was prepared to give Charles credit for more than half of the bribes promised. The firm of Welser from Augsburg and bankers from Genoa and Antwerp were among those who rushed to follow Fugger's example. Fugger did not fail to remind the emperor at suitable times that 'His Imperial Majesty could not have acquired the Roman crown without my assistance'. The expenses incurred by Charles to ensure that the imperial election would be his eventually totalled 850,000 Rhine guilders, 2.1 tonnes of pure silver, four times the amount of silver exported annually from the Americas at that time, or 62 per cent of his total annual income from the Low Countries in 1531.[7] The shrewd capitalists calculated that they would have a better chance to develop their considerable commercial activities in Spain and the Low Countries under solid Charles than under the unpredictable Francis.[8] The Fuggers secured guarantees in the silver mines of the Tirol and expected tax income from the emperor's extensive territories. They refused to redeem Francis' bills of exchange, thus cutting him off entirely. From their point of view, they doubtless made the right choice. It is less clear if, in the long run, it was so good for the people.

The XVII Provinces

On 23 October 1520 Charles was crowned Roman king in Aachen by the three archbishops who were also electors: Mainz, Trier and Cologne. In the great church of Charlemagne the new king humbly promised to defend the Church and the weak, and prostrated himself in front of the altar before being annointed and receiving the sceptre, orb, sword and crown, the regalia of the Empire. His rival, Francis, pondered other ways of enlarging his reputation. A tournament injury prevented him from intervening personally, but he urged others to attack Charles' possessions. Henry d'Albret who had lost most of his kingdom of Navarre to Ferdinand of Aragon in 1512, set out to reconquer it in February 1521. By June he had been repulsed, suffering severe losses. A simultaneous action against

Luxembourg by Robert de la Marck, lord of Sedan, met with an equal lack of success. In a counter-campaign Henry of Nassau sowed destruction throughout northeast France, then moved westwards where the French army had plundered villages in Hainault.

He laid siege to the great cathedral city of Tournai and the surrounding villages, which formed a French enclave between Burgundian-Habsburg territories. The greater part of the county of Flanders belonged to this diocese, which made relations with the bishop of Tournai particularly delicate. The town on the Scheldt had an important function in the region, especially in Flanders and Hainault. During the joint Anglo-Habsburg military campaign of 1513 Henry VIII had taken both Guinegate and the small cathedral city of Thérouanne in Artois, as well as Tournai. He had oaths of allegiance sworn to him as the 'most Christian king Henry, by the grace of God king of France and England'. His government of these towns, however, soon met with opposition. Henry's chancellor, Cardinal Wolsey, demanded the bishopric for himself, but the pope had appointed Louis Guillard, a son of a president of the parliament in Paris, and thus a protégé of Louis XII. The Flemish were not minded to accept Wolsey's authority or to make contributions to his tax collectors. The establishment of an English garrison and the construction of a citadel worried the Habsburgs and their subjects, especially when Louis XII signed a truce with Henry in 1514 and married his sister, Mary Tudor, who until then had been intended for Charles. After some years it became clear to the English that Tournai was hard to control and very expensive; in February 1519, with a certain amount of relief and for a substantial consideration, they returned Tournai to France and the French bishop as part of the London peace treaty.[9] Against this background it is not difficult to understand why two years later the Habsburgs responded to French attacks by attempting to take the dangerous French outpost that Tournai had by now become. At the end of November 1521 the city opened its gates to the emperor's troops. It was an attractive asset for him in the Low Countries, but the friendship between Charles and Francis was now broken.

Francis' influence could be felt in another remote corner of the region, through the duke of Guelders, Charles of Egmond. Duke Charles the Bold of Burgundy had taken control of this fragmented dukedom, which was strategically situated along the Meuse, Lower Rhine, Waal and IJssel rivers, in 1473. In 1477 the States of Guelders chose Adolphe as their duke, and in 1492 Charles had succeeded his father, contrary to the agreement with the Habsburgs, but with the support of the French. In 1498–99 Maximilian attempted unsuccessfully to recover the dukedom. He did not receive any support from the Low Countries, nor even from his son, who was ruler of the area. In the following years the neighbouring principalities of Brabant, Utrecht and Holland suffered from Guelders' raids, and shipping on the Zuider Zee and the great rivers was harassed. Guelders plundered the Brabant town of Tienen in 1507, and a year later invaded Holland. In 1517 a 'Black Gang' from Guelders could steal and plunder and march openly under the very walls of Haarlem and Amsterdam, without the governor's cavalry driving them away.

In the northeast of the Low Countries the divisions of power had scarcely been consolidated on a territorial level. In 1521 this gave Charles of Guelders the opportunity to install himself as lord of the Ommelanden (the country region surrounding Groningen) and to seize the Oversticht, that part of the prince-bishopric of Utrecht to the east of the IJssel. Next year he was installed in the town of Groningen and in Drenthe. He seemed to be emerging as the ruler of an extensive, united region. In Friesland he enjoyed the support of a number of the local nobility belonging to the *Vetkopers* party. Until 1516 the larger towns, Leeuwarden, Franeker and Harlingen, and their immediate surroundings were under Habsburg rule, but Guelders controlled the rest of Friesland. That summer a Habsburg offensive forced them out of Friesland altogether, apart from the towns of Sneek, Sloten and Dokkum, whence they continued to harass Holland's merchant shipping on the Zuider Zee. Not until 1522 did the Habsburg governor, Georg Schenck von Tautenburg, manage to bring the whole region under his control, although in theory it had belonged to Charles since 1515. Sloten fell in 1523, after a siege. It was thus a valid option for Francis I to support Charles of Guelders, in order to cause trouble for the emperor on different fronts at the same time.

The instability in the region meant that the duke could always find new centres of support. In 1527 the burgher faction in Utrecht, which opposed bishop Henry of Bavaria, invited a Guelders garrison inside its walls. In November the bishop appeared willing to renounce his temporal power in favour of the emperor, in exchange for Habsburg support. When the Guelders captain, Maarten van Rossum, made a raid on The Hague and exacted a levy under threat of pillage, the States of Holland were immediately prepared to pay for an army under von Tautenburg's command.[10] In October 1528 the two Charleses called a truce under which the duke of Guelders renounced all his positions in the areas of the bishop's temporal authority, the Nedersticht (the western part of the old bishopric of Utrecht) and Oversticht: thenceforth these would be under Habsburg rule. On the other hand he was allowed to govern Groningen, the Ommelanden and Drenthe in the emperor's name, as 'hereditary governor'. The Habsburg Low Countries were thus enlarged with the lands of Utrecht and Friesland, which bordered each other and the other provinces. Guelders retained an extensive sphere of influence in the northeast, between the Nedersticht and Oversticht. Francis I continued to cherish his ally who could harass the Habsburgs in the Low Countries from the north whenever Francis did so in the south.

When Francis again declared war on Charles in 1536 his troublemaker in the north came into action. The alliances had by now widened into an anti-Habsburg coalition with the German Protestants and the Danish king, Christian III. Charles did not want to recognise the latter because he was anxious to secure his own dynastic interests. He tried to put Dorothea on the throne – the young daughter of his sister Isabella and Christian II, who had been deposed in 1523 and since 1530 languished in a Norwegian prison. It was a fairly hopeless undertaking as women were barred from the succession in Denmark. It was necessary to find a suitable candidate for her hand and let him compete for the throne. Frederick, the count palatine, seemed the most suitable candidate, for Charles had many obligations to him. In the meantime, with the support of the nobles, Christian III exercised his authority in a large part of the country. Now he tried to enforce his claim by joining the anti-Habsburg coalition.

In May 1536 troops supported by Christian and Charles of Guelders invaded Overijssel and the Groningen Ommelanden. This led the people of Groningen to seek the protection of the Habsburgs and to recognise Charles as their overlord. Charles' governor in Friesland accepted their tribute and, with the help of the regent Mary, managed to oust the Danes and to take Drenthe. In the interests of trade Mary ignored the wishes of her imperial brother, and the following year signed a four-year truce with Christian III, guaranteeing the Netherlanders unhindered passage through the Danish Sound.[11]

The Guelders question became urgent again in January 1538 when Charles of Guelders died without issue. In the truce of 1528 he had appointed the Emperor Charles as his successor, but the States let their choice fall on William of Jülich who, on the death of his father in 1539, inherited the duchies of Cleves and Jülich as well as Berg and Marck. Together with Guelders and Zutphen this would form a new land-bloc on the Lower Rhine that appeared to have the power to resist the continued pressure of the Habsburgs. For the time being the emperor gave priority to other matters: the developments in the war with France, the revolt in Ghent, negotiations with the Diet and the pope, and an attempted invasion of Algiers. As long as he and Francis respected the Treaty of Nice, signed in 1538, there was no need for him to attack Francis' traditional ally, Guelders.

In July 1542, however, a full-scale anti-Habsburg offensive was launched. The Low Countries was the main target, with attacks coming from four directions. Christian III of Denmark closed the Danish Sound to the Low Countries again and sent a fleet of 40 ships with a reported 10,000 soldiers to the coasts of Holland and Zeeland. They harassed fishing and commercial traffic but were unable to set foot on land. The French attacked Luxembourg and Artois. The governor of Flanders and Artois, Adrian of Croy, and his troops managed to hold off this attack on Artois so that the French were unable to enter Flanders and join forces with the other invading forces. The French were successful in Luxembourg, however: they destroyed the town of Damvillers, took Yvoix (now Carignan) after a 20-day siege and then took the rest of the dukedom. The Guelders general, Maarten van Rossum, sent 14,000 to 15,000 foot solders and 2,000 to 3,000 knights via Brabant as reinforcements.

Van Rossum had managed to invade Brabant from the northeast, threatened 's-Hertogenbosch and plundered four towns, among them Hoogstraten and the castle of Antoine de Lalaing, the governor of Holland and Zeeland. The regent's troops were strengthened in a number of garrisons because it was difficult to know exactly where the invasion would take place. This enabled van Rossum to get to Antwerp practically unimpeded. Fearing a concentration of the regent's troops he dared not lay siege to Antwerp for long, nor to Leuven. He demanded that both cities yield to him, in the name of the king of France. Mary's troops followed him into Luxembourg, which the occupying forces then left quickly, except for the capital. Considering that approximately 50,000 men had attacked the Low Countries, the damage was fairly limited and the results meagre. Mary then launched an attack on Jülich itself, the homeland of duke William, in the hope of 'bringing him to his senses'. Jülich was unprotected and fell into her hands in less than three weeks, but Habsburg co-ordination was poor and William and his brother-in-law, the duke of Saxony, retook the duchy with the exception of the town of Heinsberg. Mary's spring offensive in March 1543 was also unsuccessful.

The breakthrough came when Charles marched into the Lower Rhine region with an army of 40,000 men from Spain, Italy and Upper Germany, under the command of Ferrante Gonzaga, his viceroy in Sicily. The alliance of William of Cleves with Francis and Christian III, and the attacks on the Low Countries made Charles determined to establish his rights in Guelders once and for all, in order to be rid of the troublemaker in the north of his lands. The stability of the region was important to Charles because of its international implications. On 12 June 1541 Francis I had agreed to the marriage of his 12-year-old cousin, Jeanne d'Albret, heiress to the kingdom of Navarre, with William of Cleves. Since his failed attempt to recover his kingdom from Castile in 1521 her father, Henry d'Albret, had complained that Francis had not asserted his rights strongly enough, so this marriage was a double challenge.[12] A further fear was that William would join his brother-in-law from Saxony in the Schmalkaldic League of Protestant German princes and hasten the spread of the Reformation through the Low Countries.

The enormous superiority of his troops and materials enabled the emperor to take Düren, the most important town in Jülich, on 24 August. One week later Roermond, in Guelders, surrendered as soon as he set up camp there. Within another week William had capitulated, and the States agreed to accept the new ruler. Charles allowed the duke to retain his original principalities. In 1543 Guelders became the seventeenth 'province' of the Low Countries. At Francis' request the pope dissolved William's marriage to Jeanne d'Albret because he had sworn allegiance to the emperor. William married again, this time a daughter of Ferdinand.[13] Five years later, in the Treaty (or Transaction) of Augsburg, the Diet decided to transfer the lands which had recently been acquired in the northeastern Low Countries from the Westphalian to the Burgundian Circle of the Empire. In addition to all the Habsburg territories in the Low Countries all their Burgundian possessions – of which Franche-Comté was the most important – belonged to this Circle. The Burgundian Circle had been established in 1512 and was not subject to the jurisdiction of the *Reichskammergericht* and in practice, after 1532, it was entirely exempt from the Circles' military and fiscal obligations to the Empire. When the question of his successor had been settled and his son, Philip, had been recognised in that capacity in the various regions of the Low Countries in 1549, Charles asked the States General in September to agree to a uniform rule covering the succession of the ruler in all the regions, through the male and female line alike. On 4 November he issued a Pragmatic Sanction (a very solemn, imperial decree) on the matter, which was intended to guarantee that the XVII Provinces would thereafter remain united.[14] Thirty years later the Revolt was to cause a definitive break between North and South.

In this way were formed lasting ties and permanent borders between any number of principalities, which would not have found this particular political framework without the intervention of the emperor. There were no borders in language, culture, economic relations or even landscape. Utrecht, Friesland, Groningen, Drenthe, Overijssel and Guelders were united with the other provinces of the Low Countries under Habsburg pressure. Charles drew Guelders definitively into the Low Countries, while Cleves, Jülich, Marck and Berg remained in the Westphalian Circle and closely connected to the Empire. The choice of those subjects entitled to vote would have lain in another direction. Being both prince of the Low Countries and emperor, Charles was able to make the division. For the good of relationships inside the Empire he allowed William of Cleves to retain his original territories, provided he abandoned his alliance with France.

Italy: the key to world hegemony

In January 1525 Charles wrote a number of observations analysing his strategic position for the first time.[15] His viceroy in Naples, Charles of Lannoy, was at that time in Lombardy fighting a large French force led by the king in person. Since the beginning of November Francis had laid siege to Pavia, where a garrison of 6,000 Germans under the command of Antonio de Leyva offered valiant resistance. In previous years the French had suffered one defeat after another in north Italy. In November 1521, the troops of the pope and the emperor, led by Prospero Colonna, had conquered Milan. Successive attempts by the French to retake the city failed. On 27 April 1522 they had lost thousands of men in a badly planned attack on the imperial camp at La Bicocca. On 30 May the Spanish and German troops of the imperial generals Colonna and Pescara stormed Genoa on two sides, after a siege lasting ten days. Until then the town had been under the command of a French governor. Owing to internal divisions in the town, the negotiations had not ended in surrender, so the imperial commanders allowed their troops to plunder it for two whole days.[16] One of Francis' greatest vassals, the *connétable* Charles de Bourbon, forswore his allegiance to the king on 7 September 1523, having first come to an agreement with the emperor.[17] The Franco-Swiss army, which then launched another attack on Lombardy, suffered severe hardships in the winter and had to retreat with many losses. Supported by an agreement between Charles and Henry VIII, Bourbon undertook an operation in Provence: it stranded after a fruitless, six-week-long siege of Marseilles in August-September 1524. Pescara led the imperial troops that attacked Languedoc from Lombardy and managed to take Toulon, but had to retreat in haste when confronted by a large, new army which Francis I himself led over the Alps. At the end of October Francis entered Milan, while the imperial troops were concentrated in Lodi, Alessandria and Pavia. A detachment under the command of the Scottish duke of Albany sent by the king towards Naples, in the hope of luring away viceroy Lannoy, who commanded the imperial troops in Lombardy, failed in its purpose. On 12 December Clement VII and the Venetians allied themselves to the French.

Such was the situation in January 1525 when Charles reviewed his position. Ten years after his spectacular conquest, and at the cost of three hard-fought campaigns, Francis was once again in possession of Milan. On the other hand, his ambition to take Naples had come to naught. However, revenues could not be collected in that kingdom to reinforce the army in the north, nor was there any money to be found in Spain. Charles wrote:

> The King of England does not help me as a true friend, nor does he honour his commitment to help me. My friends have deserted and deceived me in time of need; they do everything to prevent me from becoming more powerful and to keep me in my present dire situation.

The blame that Charles ascribed to Henry could just as well have been ascribed to himself for, in 1523, disregarding their agreement, Charles had failed to take action when the English were within 50 miles of Paris. By those friends who had deserted him, he must have meant Clement VII, whose candidacy for pope he had firmly supported two years earlier.

> In these circumstances . . . since time is passing and we too shall speedily pass away, since I should not perish without leaving a glorious memory, since what is lost today cannot be won back tomorrow, since I have not yet achieved anything that enhances my personal honour and could rightly be accused of delaying for too long; for all these and many other reasons I see no grounds for postponing a grandiose undertaking any longer. . . . I cannot think of anything that would improve my affairs in general as much as my expedition to Italy.

The young emperor thus explains the basis of his thinking. It seems to reflect the influence of romances of chivalry more than the sensible advice of his advisors. His greatest concern is for peace, but his enemies deprived him of the opportunity for it, so now he must enter upon a great, honourable and glorious venture – an expedition to Italy, such as his rival Francis had twice successfully undertaken. Charles would first have to be recognised as king in Naples and then move north to have the pope crown him emperor. To finance all this a call would have to be made on the dowry of Isabella of Portugal, whom he now decided to marry. The *cortes* of Castile had sung her praises, not least because she was of marriageable age, unlike his former betrothed, Mary Tudor, the daughter of Henry VIII. The *cortes* could therefore make a sizeable contribution to the 'great plan'. At the same time Charles would have to ensure that Henry remained an ally and that Mary did not marry in France.

It would be more than four years before Charles was able to embark for Italy where he would hold his triumphal procession which, in the circumstances, would not be a *Romzug*, a march to Rome, in the tradition of the

German emperors. Completely inconceivable quirks of military fate would decide the fortunes of the emperor, of Francis I and of all those who were dependent on them. The French army and their king had spent the winter encamped outside Pavia, which was well defended. Most of the imperial troops were originally encamped at Lodi, more than 20 miles to the northeast. In the middle of January 1525 they included 22,000 infantry, 800 heavy cavalry and 1,500 light cavalry. The French units were then more numerous, but during the following weeks desertion took its toll. The French had 53 cannon, against the 17 of the imperial forces, which in turn had more small arms. On the side of the river Ticino the encirclement was not yet complete; towards Lodi the imperial camp lay behind the French with only a small river, embankments and trenches separating the two armies. The French were thus hemmed in, with the enemy in the town and at their rear, and had little freedom of movement. The imperial army's attempts to lure the besiegers into a pitched battle were unsuccessful. The long months of immobility gnawed away at the morale of both armies, and at the emperor's finances. At the beginning of February, 5,000 of the French army's Swiss mercenaries returned home to Grisons, while two weeks later a group of Italian mercenaries slunk off.

In the night of 23 February the emperor's generals, Lannoy, Bourbon, Pescara, Frundsberg and Vasto, apparently in retreat, attempted to challenge the French in the nearby walled park of Mirabello. Francis did indeed rush after them with his cavalry but found himself in front of his own artillery, which he had to order to cease fire. He broke through the imperial cavalry, then ended up in the line of fire of the Spanish arquebus. They shot at the heavily armed cavalry, which was soon surrounded by a force of much more mobile lansquenets. The king's horse was hit, the king himself continued to fight on foot but was soon taken prisoner. In the meantime, the garrison made a sortie and drove off the Swiss infantry, which had been under Francis' command.[18] The French army was routed, the nobility suffered heavy casualties and there was total chaos. It was the first time that a king of France had had to abandon a siege, and the second time since 1356 that a French king had been taken prisoner by his great rival. Pescara was badly wounded but tried to regain control of Lombardy; Leyva again took possession of Milan. Anti-Habsburg sentiment raised its head again and, as usual, it was months before instructions came from Spain.

The chief architect of Charles' Italian policy was his grand chancellor, the Piedmontese Mercurino di Gattinara. Although in the court council he had to cope with indifference and even unwillingness, especially on the part of its Spanish members, he convinced the emperor of the absolute necessity of pacifying and gaining supremacy in Italy. After all, Italy was where the great imperial ambitions of the French king lay, which were always bound to clash with those of the Holy Roman Emperor, the mightiest defender of the Catholic Church, king of Naples, Sicily and Sardinia. It was Gattinara, too, who persuaded Charles not to exercise his power in the northern regions of Italy directly, but rather through alliances with local lords who enjoyed the support of the most influential parts of the population.

This form of indirect rule was in sharp contrast to the French modus operandi. In Genoa they appointed a governor who ruled the area as if it were a French province, imposed taxes dictatorially, interfered in the administration of local law and land grants, and divided the region as the king saw fit. In the sensitive relationship between the rival ports of Liguria, the French tried to play Savona against Genoa by removing the former from the authority of the capital of the *patria*. This all helped to stir up bad blood in the Genoese, and was a reason for them to choose Habsburg rule. The Habsburgs recognised the Republic's freedom to choose its own doge, to administer its own justice and to transact business. The merchants saw the advantages of maintaining good relations with their immediate hinterlands of Piedmont and Lombardy, with their grain suppliers in Naples and Sicily and with their trading partners in Catalonia. In 1524 the Genoese there, as in all the emperor's other territories, were given the same rights as the local inhabitants.[19]

Italy was a central theme in the negotiations between Charles and Francis during the latter's captivity: Charles demanded that Francis immediately renounce his claims to Milan, Genoa and Asti. The demand did not form a real obstacle and was agreed in the Peace of Madrid, which the two monarchs concluded on 14 January 1526. Barely one month after Francis was released, Lannoy and Praat, Charles' envoys to the royal council in Cognac, heard on 16 May that the king did not consider the treaty as binding because it had been made under duress. Within the week a new alliance, the League of Cognac or Holy League, was forged between the former allies – the pope, Francis, Venice, Francesco Sforza and the Medici government in Florence. One of their demands was that Sforza be restored as duke of Milan, and war in Italy was threatened. Francis promised to send a fleet to Genoa and take the city and then to move on to Naples: the pope was to decide who should have Naples and Milan.[20] The first action of the Holy League – which apparently did not want to leave Charles time to think – was to occupy Lodi on 24 June. On 25 July, however, Sforza was forced to surrender the fort of Milan. Help from the French failed to appear. At the end of November, Frundsberg led his German troops southwards through friendly Ferrara and Lannoy attacked Tuscany. The pope was trying to fend off an attack from the Colonna clan of Rome.

Lannoy and Bourbon now led the imperial army into the Papal States. As usual, the army was not paid but had been given the prospect of being recompensed in Rome: this meant that the pope would be pressured into giving money. Although Lannoy had received instructions from Charles to spare the pope, and they had signed a truce on 15 March 1527, there was no stopping the troops in their hunger for booty. Clement seemed to be hesitating and on 25 April once again took the side of the League. The soldiers saw him as the emperor's enemy. On 6 May they stormed the Eternal City. During the attack Bourbon lost his life, and the soldiers any form of control. The pope and 14 cardinals sought protection in the Castel San Angelo, while the city was the object of unbridled looting, the Sack of Rome. Not until 6 December could Clement escape to Orvieto, disguised as his own major-domo. Unintentional and unplanned, these events once again gave Charles an enormous strategic advantage: the League was coming apart and the pope could be persuaded to choose his side. On the other hand, the pope's long imprisonment and the devastation of the holy city created a wave of condemnation throughout Christendom, which was a cause of great embarrassment to the emperor.

Francis at once assured himself of an alliance with Henry VIII, who gave him financial support for a campaign in Italy. Moreover, Henry renounced his ancient claim to the French throne and there was talk of a marriage for Mary Tudor, if not with Francis himself (who, according to the Treaty of Madrid, was betrothed to Charles' sister, Eleanor) then with his son. Both kings rejected a general council, thus frustrating Charles' favourite project.

In the meantime, a Holy League fleet blockaded the coast of Liguria: Genoa was starving and unemployment was high. In July 1527 the French field marshal Lautrec marched into the region. Andrea Doria and his fleet rallied to the side of the French: they captured the ships bringing grain from Corsica and some galleons belonging to the Republic. The Adorni, Spinola and Fieschi clans, which were favourably disposed towards the emperor, were blamed for the general malaise. In May, hundreds of citizens swore an oath to a 'Union'; the text of this oath had been prepared two years previously. The aim was to replace the partisan clans of the Adorni and Fregosi, which took it in turns to govern, with a republican system that would allow wider participation and greater legal certainty. Opponents of the Union were mostly members of the nobility, while the majority of its supporters were representatives of the people. It was the personal authority of Andrea Doria that converted first the nobility and then the popular faction to the idea of making not the opposition leader, Cesare Fregoso, but an influential outsider, governor of the town. It was hoped in this way to be rid of the tyranny of the leaders of the factions. On 18 August the doge,

Antoniotto Adorno, his adherents and Charles' ambassador, Soria, left the city. On 22 August a new governor, Trivulzio, appeared with the permission of the French: he had been purposely brought in from outside to be above the factious parties.

Soria had always kept his sovereign informed of the dangers of the situation. On 30 August he wrote that a year-long blockade of the harbour, the hunger, the threat of Lautrec's army and the absence of imperial troops had made capitulation unavoidable. Three weeks later he realised how mistaken it had been to rely on one faction because it was friendly to the emperor:

> The entire town would be very pleased if Your Majesty appointed a governor to govern in your name, one who would serve God and Your Majesty. For the leaders of the Adorni and Fregosi do not know what justice is and bring ruin upon the city.[21]

At the time chancellor Gattinara was in Genoa: he managed to escape the coup on a brigantine. Through the offices of a hermit he had negotiated secretly with Andrea Doria about the terms on which the latter would enter the service of the emperor. Apart from reasonable demands concerning remuneration and the safety of his family, he had asked Charles 'to subdue the city and territory of Genoa and not to leave them any longer in the power of the Adorni or Fregosi'.[22]

Gattinara decided then that this could best be effected if Doria was in the emperor's service. Doria's attitude towards the Holy League had become ambiguous. Early in 1528 an attack on Sardinia failed because 'he already had other plans in mind', according to the Florentine chronicler, Francesco Guicciardini. Afterwards he should have sailed to Naples to blockade the harbour, in accordance with the plans of the League, but he turned his galleons back towards Genoa. Genoa was afraid that Francis I wanted to expand Savona to be his largest commercial port and naval base, which would severely damage Genoa's position. The town government had asked the king to recognise its 'freedom'. Doria, too, wrote a personal letter to Francis, strongly urging that Savona remain subordinate to Genoa. The king rejected both requests and Doria asked for his contract to be suspended. His nephew Filippino would lead the fleet to Naples in his stead. By now the town council had approved a new constitution. Even though Francis had proposed restoring Genoa's position of superiority at the end of May, Doria offered his services to the pope and emperor. Clement would not side with Doria because he distrusted Francis, so Philibert of Chalon, who was then commander in Naples, closed the deal with the admiral between 9 July and 12 July on behalf of the emperor.[23] His fleet had already sailed from the Bay of Naples on 4 July.

On 22 January 1528 heralds of the kings of France and England had solemnly declared war on Charles at his court in Burgos. Together with a Venetian force, Lautrec managed to advance southwards quickly along the Adriatic coast, partly because the duke of Ferrara had again chosen the French side, as indeed had his neighbour, the marquis of Mantua. The French and Venetians pushed the remainder of the imperial troops out of the Papal States; in March they had control of Apulia and continued on towards Naples to which they began to lay siege. At the same time the fleet, under the command of Filippino Doria, blockaded the harbour.

By now Charles of Lannoy was dead and Ugo de Moncada, the viceroy of Sicily, took over his command. His greatest problem was to provision Naples, a town of more than 100,000 inhabitants. In an attempt to lift the blockade Moncada, too, was killed. The withdrawal of the Genoese fleet on 4 July brought some relief. Soon the garrison had more success in its sorties, because plague had broken out in the camp of the besiegers. By August the French troops were reduced to a third; Lautrec was among the victims. On 9 September Philibert of Chalon was able to inform Charles that the enemy had been practically driven out of the kingdom of Naples. Three days later Andrea Doria drove the French out of Genoa, and on 21 October the French garrison in Savona surrendered. An autumn attempt by the duke of Saint-Pol to retake Lombardy and Genoa with a force of 10,000 was a miserable failure. On 29 June 1529 he himself was taken prisoner.

Since his election to the papacy in the spring of 1523 Clement VII had continually changed allegiances, mostly choosing the French because they were the weakest. Now he made a decision: 'I have made my choice: I have chosen the side of the emperor, and thus will I further live and die'.[24] On 29 June he reached an agreement with Charles. The occupied areas around Ravenna, Reggio, Modena and Cervio would be returned to the papacy; Charles would guarantee the return to power in Florence of Clement's nephew, Alexander de Medici, with the hereditary title of duke. He had been driven out of Florence in a popular uprising during the last days of the Sack of Rome. By now quite old, Alexander would consolidate his alliance with Charles by marrying his natural daughter, Margaret: in view of her age, the marriage would not take place until November 1535. Margaret had been conceived during the siege of Tournai in 1521: her mother was a girl from Oudenaarde, Joanna van der Gheynst, whose later marriage to an official of the Chamber of Accounts of Brabant was arranged by Charles. Margaret had been brought up at the court of the regents Margaret of Austria and Mary of Hungary. For his part, Clement granted dispensation to those responsible for the Sack of Rome; he promised to crown Charles emperor, to invest him with the kingdom of Naples, and never again to side against him. He agreed that Charles and

Ferdinand should have one quarter of the Church's income in their lands to use in the struggle against the Turks, and promised his support against the Lutherans; lastly, he promised to call a general council within a year of a peace being concluded between the Habsburgs and Valois. Now that the pope had been converted to the imperial camp he no longer needed Henry VIII as an ally, and rescinded the divorce proceedings between Henry and Charles' aunt, Catherine of Aragon.

All Charles' objectives had now been met. The road to hegemony in Italy was finally open to him: it would bring long-term peace and stability to the peninsula. His dream of a coronation journey to Italy, which he had planned since January 1525, could now be realised. He had been preparing for it in Barcelona since the end of April 1529, and on 12 August Andrea Doria welcomed his sovereign in the town that he now governed as 'permanent magistrate' in Charles' name. Negotiations between Charles and the pope in Bologna began in November and went on for months. Charles felt strengthened by the peace that had been reached with France in August, because his Italian adversaries had now lost their most important ally. Gattinara, the architect of the policy of pacification in Italy, now worked on an agreement with the Venetians who were to return all the occupied areas to the pope and emperor and to pay reparations. Like the pope, and indeed all the north Italian princes, they promised to declare war on any foreign ruler that threatened the peace in Italy. Charles agreed to the return of Francesco Sforza to the duchy of Milan on condition he paid 500,000 *scudi* as compensation for his treachery, and a further 400,000 for his investiture. The submission of Florence on 12 August 1530 came only after a difficult siege of eleven months, for the city was equipped with most ingenious fortifications, some of them designed by Michelangelo. Charles' general, Philibert of Chalon, recently appointed viceroy of Naples, died in a skirmish ten days before. Now the entire peninsula was tied to the emperor, directly or indirectly, through an alliance or a peace treaty. At last Charles was free to undertake what he saw as his greatest mission, the defence of Christianity against heretics and Muslims. Before that, on his thirtieth birthday, he would be solemnly crowned emperor in Bologna – not in Rome where traces of the Sack were still visible. He would be the last Holy Roman Emperor at whose coronation the pope would officiate.

France – again and again

In the space of nine years Francis I had mounted six major campaigns in Italy, each time with forces varying from 10,000 to 25,000 men. His opponent was obliged at least to equal his efforts. Since 1494, and especially during the disastrous 1520s, north and central Italy had been transformed into an almost permanent base of operations for constantly underpaid, regular and irregular forces. Predominantly foreign mercenaries looted the countryside and occupied the towns. Milan saw armies come and go. Genoa, and Rome even more so, were plundered systematically. Plague, syphilis and dysentery spread throughout the land. The blockade of ports, most importantly Genoa and Naples, and of trading routes, was a cause of starvation and economic recession. The bleeding of this most prosperous region was one of the reasons that for centuries it would have to cede its leading position to the lands around the North Sea. By 1529, those responsible for this disastrous situation – Charles VIII, Louis XII and Francis I, whose hunger for dynastic and personal glory unleashed these scourges on their own subjects and those of the other lands involved – had only increased taxation, lost domains, and an ever-growing mountain of debt to show for their grand ideas.[25]

These nine years of large-scale warfare between the Habsburgs and Valois were interrupted by Francis' nearly 14 months of captivity after the battle of Pavia. Charles treated this spectacular piece of good fortune cautiously. He did not give the impression of being aware of the strategic opportunities he held in his hands. He even ordered his military commanders to cease hostilities as long as the king was in captivity. Henry VIII, on the other hand, did not waste time. 'The time has come for the emperor and for me', he said, 'to obtain satisfaction from France. There is not a moment to lose.'[26] He suggested to Charles that they should carry out the joint invasion plans made in 1521. The idea then had been a combined attack, Henry from Calais and Charles in Languedoc, with a view to the definitive elimination of the French monarchy. In September 1523 Henry did invade Normandy and got to within 50 miles of Paris, but Charles did not have the necessary resources and withdrew, so that the entire operation came to naught. Next year Bourbon and Charles campaigned in southern France, though without any lasting success; this time it was Henry who failed to show up.

After Pavia, Henry again pressed his old claim to the French crown, and was eager to divide the territory. Charles vacillated, then rejected Henry's plans. He deliberately let slip the unique opportunity afforded by the king's captivity and the destruction of his army to weaken his great opponent for ever. His reluctance persuaded Henry to make a separate peace on 30 August with the regent of France, Francis' mother, Louisa of Savoy. She had already approached Sultan Sulaimān with an urgent request for help, lest otherwise the emperor become 'master of the world'. In the summer of 1526 the Turks did indeed mount a concerted attack on Hungary, and took most of the country. Louis of Hungary, husband of Charles' sister Mary, was killed in the battle of Mohács. Through his hesitation Charles lost his enormous advantage in the balance of power in western Europe. His negotiations with Francis were not progressing either. Did strategic considerations stop him from delivering the *coup de grâce*, now that the prize was within his grasp? Was he prepared to bear the loss of his English ally and of Hungary for the sake of these considerations?

By then it was clear that, even if an Anglo-Habsburg invasion of France were successful this time, in the long term it would only lead to new problems with Henry, revolving round the division of France and command of the occupied area. Moreover, it was likely that internal opposition would cause them even more worries. It is most probable that the still politically immature Charles had no idea of what to do in such a situation, and had too much respect for his royal captive to eliminate or even to weaken him by holding him permanently, for example. That was the fate of Charles' brother-in-law, Christian II of Denmark, some years later. It is possible that under the pressure of the Turkish advance, and aware of Sulaimān's promise to support Francis, Charles managed to persuade him of the importance of making the defence of Christianity their joint, primary objective. We know, moreover, that differing viewpoints prevailed in Charles' council, depending on the degree of trust in the French king's word: Lannoy, who came from a traditionally pro-French family and had personally escorted the prisoner, tended to accept his word; Gattinara's doubts were evident.

Charles formulated very limited demands for Francis' release, all of them relating to the dynastic conflicts which had been smouldering for years: the return of the duchy of Burgundy and some smaller territories, the sovereignty over Flanders, Artois and Tournai, the renunciation of claims to Milan and Genoa, the creation of a kingdom of Provence for Charles de Bourbon and joint participation in a crusade. The peace treaty concluded by Charles and Francis in Madrid on 14 January 1526 conceded nearly all Charles' demands, except that Francis made the return of Burgundy conditional on the agreement of his subjects. He would marry Charles' eldest sister Eleanor, and leave his two sons as hostages to guarantee that he would faithfully carry out the terms of the treaty. Provence did not become a kingdom for Bourbon, but he was offered reasonable compensation for the loss of his lands. Francis had secretly stated that he would never give Burgundy up, and within a month of his release on 17 April 1526 he declared the treaty invalid because it was made under duress. On 22 May he signed the Treaty of Cognac with ambassadors from the pope, Venice, Florence and Francesco Sforza, now expelled from his dukedom of Milan.

The League asked Charles to release the royal princes in exchange for a reasonable ransom and to give up Milan. Charles' victory had made Italy more fearful of his hegemony. He had won a battle, but not the peace. Francis' breach of the promises he had made in Madrid was a blow to Charles' plans. He had had visions of an early coronation by the pope, a firm stand against the German Protestants and a crusade against the Turks. Now the continuing war with France forced him to send troops to Italy again.

Only after new French losses at Naples and Genoa in December 1528 was a truce possible between the Habsburgs and Valois. It resulted in further peace talks, this time entrusted to queen Louisa of Savoy and her sister-in-law Margaret of Austria (who had once been married to Philibert of Savoy), the emperor's aunt and regent of the Low Countries. In July 1529 the two ladies conferred in a very cosy atmosphere in Cambrai, a cathedral city belonging to the German Empire, situated on the French border. Francis remained close by to be kept informed of developments while Charles, with complete faith in his aunt's diplomatic skills, sailed from Barcelona to Genoa. His main object was to achieve a peace with France; that would lead to peace in Italy.

Margaret achieved all her objectives and in the peace treaty of 3 August she made only one deviation from the Treaty of Madrid: it was a concession of great symbolic value, however, relating to the duchy of Burgundy, which the French held dear. In the early Middle Ages Burgundy had been a kingdom, and for that reason the duke of Burgundy ranked first among the peers of France, the most important princes after the king. For Charles the significance of Burgundy lay rather in the origins of his dynasty: in the east it bordered Franche-Comté, the free imperial county of Burgundy, which still belonged to the Habsburgs and was governed by Margaret. The duchy of Savoy, lying to the south, was strategically of far greater importance than Burgundy because of its links with the Swiss cantons and Italy, thus making it a bone of contention between the Habsburgs and Valois. In short, Charles' abandonment of his demand for the return of Burgundy should be seen as a symbolic concession, especially since in the previous years he had never made any serious attempt to recover it even though he had attacked other parts of the kingdom. He still retained the right to pursue his claims to Burgundy by other means. But his concession confirms the view that it was not Charles' intention to divide France; nor did he really press for the establishment of a kingdom of Provence – its prospective king, Charles de Bourbon, had in the meantime been killed in Rome.

In other respects the Peace of Cambrai confirmed the Treaty of Madrid.

It provided for the release of Francis' two sons, who had been held hostage in Spain since 1526 to guarantee their father's observance of the treaty. Because he had breached the treaty so flagrantly, and because he was allowed to keep Burgundy, Francis was obliged to pay a ransom of two million golden *écus*, to exclude his allies in the League of Cognac from the treaty (thus betraying them), to abandon once again all his claims to Italian titles and to give up his rights of sovereignty over Artois, Flanders and Tournai. This time the conditions had to be fulfilled before the princes were handed over and before Eleanor – after a betrothal of more than four years – could set off as future queen of France. It did not happen until 1 July 1530, because it was difficult to collect the ransom in a country exhausted by war, and there were months of tough negotiations in Bayonne to agree the weight and quality of the coins in which it was paid.[27]

Nothing came of the joint crusade of Christian monarchs that Charles continually pressed for and had included in his treaties. Henry was in a precarious relationship with the Church following his divorce, and Francis was in league with the sultan and his vassal in Hungary, Zápolya, the *voivode* of Transylvania.[28] So it was that in 1535 Charles took action alone against the infidels; the pirates in Tunis, who hampered Spanish trade, were his target. It would have been an unacceptable loss of face for Francis if he had attacked the emperor in the rear during that crusade. A new reason for tension arose, however, when Francesco Sforza, duke of Milan, died in November 1535 without issue. The dukedom was within the gift of Charles, as Holy Roman Emperor, but Francis still hoped for this prize, if not for himself or the dauphin, then for his second son, Henry.

1536–1537

Francis did not yet dare to confront Charles directly, who was making a triumphant journey through Italy. He opted instead for indirect pressure. In February 1536 he occupied the duchy of Savoy on a flimsy excuse. Duke Charles III was brother-in-law (through his marriage to Beatrice of Portugal) and ally of the emperor, and from Savoy it was easy to threaten Milan. In March French troops advanced as far as Piedmont, whose towns they held for a number of months. In an address to the pope and College of Cardinals in Rome, Charles condemned the invasion of Savoy, yet suggested that Milan be given to Francis' youngest son. For the third time he proposed a duel between king and emperor if this did not happen. If Francis won he could have Milan; if Charles won he could have Burgundy. Francis agreed to this, although he could not see how he could have impugned his opponent's honour. Both men continued to nurse their old dreams, but again it did not end in a duel. Pope Paul III offered to mediate, but the fighting cocks were by no means ready for that.

Charles had raised an army of nearly 45,000 men for a second expedition to the north African coast. The destination was Algiers, where Barbarossa had settled when he was forced out of Tunis. Now Charles deemed it appropriate to use these troops to counter new attacks from France. He could have decided to force the French garrisons out of the towns they still occupied in Piedmont, in order to defend Milan and liberate Savoy from there. He chose another strategy, however, which might have made it possible to drive the French out of Savoy from the west, if he could first take Provence. Apparently he had not forgotten his campaign with Charles de Bourbon twelve years previously, for he referred to it explicitly. Moreover, he fell back on his old strategy of attacking on two fronts, ordering Henry of Nassau, his commander in the Low Countries, to operate in the north.

Charles' strategic concept was not very clear, unless it was that Andrea Doria and his galleons would take the port of Toulon and supply and support the troops from the coast. The French, on the other hand prepared their defences very carefully. At the start of the invasion on 25 July General Montmorency had some 30,000 men under his command, and this number was to grow. He had set up camp on a hilltop near Avignon, the king was safe some distance away at Valence. The towns' defences were inspected and Marseilles, Arles, Tarascon and Beaucaire, which controlled the Rhone, were strengthened. Aix's defences were thought to be too weak and the town was evacuated. A scorched earth policy was followed throughout the region to deny the invading forces any opportunity of living off the land. Five weeks into the campaign the imperial army had taken a number of small coastal towns and Aix, which had been left undefended, but it did not make headway. A siege of Marseilles was unthinkable, as Bourbon had discovered in 1524. The French avoided open battle but carried out guerrilla attacks, seriously impeding the transport of food. The invading army was huge and the shortage of supplies took its toll of thousands of victims of hunger and dysentery, among them the distinguished commander Leyva. The emperor himself described the urgency of the situation in his letters:

> The shortage of food has formed the greatest problem because we cannot count on help from our fleet as we have moved inland. The French king has forced the country people to leave, taking with them what they can. His troops have devastated and burnt everything, they even destroyed and wrecked the mills. All our efforts have been directed towards looking for food, for a large part of the army has had neither bread nor meat for several days.[29]

Charles feared that the attack on Genoa in August, which had been repulsed, would herald a new invasion and turmoil, which would cut off his return; he decided to retreat. In his letter of 31 August to count Cifuentes, his ambassador in Rome, he stated that he would

> follow the same route through Nice as on the outward journey, leaving troops in Toulon, Hyères, Fréjus, Cannes and Antibes with enough supplies, artillery and munition to be able to hold these towns with the help of a good number of ships off the coast of Provence and the Genoese Riviera.

However, a few days later he scrapped this paragraph and noted in the margin, 'Cancelled, because we have decided not to hold any place in this region.'[30] So, within a very short time, the expedition appeared to be a complete failure which, in the same letter – sent also to Henry of Nassau in a slightly different form – the Emperor tried to disguise by pointing to the heavy French losses:

> The king cannot fail to feel the consequences of this war in his own kingdom, for both here and in the regions bordering Flanders the land has suffered enormous losses and damage. It has, after all, had to support four armies, two of ours and two to fight us. His vassals must be exhausted. This area is exhausted too, for almost everything has been destroyed. In other areas he must have had enormous expenses also, and he cannot still be in a state to make war on others rashly.[31]

In the north, Nassau had taken the small town of Guise, then pushed on to Péronne, but he had to raise his siege there. The most important effect was that it stopped the king sending his troops in pursuit of Charles, who instructed his regents in Spain to make the northern borders extra secure.[32] Charles stayed in Genoa from 17 October until 15 November: he was as concerned about the militarily strategic importance of the city as about its role as a financial centre. Vast quantities of silver from the Americas flowed from Barcelona to Genoa, and thence to the rest of Europe. The government of the Republic asked the emperor to guarantee its security, food supply, economic relations with Milan and France, and to respect its privileges.[33] When cordial relations had been consolidated between town and emperor, Charles undertook the journey to Spain. In France, Montmorency was made *connétable*, a position that had become vacant when Bourbon defected to Charles' side. The farmers in Provence and the inhabitants of Aix were left to make good their losses.[34]

Hostilities were resumed in 1537 in Artois. Nassau took the county of Saint-Pol but had to end his siege of Thérouanne when a truce was declared at the instigation of Mary of Hungary and Louisa of Savoy. Francis gave priority to a new campaign in Italy where in October he managed to occupy Piedmont as far as Montferrat. When their resources were exhausted both sides had to call a truce in Italy as well. The Habsburg attack on Artois caused a delay to Francis' army crossing the Alps, on the other side of which, in Apulia, the Turks had landed in July. A joint Franco-Turkish attack on Italy thus never materialised. The Turks did take Corfu, part of the Venetian empire, thus driving the Republic in September to enter into a 'Holy League' with Charles against them. On 27 September 1538 the Turkish fleet forced Andrea Doria's fleet to withdraw at Preveza, on the Greek coast south of Corfu, and the Venetians again abandoned their martial attitude.

Through the mediation of Paul III, Francis and Charles agreed to a peace treaty in Nice in May 1538. Under its terms, Francis agreed to leave Savoy and Piedmont as soon as his youngest son, the duke of Orleans (who since the death of the dauphin was now second in line to the throne), had been invested as duke of Milan and had married a daughter of the Roman king, Ferdinand. Charles and Francis met in Aigues-Mortes, where they discussed joint actions against the Protestants and Muslims – Charles' favourite subject. All their good intentions could not prevent Turkish successes in the Adriatic and Moldavia, however. The renewed ties of friendship between the two monarchs made it possible for Charles to go to the Low Countries overland, crossing right through France from November 1539 to January 1540. The royal princes and *connétable* Montmorency escorted him as far as Valenciennes. Francis and Eleanor gave splendid receptions for him in Loches, in the brand-new castles of the Loire, in Fontainebleau with its magnificent art collection, and in Paris. Charles would never take any initiative to realise such artistic achievements. So lavish were the feasts and tournaments that the peace talks got no further.

Charles continued to brood over the possibility of making a lasting peace with Francis. In March 1540 he suggested that Francis' youngest son, Charles, should marry his daughter Mary, then 12 years old. As her dowry the couple would be given hereditary government of the Low Countries, though under the emperor's sovereignty during his lifetime and reverting to the Habsburgs should they die childless. The emperor would cede his ancestral rights to the duchy of Burgundy in favour of his son-in-law. In return, Francis would again have to relinquish his claims to Savoy and Piedmont and, once more, support Charles in his struggle against the Protestants and Turks. In the light of the difficulties of the conquest of the northeastern provinces and of the 80-year war that Spain would fight for the Low Countries, Charles' offer of the XVII Provinces seems extremely generous. In his speech from the throne in 1542 he put it so:

> At the time I negotiated with the king of France . . . about the establishment of a permanent peace between us. For the sake of Christendom, its kings and

peoples, I made him an offer of such great and profitable regions that in all reasonableness and sincerity he could not have refused.[35]

In his memoirs of 1550 he repeated this in almost identical words. Francis wanted so many amendments, however, that they negotiated until June without reaching any agreement.[36] On 28 October 1540 Charles bestowed the duchy of Milan on his own son. In practice, it was governed by Charles' good friend and general, Ferrante Gonzaga, viceroy of Sicily and brother of Federigo, the duke of Mantua. By doing this Charles frustrated the ambitions of both the Roman king, Ferdinand, who was anxious to acquire that part of the Roman Empire for his own dynasty and, of course, the king of France. In 1543 Paul III tried to buy Milan from Charles for his own son, Pier Luigi Farnese, the new duke of Florence. Charles thought that the offer of 1,000,000 ducats should have been at least twice as high; moreover he recognised the strategic disadvantages of the offer and so rejected it.[37]

1542-1544

In the meantime Francis renewed his efforts to achieve his objectives by military means and by close collaboration with Suleimān. On 12 July 1542 he declared war on Charles on the pretext that two of his negotiators with the sultan had been murdered. His attacks on Luxembourg and Perpignan were repulsed. His actions brought the traditional allies, Henry VIII and Charles, together again, and on 11 February 1543 they once more agreed to make a joint attack on Francis. In July they declared war. Henry sent troops to Calais, to wreak havoc in the county of Boulogne. In September the French managed to occupy Luxembourg with the help of a Guelders army. When Guelders had been subdued Charles and his army went south, towards Artois. On 2 November they confronted Francis' army at Landrecies, on the upper reaches of the Sambre. The results of any battle must have been difficult to foresee, but Francis sounded the retreat. Charles then hurried on to occupy Cambrai. The town and surrounding villages were an imperial fief, but the bishopric stretched far into the Low Countries. The bishop tended to side with the French, thus damaging the homogeneity of the XVII Provinces.

In August, French and Turkish troops besieged Nice, which was still in the hands of Charles III of Savoy. When it fell, the French pushed on to Piedmont. The Turkish fleet, under the command of the infamous Barbarossa, plundered its way along the coast as far as Toulon. On the king's orders the inhabitants had to vacate their homes for Turkish officers, allow the force of 30,000 men to set up camp nearby and supply them with food. For eight months, until May 1544, a piece of French territory was a base for the Turkish fleet. It led to protest in the surrounding area and outrage throughout Christendom. The Habsburgs could do little more than carry out limited naval action and try to defend the coast from the superior forces of the French and Turks and the threats they posed in the western Mediterranean.[38] In April 1544 the imperial troops in Piedmont suffered an ignominious defeat when they unexpectedly came upon Franco-Swiss troops at Ceresola and were forced into battle. The French lacked financial resources, however, and were unable to exploit their victory. In June, their commander, Piero Strozzi, was again defeated during an attack on Milan.

Once Charles had his hands free in Guelders he asked the support of the German princes to attack the French, who were so shamelessly in league with the Turks. Two prominent Protestant princes, Duke Maurice of Saxony and Albrecht Alcibiades of Brandenburg, each with about 1,000 cavalry, joined the imperial army at Saint-Dizier. According to plan, Henry VIII simultaneously invaded Picardy and laid siege to Boulogne. Charles' commander, Ferrante Gonzaga, had by now retaken Luxembourg and joined the imperial army, which, with units recalled from Italy, numbered some 45,000 men. The plan was that the two great armies should advance on Paris, but both were held up by sieges for several weeks: Saint-Dizier, a walled town with modern fortifications, held out until 17 August, Boulogne until 14 September. The shortage of supplies, and above all of money, was felt after a couple of months, which was quite normal in such a large military operation. Francis had counted on this: he gathered a force of 45,000 men and strengthened the defences of Paris; but he also tried to arrange a truce immediately.

Francis managed to avoid a pitched battle. His army was on the move south of the Marne while that of Charles headed west on the northern bank. These enormous forces marched in parallel for 100 miles. In his memoirs of 1550 Charles reflected that if his troops had been able to go further and cross the Marne by the stone bridge at Épernay, then the battle he had wanted could have taken place there. His troops were exhausted from the previous days' marches, however. The French had an extra day to fortify the place, and then it was not wise to attack.[39] The greatest damage was done by French troops plundering the town of Lagny because they considered its inhabitants 'rebels and enemies of the king and his authority'.[40] The advance of the imperial troops as far as Château-Thierry, 50 miles from Paris, caused panic in the capital and increased pressure on the king to negotiate. Charles, also, was afraid of being pressed for time, and especially for money, and at the beginning of September he started to parley. He barely informed Henry of his plans and rather let his ally down – although it was reasonable to suppose that Henry would not reach Paris before winter and that his men would want to return home.[41]

So it was that on 18 September 1544 Francis and Charles made a separate peace at Crépy. They would both renounce their conquests and their conflicting claims as soon as Francis' younger son Charles, duke of Orleans, had married either Charles' daughter, Mary, or Ferdinand's daughter, Anna, whichever the emperor eventually decided. Keeping to his plan of 1540 he would give Mary the Low Countries and Franche-Comté and Anna the duchy of Milan as a dowry, if the groom were also given four dukedoms in appanage. Once more it was agreed that both Catholic monarchs should strive for the reformation of the Church through a general council, and that they would fight Protestants and Turks together. Under the secret part of the treaty it was agreed that Francis would provide 10,000 foot soldiers and 600 heavy cavalry to fight against these enemies of the faith whenever the emperor asked.[42] With past history in mind, some doubt about the likelihood of such a promise being kept is not out of place. In view of the enormous show of strength preceding it, this treaty was a very meagre result, containing nothing that had not been discussed or even solemnly promised several times before. There is a vast discrepancy between the firm plans devised in the spring, the strenuous efforts to implement them and the ease with which they were dropped, which does not seem credible to the present-day observer. The proposed offer of the duchy of Milan or the Low Countries as a dowry, an offer first made in 1540, is also astonishing. Milan had one-third of the population of the Low Countries and was ravaged by 50 years of war. Its strategic position in relation to Italy, and Francis' exceptional desire to possess it, must have been the deciding factors.

The Treaty of Crépy met with serious resistance on both sides. Charles' council objected to giving up those areas that were of strategic importance to his empire. The French crown prince, Henry, was opposed to the division of the kingdom and the conferment of Milan on his brother. The unexpected death of the latter in September 1545, and of Francis I on 31 March 1547, gave the new king, Henry II, a free hand.

1551–1553

Henry II's anti-Habsburg policy was no less tough than that of his father. He did not have the basis of personal camaraderie and mutual respect that always remained between Francis and Charles despite their keen disappointments. His four-year captivity in Spain may have had a negative effect on Henry's feelings. He collaborated with the Protestant princes in Germany and with the Turks. He strengthened his position in Italy by siding with Ottavio Farnese, whose possession of the duchy of Parma was questioned by Charles. In spite of a long siege there in 1551 Charles had to withdraw his troops on 15 May 1552. At the end of July an uprising in Siena forced the Spanish garrison out, and the republic asked for support from the French. The most important theatre of battle would now be in the north, on the border between France and the Low Countries. The summer of 1551 saw acts of piracy against shipping from the Low Countries on the North Sea and along the Atlantic coast. The following year Mary of Hungary fitted out a fleet with 6,000 men to safeguard commercial traffic to and from Spain.[43] On 26 September Henry made a formal declaration of war, but continued to negotiate with margrave Albrecht Alcibiades of Brandenburg and Maurice of Saxony. He agreed on subsidies for the army that the Protestant princes would lead against the emperor, while he would take the battle into Lorraine and the Low Countries.

In April 1552 Maurice advanced along the Danube while Henry invaded Lorraine with 35,000 men. Within a month he had taken the cathedral cities of Toul, Metz and Verdun which were dependencies of the German Empire, as well as strongholds in Luxembourg. He carried out raids in Artois and Hainault. Charles' attention was fixed on Italy, and this dual attack took him completely by surprise. He was in Innsbruck, his army in Lombardy, and Ferdinand was occupied with the defence of Hungary. It was months before he could respond from his awkward position, recall his troops from Italy and raise more lansquenets in those parts of Germany that were still Catholic. He even persuaded Albrecht Alcibiades to take part in an attempt to recover the towns of Lorraine.

The army of 55,000 men and 150 cannon with which Charles advanced on Lorraine in September was probably the largest ever mobilised in Europe until then. He explained at length in a letter to Philip that it was essential to win back this part of the Empire: not only did it open the way to the German lands, it was also strategically important for communications between the Low Countries and the south.[44] There was a garrison of 6,000 men at Metz and the defences had been considerably strengthened during the summer, complying with the highest requirements of the period. The siege began on 19 October when trenches were dug, very late in the year. The cold took its toll of the army, and of the emperor too. Severe attacks of gout kept him to his bed for long periods. Despite constant bombardment and successfully making a breach, the duke of Alva dared not give orders to attack, fearing he would come under side fire from the besieged. While the imperial army was thus tied down before Metz, Henry

II attacked Artois and Hainault and laid siege to, and then took, Hesdin. Although Charles was very sensitive of the damage to his reputation if such a large army under his personal command had to lift a siege,[45] nevertheless the winter, sickness, death and desertion among the troops forced him to retreat on New Year's Day 1553. 1552, a calamitous year in which he lost Parma, Siena and Hesdin, ended in even greater disaster.

With the help of Mary of Hungary, with whom Charles spent the winter in Brussels in a state of great despondency, Habsburg troops were able to retake Thérouanne and Hesdin in 1553 and push the French back from the border regions. The city and cathedral of Thérouanne were demolished for its so-called treason. Mary was saddened that Henry had destroyed her castle and hunting lodge at Binche and her fort of Mariemont. It was the king's personal revenge for the destruction the year before of his castle of Folenbray, on Mary's orders.[46] In August 1553 French and Turkish ships took Corsica from Genoa and made communications in the western Mediterranean very unsafe.

Right, ambition and necessity

It was not until 1559, with the Treaty of Cateau-Cambrésis, that the Habsburgs brought their wars with the Valois to a satisfactory conclusion. The wars had started in Italy in 1494 (although the Habsburgs were not involved directly) and the wars between France and the dukes of Burgundy had begun as early as 1465. The protagonists constantly asked themselves how so much violence could be justified. In the sixteenth century conflicts were increasingly fought through the mass media – in those days, printed pamphlets which had an unmistakable influence on public opinion. Charles appears to have disliked this form of propaganda.[47] In order to justify his attacks on Milan, Francis pointed to his dynastic rights, which Maximilian had recognised when he invested Louis XII with the duchy in 1512. He called upon his dynastic rights, too, to justify his repeated attacks on Naples, Luxembourg and Artois. His surprise attack on Savoy in 1536 was justified by his mother's hereditary claims. All these claims were, of course, open to dispute because they were seldom clear-cut, but it was still felt necessary to formulate them. The main aim was to gain permanent control of the land.

Charles fought few wars of conquest: in 1521 the conquest of Milan and the capture of Tournai, in 1522 the complete subjection of Friesland, and in 1543 the submission of Guelders. In Milan he pursued the claims of his predecessors as Roman kings, in Guelders those of duke Charles the Bold of Burgundy, confirmed by treaty in 1528; in 1515 he had bought the rights to Friesland from its ruler. Only in the cases of the cities of Tournai and Cambrai was there any question of territorial possession that could be justified purely as compensation for damages suffered as a result of wars of aggression. For it was always the French who started the aggression: against Naples from 1494, Milan in 1498, the attack on Luxembourg in 1521, 1527–28 the League of Cognac, 1536 the invasion of Savoy and Piedmont, in 1542 invasions of Artois, Luxembourg, Brabant and Navarre, and in 1552 the invasion of Lorraine, Luxembourg and Artois.

The wars Charles waged were essentially defensive wars. It is true that on a number of occasions he made plans with Henry VIII to invade France jointly and divide it between them: in 1524 he campaigned on that basis in Provence, with the original intention of winning the region as compensation for Charles de Bourbon. Conquest was clearly not his intention in Provence in 1536, nor in Champagne in 1544: his aim was to punish the aggressor and put pressure on him to make a favourable peace. Charles' main justification here was to regain his honour when it had been impugned, as the traditional ethics of chivalry required.

The kings' ethics cannot be blamed for France regularly beginning the wars. France was the largest, richest and most populous state in western Europe, and keen to expand. From 1494 to 1520 it met no opposition worth speaking of. The surrender of Naples was largely due to the logistic difficulties of controlling the region from France. So the struggle centred on Milan. The growth of the Habsburg possessions as a ring round France and in Italy was a structural hindrance to France's attempts to expand in north Italy, as it had been able to do for more than twenty years. When the Habsburgs began to form a real opposition they became the block over which France's drive to expand constantly stumbled. It is interesting to see a certain regularity in the frequency of the French attacks (apart from the 1520s): most wars lasted from two to three years, with an interval of five to seven years between them. Apparently this was the length of time necessary to recover and to find sufficient military, demographic and financial resources for the fight.

Table 3.1 Frequency of wars between Habsburgs and Valois

	Duration of war in years	Interval between wars in years
1515	1	
1521–25	4	6
1527–29	3	2
1536–37	2	7
1542–44	3	5
1551–53	2	7

Obviously there was an enormous difference between the justification of war as defined by theologians and the political reality. In every case insufficient use was made of diplomacy to solve conflicts, and the resources employed were infinitely heavier than could be considered reasonable for the official objectives of the struggle. How much human suffering was necessary to satisfy the honour and reputation of the king and the emperor was a question that their contemporaries dared not ask.

Notes:

1. Alvarez Fernandez, *Corpus documental*, I, 82.
2. *Ibid.*, 71–4.
3. Haliczer, *The Comuneros of Castile*, 139–41.
4. M. Alvarez Fernandez, *Carlos V. Un hombre para Europa* (Madrid, 1976), 28.
5. Kleinheyer, *Die kaiserlichen Wahlkapitulationen*, 45–50, 101–3, 127–8; text: A. Kluckhohn, ed., *Deutsche Reichstagsakten, Jüngere Reihe*, I (Gotha, 1893), no.387, 864–76.
6. M. le Glay, ed., *Négotiations diplomatiques entre la France et l'Autriche 1491–1530*, 2 (Paris, 1845), no.40, 125.
7. Quote from H. Rabe, *Reich und Glaubensspaltung: Deutschland 1500–1600* (Munich, 1989), 149; P. Chaunu, *L'Espagne de Charles Quint* (Paris, 1973), 226; for revenue in the Low Countries: M. Baelde, 'Financiële politiek en domaniale evolutie in de Nederlanden onder Karel V en Filips II (1530–1560)', *Tijdschrift voor Geschiedenis*, 76 (1963), 15.
8. A. Pacini, *I presupposti politici del 'Secoli dei Genovesi': la Riforma del 1528* (Genoa, 1990), 80, 101–14.
9. C. S. L. Davies, 'Tournai and the English Crown, 1513–1519', *The Historical Journal*, 41 (1998), 1–26, especially 3–17; Knecht, *Renaissance Warrior*, 170.
10. J. D. Tracy, *Holland under Habsburg Rule 1506–1566* (Berkeley, 1990), 69–89.
11. Gorter-van Royen, *Maria van Hongarije*, 197–227.
12. Knecht, *Renaissance Warrior*, 176, 396.
13. *Ibid.*, 486–7.
14. J. G. Smit, *Vorst en Onderdaan. Studies over Holland en Zeeland in de late Middeleeuwen* (Leuven, 1995), 252–3.
15. Brandi, *Kaiser Karl V.*, 190–2.
16. Pacini, *I presupposti politici*, 86–101.
17. Knecht, *Renaissance Warrior*, 200–15.
18. *Ibid.*, 216–25.
19. Pacini, *I presupposti politici*, 115–45.
20. Knecht, *Renaissance Warrior*, 256.
21. Pacini, *I presupposti politici*, 256–66, 264 n.254 (quotation).
22. *Ibid.*, 260.
23. *Ibid.*, 312–23.
24. Knecht, *Renaissance Warrior*, 279.
25. *Ibid.*, 193–7, 342–7.
26. *Ibid.*, 229.
27. *Ibid.*, 285–6.

28. *Ibid.*, 295–6.
29. Fernandez Alvarez, *Corpus documental*, I, 522: Charles to the count of Cifuentes, 31 August and 5 September 1536.
30. *Ibid.*, 523 and n. 345.
31. *Ibid.*, 524–5.
32. *Ibid.*, 525–31: Charles to Isabella, 8 September 1536.
33. A. Pacini, *La Genova di Andrea Doria nell'Imperio di Carlo V* (Florence, 1999), 372–3.
34. Knecht, *Renaissance Warrior*, 334–41.
35. Fernandez Alvarez, *Corpus documental*, IV, 509 n. 100.
36. Knecht, *Renaissance Warrior*, 393–405.
37. Fernandez Alvarez, *Corpus documental*, II, 125, 135, 165–6: June–October 1543.
38. *Ibid.*, II, 160–9: August and October 1543.
39. *Ibid.*, IV, 521–3.
40. Knecht, *Renaissance Warrior*, 492.
41. J.J. Scarisbrick, *Henry VIII* (New Haven and London, 1997), 439–51.
42. Brandi, *Kaiser Karl V.*, 448.
43. L. Sicking, *Zeemacht en onmacht. Maritieme politiek in de Nederlanden 1488–1558* (Amsterdam, 1998), 106–46.
44. Fernandez Alvarez, *Corpus documental*, III, 542: Charles to Philip, Metz, 25 December 1552.
45. *Ibid.*, 543.
46. Gorter-van Royen, *Maria van Hongarije*, 294.
47. Brandi, *Kaiser Karl V.*, 404.

4
Protector of the Catholic Church

The great misunderstanding

On his election as Holy Roman Emperor Charles was immediately confronted with his responsibilities to ensure the destruction throughout all his territories of those works which the pope had branded as heretical. In 1515 Leo X had already pointed out that printed works could spread heresies and he wanted bishops and inquisitors to censure them. In the Low Countries Charles and Regent Margaret issued edicts on the matter in 1517, 1519 and 1520, but found that, despite heavy sanctions, they were not sufficiently observed. On 20 March 1521, Charles issued a new ordinance following the excommunication of Martin Luther by Leo X. In it he referred to himself as the 'greatest protector and upholder of the Universal Church', because of his position as emperor. Heretical books were to be burnt to the sound of trumpets at those places where normally public punishments were carried out. Informants were promised one third of the fines imposed.[1]

In the German Empire the situation was rather more complicated. In the Low Countries Charles himself was ruler of each principality, just as he was king of each of the kingdoms of Spain. In the German Empire, however, the emperor did not have the power to enforce his will on his subjects directly: to exercise his authority he was dependent on the government of the town or territory in question. Spurred on by the papal legate, the emperor was keen to order that all books by Luther be burnt in the German Empire as well. But Martin Luther, the Augustinian monk and professor of theology at the distant University of Wittenberg, enjoyed the protection of no less a person than Frederick the Wise, duke of Saxony and founder of the University. He asked the emperor not to proceed against his subject Luther without first giving him a hearing. Charles was anxious to get the matter over with as soon as possible because 'much unrest and heresies could grow from it'. He summoned Luther under safe conduct to be heard by 'learned and very wise men' at the next Diet in Worms. Because Luther had been excommunicated it was necessary to persuade him to recant his questionable works and submit again to the authority of the pope.[2]

Charles was barely 21 years old, and had just been crowned Roman king in Aachen when he confronted the theologian who had publicly burned the pope's letter of excommunication along with a copy of Church Law. The previous five years had seen the spread of more than half a million copies of Luther's works, in the form of hundreds of pamphlets as well as the more important books, *Address to the Christian Nobility of the German Nation*, *On the Babylonian Captivity of the Church of God*, and in particular, *On the Liberty of a Christian Man*. During his journey to Worms, Luther preached to full churches in every town.[3] Charles and his advisors had intended to follow the traditional procedure of pronouncing the imperial ban, putting Luther outside the secular law as well. In view of the papal excommunication there could be no question of a sensitive consideration of Luther's arguments and views on spiritual matters. Luther recanted nothing because no proofs from the Scriptures had been put forward to counter his theses while 'the pope and councils are not credible because they are known often to have erred and contradicted themselves'. On 19 April the Diet condemned him, because, according to the verdict given in French in the name of the emperor, 'any thing else would be a disgrace to me [Charles] and to you, the noble and illustrious German Nation, since through privilege and special election we have been appointed defenders and protectors of the Catholic faith'.[4] Even today, Luther's words, 'Here stand I. I can do no other. God help me. Amen', quoted in thousands of pamphlets after the Diet, strike a far more sympathetic note.

The imperial court had seriously underestimated the scope of the religious movement in the German lands. On 8 May and 26 May 1521 Charles published an Edict in Worms against both Luther and the possession and circulation of his works and his image: it demanded nothing less than the complete destruction and public burning of all his works. New works had to be approved by the bishops or their substitutes in agreement with the nearest theological faculty.[5] The authorities were apparently still unaware of how widely the works had already been disseminated, or of the enormous, continuing public interest in reformist thought.

Luther's case, which lasted barely two days, was not the only business of the Diet of Worms in 1521. A long list of 'Complaints of the German Nation against the Holy See' was also presented. These complaints had been under discussion long before Luther appeared on the scene: they dated from 1417, when the German council fathers had formulated an extensive list of abuses at the Council of Konstanz. They were primarily concerned with Rome's interference in the affairs of the German Church, especially the Curia's appointments to Church positions, its intervention in matters within the jurisdiction of German bishops, and its financial practices. These complaints could have then formed a basis for internal reform of the Church's organisation, allowing Rome less opportunity to meddle with the German 'nation'. At the same time there were similar aspirations in France and England to greater freedom for the 'national' church, and these did actually take shape through royal legislation and concordats with the pope.

In Germany, the peculiar structures of power impeded any such reform in the sense of a greater independence from Rome. Successive emperors, with their imperial coronation in mind, kept a wary eye on the pope while, as princes in their own hereditary lands, still managing to reach agreements to their own material advantage. In 1445 Frederick III, for example, acquired the right to 10 per cent of all church benefices in the Empire. The people bore the burden and, like the local clergy, were also confronted with the pope's seemingly arbitrary intervention and appointments. The German clergy and the faithful showed an increasing aversion to it all. At the Diet at Augsburg in 1518 Maximilian's request for a tithe for his struggle against the Turks was turned down forcefully, the argument being that taxes for the benefit of the Roman Curia already pressed heavily on the 'common man'. At the same assembly Erard de la Marck, the bishop of Liège, lodged a sharp complaint about the Curia's interference in his diocesis.[6] The deeply rooted annoyance felt by clergy and laity alike was not understood by the emperors in Germany, as it was in other western monarchies. The special relationship between the Roman emperor and the papal Curia helps to explain this lack of understanding, which made the emperor an object of the same criticism to which the papacy was exposed.

When summoning them to the Diet at Worms Charles had invited the estates to list their complaints and present them. After 100 years of neglect, 40 pages and 102 articles of grievances against Rome and the native clergy placed an originally internal problem in the political forum. It was not so much a matter of theological problems as of legal friction between different levels in the Church organisation and between the clergy and temporal bodies. For the next ten years these 'Complaints of the German Nation against the Holy See', with a number of adaptations and reactions, would return to the agenda of the meetings of the Diet and of other representative bodies such as regional assemblies, synods and consultations between towns. Among both the spiritual and temporal estates there was a genuine desire to settle the mutual complaints and a wish for reform in a reasonable and businesslike way. In the summer of 1524 the German clergy played a constructive part in preparing for negotiations on the matter for the planned autumn Diet in Speyer.[7] In fact this never took place, because of the outbreak of the Peasants' War (nor did the Diet of 1525). So it was that the complaints appeared on the agenda of the Diet of Speyer in 1526, where the atmosphere was entirely different owing to the acts of violence that had been committed during the revolt, particularly against church property. A large number of princes, even Catholic ones, had attacked religious institutions. The clergy vented their grievances against the temporal estates more strongly than before. The rebels' complaints also found a place on the agenda of negotiations. The slowness of the decision-making process complicated the problem. More and more documents were added to the records, the Peasants' War highlighted the differences, and in the meantime the movement for reform continued to grow.

The Diet of Worms of 1521 is well known in history for the confrontation between the emperor and Luther, and for the latter's punishment. The emperor and his entourage considered this just a minor matter to be resolved quickly and formally, their major concern being to strengthen Charles' political position in the Empire. Charles took a conciliatory line with Frederick of Saxony and Joachim of Brandenburg who, as electors, had hesitated the longest before giving him their support. It was also essential to make arrangements for the government of the Empire during his forthcoming absence. Many towns in Spain had rebelled and his return to the peninsula was a matter of some urgency. This was the reason for his insistence on the formation of a regency council, the *Reichsregiment*, on the pattern of the one imposed on Maximilian by the Diet in 1500 which had been disbanded in 1502. The main aim of the estates now was to stop the emperor from putting his general European interests before those of the Empire. The emperor, on the other hand, did not want a permanent body to be created, only one that would govern during his absence.[8] The *Reichsregiment* established at Worms was the most important governing body for the ten years before Charles' return to Germany. In addition to the emperor's deputy – Charles appointed his brother Ferdinand to this position – the *Regiment* had 22 members, elected for a limited term from the various estates.[9]

Charles was away from Germany for ten years, and in that time he lost sight of the question of reformation in Germany. Even the Peasants' War, which threw Germany, Switzerland and the hereditary Habsburg lands into turmoil between 1524 and 1526, failed to gain his attention. However, in 1524, he did oppose the plans of the Diet to hold a National German Council, because by then he favoured a general council. He hoped that Germany's religious problems could be resolved within the framework of general Church reform. His demand put pressure on Clement VII, who had joined the anti-Habsburg League of Cognac in 1526.[10]

In the meantime there had been such radical changes in relationships in Germany that it was increasingly difficult formally to maintain the rigidly repressive policy of the Edict of Worms. It had indeed proved impossible to put such a strict policy into practice. The ever-growing support for the reformist movement could no longer be ignored. The Diet of Speyer in 1526 in fact rendered the Edict – which had not yet been enforced – inoperable by accepting that, in anticipation of a council, 'in religious matters every section of the Empire could behave in a way that it hoped and believed could be justified before God and His Imperial Majesty'. The representatives were obviously affected by the Peasants' War, which in many places had evangelical undertones, and they were afraid of new outbreaks. The Diet, however, was not an unchanging legislative body: its composition varied somewhat according to circumstances, the participating estates and the presence or absence of the king or emperor. In 1529 King Ferdinand had a majority in the Diet of Speyer weaken the 1526 resolution and the Edict of Worms again took effect, but the results were exactly the opposite of what was desired. The evangelically minded estates now declared that a majority decision of the Diet could not be binding on 'matters concerning the honour of God and our spiritual welfare and salvation'. This meant that the legal basis for the intervention of the state in religious matters had now fallen away. This formal 'protest', led by the elector of Saxony and the landgrave of Hesse, and supported by imperial towns of south Germany – the 'protestants' – was the impulse for the formation of a political alliance to protect reformist religious beliefs, the League of Schmalkalden.

Charles was at last forced to realise that his years of urging the pope to call a general council had not brought results. The long delays in Rome undermined the German Protestants' trust in the emperor's commitment. They proposed that a council be held on imperial soil and presided over by the emperor. This was not an option for Charles; he could see that the French would never accept him as president of the council. Moreover, Clement VII feared that a council would strengthen Charles' hegemony in Italy while appearing only to solve his problems in Germany. Certainly the pope and his cardinals had reason enough to view any reformation of the Church 'in its head and members' with the greatest suspicion: their own actions would of course be exposed to severe criticism. Clement never convened a council, thus helping to undermine the position of the emperor, who had long held out to the German Protestants the prospect of reformation through a general council.

During the Peasants' War (1524–26) the split between the traditional Church in Germany which, as a large landowner and through the recruitment of its prelates, naturally tended to favour the nobility, and the ordinary faithful, had been shown to be very deep. There were other cultural differences between the more urbanised Rhineland and south and the still very rural central and east Germany. In the Low Countries a number of religious movements supporting religious revival, pious literature in the vernacular, inner devotion and reformation of the monasteries with a view to a strict observance of the Rule (observantism) had been active since the fourteenth century. There was little of this in Germany. The fundamental differences between the Church and religion in Germany were essentially due to the absence of reforms that had been introduced gradually and earlier in other places. This delay in institutional adaptation would lead to an even more radical theological breakthrough in Germany.

All these developments had taken place almost without the emperor's knowledge. After his departure from Germany in 1521 he had not realised how much opposition his repressive policies aroused nor how much support the movement for reform won. Not until 1529–30 was there a radical change of direction in Charles' policies in general, and thus, too, in his religious policy. The peace with France and his hegemony in Italy meant that his hands were no longer tied. Growing pressure from the pirates from north Africa and the western Mediterranean made his Spanish subjects nervous. They demanded drastic action to get rid of them. Then, in 1529, the Turkish armies occupied a large part of Hungary and threatened Vienna, the very heart of the Habsburg possessions. The dynastic interests of the Habsburgs and the emperor's universal responsibility to defend Christendom compelled Charles to move against them.

In June 1529 Charles had made a peace with Clement VII in which both he and Ferdinand agreed to fight against the heretics and to return to the pope those areas that had been occupied by Venice; in return, Clement granted Charles the enjoyment of Church benefices, the right to the investiture of the kingdom of Naples and the promise that the Curia would deal with the divorce between Henry VIII and Catherine of Aragon, Charles' and Ferdinand's aunt. A month later Charles embarked in Barcelona for Genoa, whence he commenced a triumphal journey through the newly conquered regions. He stayed in Bologna from December 1529 to the end of the following March, conducting delicate negotiations with Clement. The pope had first to give absolution for the havoc caused by the imperial troops in Rome in 1527, including his own captivity. It was a difficult matter to summon a council for church reform and matters of the faith, and no progress was made in that direction. In exchange for crowning him emperor the pope demanded that Charles restore Francesco Sforza as duke of Milan and that he help to regain the Republic of Florence so that the pope's nephew, Alexander de Medici, could be restored to power there. It was only at the beginning of February that the decision was made not to hold the coronation in Rome but in Bologna, which was also in the Papal States. Painful memories of the Sack of Rome would be avoided. Charles hesitated for a long time: the deciding factor was that Ferdinand had been urging him for many months to come to Germany to counter the threats from the Protestants and Turks. A journey to Rome, and then to the kingdom of Naples, which had been ravaged by the recent French invasion, had to be postponed.

In a long letter from Bologna, dated 11 January 1530, Charles carefully explained his reasons to his brother. At that point he was unsure about the possibility of postponing his journey to Germany for some months, in order to have the coronation in Rome and then to proceed to Naples. For page after page he deliberated the question; clearly, he had not yet realised the urgency of the religious problems. His approach to the situation shows how little insight he had into German relationships:

> If there is any remedy for the great heresies that get worse by the day in Germany, it is that I come in person, or at least that it is known I am on the way. In that connection, one must act resolutely and unhesitatingly against disobedience, and must take side against those who, in their malevolent meanness of spirit, are eager to make someone else [other than you, Ferdinand] Roman king.[11]

Give and take

The whole confused business eventually appeared on the agenda of the Diet at Augsburg in June 1530, where all the complaints were included in the general religious discussions. It was the first time that the religious question was discussed openly in the Diet. The proclamation of the Confession of Augsburg had clearly aligned the evangelical movement and provided the opportunity for excluding fundamental tendencies, like the Anabaptists of Münster. The presence of the newly crowned emperor raised great expectations, but after such a long delay it was very hard to deal with Church and religious questions. Only in the spring of 1530 did Charles begin to give serious thought to the problems of the German Empire. Bernhard Cles, archbishop of Trent and one of Archduke Ferdinand's leading counsellors, was an important advisor to Charles on the road to Augsburg.

In calling the Diet the emperor had desired all participants to 'put in writing their views and ideas on the digression and discord and also on the abuses ... so that the digression and discord could be considered and understood as well as possible, and they could be restored as soon as possible to a unanimous Christian agreement'. So the Complaints of the German Nation against the pope and Roman Curia, which had first been lodged in 1521, and the objections of the temporal estates to the spiritual, were once again presented. The emperor had to achieve agreement on the religious question because he needed wide support for the election of his brother Ferdinand as Roman king – an honour which had become available on his own coronation as emperor – and for the defence against the Turks.

On 25 June the chancellor of the elector of Saxony solemnly read the Confession of Augsburg to the emperor and the Diet. It gave the Protestants a status that could never be taken from them. The Catholics did not deem it necessary to formulate a confession of faith because they felt they were already on the right path. At the emperor's request a refutation, the *Confutatio*, was drawn up by Catholic theologians. As it was read out in the Diet in his name, the emperor lost some of the strength of his impartiality, in Protestant eyes. This seems entirely understandable, especially in view of the terms in which Charles referred to the Protestants in a letter written to Clement VII on 14 July: 'the villains ... the abscess'. Melanchthon replied to the *Confutatio* with his *Apology*, but since neither text was included in the formal discussions nor in the closing act of 19 November the two documents, which were essential for the discussions between the religious persuasions, were not given any constitutional importance. Consequently, political propaganda carried much weight in the projected religious discussions.[12]

For many months a special committee of the Diet examined all the complaints in an attempt to find a legally sound basis for a solution. It was the first time that the advocates of the Confession of Augsburg were accepted as equal partners in the discussion. The result was mainly concerned with the disputes that were thought to have caused the most trouble in the preceding years, viz. the application of Church penalties such as excommunication and interdict, and the revenues and privileges of the parochial clergy. The committee of complaints tried to make a clear distinction between Church and worldly matters in an effort to pave the way to an agreement. It recommended that the clergy should confine its jurisdiction to Church and spiritual affairs and that the secular authorities, on the other hand, should not impede the execution of a Church verdict. Agreement could not be reached on the subject of the lay chalice, the canon for the Mass or the marriage of priests.

In November the emperor had those articles on which the spiritual and temporal estates had reached agreement bound into a concordat. With it the Catholic representatives to the Diet recognised the need for a new definition of the relationship between the Church and the world. The legal ruling had gone too far, however, for some Catholics, notably the elector of the Palatinate and the duke of Jülich, while the Protestants, who were interested in fundamental spiritual questions, rejected it as not going far enough. This was why the concordat was never enacted into law.[13] The emperor had first invited the Diet to reach a consensus on spiritual matters. The differences of opinion seemed to be irreconcilable on the political level, because some Catholic princes rejected the proposals of the concordat and the Protestants pressed for political tolerance for the evangelical movement.

The recess declaration of the Diet of Augsburg again confirmed the Edict of Worms, in the hope of putting an end to further expansion of the Reformation. Freedom of religion would have to be guaranteed to Catholics living in evangelical areas. Illegally acquired Church property would be restored to its rightful owners. It was proposed that within a year a general council would make a decision on the complaints that had been raised. The criminalisation of the Reformation was accentuated by its being perceived as violating the national peace – a crime for which heavy penalties, including military intervention, were possible under imperial law. Although the emperor did indeed consider taking military action against the Protestants the Catholic princes dissuaded him, arguing that the outcome was highly uncertain, in part because it was possible that many of the mercenary soldiers would defect to the other side. A massive number of cases against the Protestants had already been brought before the *Reichskammergericht*, accusing them of unlawful appropriation of Church property and revenues. In 1534 this led to the most important of them rejecting the jurisdiction of the court that had only been established in 1495; in 1542 they also rejected the Empire's highest judicial authority, thereby repudiating one of the very foundations of the Empire's unity.[14]

In direct reaction to the renewed declaration of religious persecution, the Protestants formed the League of Schmalkalden in February 1531. It was a defensive alliance of princes and towns, such as had existed for hundreds of years in the Empire, and which had been a target of government reform since 1495. The lack of authority of both emperor and Diet resulted in a restoration of traditional forms of government, which in essence negated any effective form of higher authority.

Charles worked with greater urgency than before to arrange a general council in the hope that the battle of the faith in Germany could be brought to an end. He accepted the initiative of the electors Albrecht of Mainz (the primate of the Catholic Church in the Empire) and Louis of the Palatinate to continue to negotiate with the Protestants in order to avoid a permanent political and religious split in the Empire. In the expectation of a general council the Protestants were willing to talk about the restoration of the general national peace, as long as the proceedings against them were suspended. They saw no point in discussing dogma. On 8 July 1531 Charles mandated the two Catholic negotiators to suspend all cases sub judice against the Protestants, but at the same time forbade them to inform anyone or make his decision public knowledge.[15] Obviously the emperor still hoped for some arrangement, but wanted to keep all his options open and did not want to deal directly with 'heretics'. Even the agreement reached on 3 August 1532 at the negotiations in Nuremberg was not included in the closing act of the Diet: formally, it was no more than a declaration of the towns and the Catholic and Protestant princes concerned. Charles pledged all the estates of the Empire to the peace in 'matters of religion', without any further explanation. His agreement to suspend all actions relating to Church property that were before the courts was only communicated verbally and he did not inform the judiciary. He distanced himself from the mutual promise of peace, which meant that he could withdraw from it any time he wanted. In this way he added to the lack of constitutional clarity: he encouraged negotiations but declined to recognise their outcome officially. In practice, the Protestants were given provisional recognition, in spite of the fact that they had been formally denounced in the resolutions of the Diets of 1521 and 1531. They were given space to organise themselves in the political and Church sphere. This conscious lack of clarity was considered to be in the best interests of the Empire, but in fact it led directly to its split.[16]

Both sides had their own ideas on the general council that was constantly promised. The Protestants insisted that a council be presided over by the emperor, not by the pope, that it be held in 'German lands', and that it would only concern itself with the word of God. Charles, for his part, insisted that no concessions would be made in the matter of communion in both substances for the laity, and that the spread of the 'heresies' should be limited. The archbishop of Mainz had urged him most strongly to give way on this point, not to satisfy the Protestants, but because he feared that any deviation from the *communio sub utraque specie* could once again lead to an uprising of the 'common man', as it had in 1525. The twelfth and last article of the 'Nuremberg Postponement' had been decisive for the emperor: as long as he guaranteed peace in religious matters the Protestants would lend their full support to the defence of the land against the Turkish advance.[17] In order to avoid more trouble he was prepared to give the 'heretics' more time, but only on certain conditions, and in the expectation of a decision to hold a council. The German Protestants saw in the 'Postponement' another step towards their recognition. Charles did not consider giving any such concession to the reformers in the Low Countries, because he could exercise his authority there directly in all of the provinces.

With his return to Spain in March 1533 Charles' problems in the German Empire were pushed into the background. The status quo remained unchanged, thus actually facilitating the steady expansion and consolidation of the Reformation. Pope Clement VII and the majority of the cardinals had no inclination to call a council, and Charles' hopes for a solution became dimmer. Paul III, who became pope in 1534, may at first have been prepared to take an initiative in this direction, but was dissuaded from it by Francis I. He rejoiced at the dissension in Germany because it weakened his rival just when he was preparing further attacks. In May 1532 four German princes, Elector John of Saxony, Landgrave Philip of Hesse and Dukes William and Louis of Bavaria, who continued to oppose Ferdinand's election as Roman king, made a pact with Francis, who gave them money. With this support Philip managed to drive the Habsburgs out of the duchy of Württemberg in January 1534.[18] Charles ignored this flagrant attack on his patrimonial position in the Empire, for he was fully occupied with the conquest of Tunis. In 1536 he had to counter French attacks in Savoy, Piedmont and the southern Low Countries.

In such a climate the efforts of Paul III to organise a general council in Mantua in 1537 came to naught.[19] The German Protestants made demands that were unacceptable to Rome, and the other Christian kings had no desire to work on a solution to something they saw chiefly as Charles' problem. Charles' main aim was still to postpone the matter so that he was free to deal with his external enemies, France and the Turks. On 31 May 1537 he wrote to his brother, Ferdinand, the Roman king:

> In Schmalkalden the princes and others who have lost their way have acted extremely improperly and absolutely, but if we maintain a strong, close relationship with the Catholic princes and estates they will be on their guard against any actual attack, as you rightly remarked. For this purpose I send you a mandate to allow the archbishop of Lund [John of Weeze] and Dr Matthias [Held, vice chancellor of the Empire] to negotiate and do all that they find needful and necessary for the good, or at least to ensure that those who have lost their way do as little harm as possible, so that they cannot cause any trouble or use violence just at this time when we are so occupied with our resistance to the Turks and the French king. As a last resort we should grant them [the Protestants] a postponement during which the trials relating to Church property may be suspended for a little longer. But be sure that neither you

[Ferdinand] nor the archbishop and doctor expressly agree to things which could trouble our conscience or damage our honour: it must be a toleration such as was agreed in Nuremberg. It is of great importance that the contents of this article remain a close secret so that those who have strayed do not come to learn of it beforehand, either directly or indirectly.[20]

In spite of Charles' expressed desire for peace, the divisions within Germany deepened. A number of Catholic princes, including the dukes of Bavaria, Saxony (not the elector John) and Brunswick and the archbishops of Salzburg and Magdeburg, but no electors, established an alliance on 10 June 1538 to resist the League of Schmalkalden. The latter formed alliances with the Protestant King Christian III of Denmark and with Francis I. In the face of such an explosive situation, Charles fell in with the suggestion, now put forward by elector Joachim II of Brandenburg, for making another attempt at a religious peace. In the absence of a general council, Joachim had introduced into his margravate a reformation of the Church that was something midway between Wittenberg and Rome. He was not the only one in Germany who, in the spirit of humanism, strove to settle the differences of meaning in the bosom of the Church, although he was dissatisfied with Rome's lack of action.[21]

On 19 April 1539 the 'Postponement' of 1532 was given an extension in Frankfurt, on the understanding that the freedom of belief would now include all those who supported the Confession of Augsburg. It was conditional on the Protestants giving up their demand for further secularisation of Church institutions and no new members being admitted to the League of Schmalkalden. On 1 August theologians were to start discussing how far differences in dogma could be solved. When Charles opened the Diet at Regensburg on 5 April 1541, he established a 'Colloquium', chaired by Frederick, the count palatine. Three Catholic and three Protestant theologians would serve on it, together with three lawyers from different estates and Charles' first advisor and keeper of the seal, Nicholas Perrenot, lord of Granvelle. The year before, he had led the extremely delicate discussions on religious questions, which had resulted in a negotiation document of 23 articles. In May, the reformist theologian, Melanchthon, and Eck, the extreme councillor from Bavaria, agreed on a joint formulation of the doctrine of justification – the view of God's judgement on human wickedness. This caused the emperor great pleasure, not so much for the content as for the fact that an agreement had been reached. The negotiators were unable to agree on the questions of the Eucharist, confession and transubstantiation, or on the role of the Church hierarchy. Their resolutions were not supported in separate assemblies of the Catholic and Protestant estates, and both Luther and Rome eventually rejected their efforts to reach a compromise. The official closing act of the Regensburg Diet on 29 July 1541 confirmed the resolution of 1530, which placed the reformers outside the law, even if the 'Postponement' of 1532 was again extended.

The precarious position of Ferdinand, the Roman king, in Hungary, once again forced Charles to buy the military support of the Protestant princes with concessions which, although perhaps limited at the time, were not only renewed but also extended. In a separate, secret Declaration he emasculated the official resolution of the Diet, in fact according the Lutherans a special status. He allowed them to hold their churches and monasteries for the Christian Reformation. They would be allowed to keep the revenues from Church estates and apply them to schools and charitable ends. Those who fled for reasons of faith would be allowed to find shelter anywhere. People of the evangelical persuasion would forthwith be admitted as judges and assessors in the *Reichskammergericht*. The actual division of the Diet into two religious parties was further hastened by a second Declaration, also secret, in which the emperor yielded to the demands of the Catholic estates. This obviously caused a great deal of legal uncertainty.

During the following year, 1542, Ferdinand, the Roman king, added to the confusion by confirming his brother's two Declarations and negotiating with the Catholics and Protestants separately about the defence against the Turks.[22] In the meantime, Elector John Frederick of Saxony and Landgrave Philip of Hesse took the duchy of Brunswick-Wolfenbüttel, the last Catholic territory in the north of the Empire. They made the duke and his sons prisoners. It began increasingly to look as if the status quo in Germany could never be restored. During the Diet of 1544 there was already talk of an interim arrangement, still in anticipation of the decision to hold a general council. At last, in December 1545, this council met for the first time in the imperial city of Trent. Political developments had paved the way, especially the obligation to co-operate that Charles had imposed on Francis I in September 1544 in the Treaty of Crépy and the truce with Sultan Sulaimān that he had achieved in October 1545, thanks to the enforced co-operation of the French. Paul III was now also favourably disposed towards Charles, who had given the strategically placed towns of Parma and Piacenza to his son, Pier Luigi Farnese.

Authoritarian Reformation

It soon became clear that Charles' wish to give priority to the reformation of Church institutions would not be respected by the council fathers. Indeed, in January 1547, they rigorously condemned the doctrine of the reformers, in particular Luther's doctrine of justification by faith, so that the German Protestants no longer felt inclined to take part in a council that was chaired by the pope and that was so hostile towards them. The Schmalkaldic League offered them enough political and military protection when they rejected the council. In March 1547, when the Curia decided to move the location of the council to Bologna, in the Papal States, they no longer saw any reason at all to take part in it. It was to break this political resistance that Charles, after the failure of yet another round of religious discussions that he had encouraged, considered a war against the Schmalkaldic League justifiable. He accused Elector John Frederick of Saxony and Landgrave Philip of Hesse of breaking the national peace through their occupation of Brunswick and the capture of the duke and his two sons. On this basis he put the two most prominent Protestant princes under the imperial ban, outlawing them. On 9 June 1546 he explained his reasons for this in a letter to his sister, Mary:

> We have no other recourse than to resist these apostates strenuously and to use all means to force them to some sort of acceptable conditions. Even if nothing is achieved, at least it should stop everything being irrevocably lost.... If we do not take a strong line the risk to the faith is enormous. The consequences could be so harmful that there could be no turning back, namely the estrangement of the rest of Germany from our holy faith.'[23]

Charles further explained that he hoped to divide the Protestants in the Empire by eliminating their leading princes. He was not concerned explicitly with the persecution of the Protestants as such, and nothing in his later behaviour points in that direction. He tried to remove the political obstacles that hindered his efforts to restore his authority and peace in the Empire. In this he was acting in anticipation of a definitive settlement of the religious question in a general council.

The idea of using military force to persuade the Protestant estates to take part in the general council and to abide by its decisions dates from 1545. The resolutions of the Diet in that year do not even refer to a general council because none of the parties concerned had any confidence in it, in the very year that the Church assembly actually met for the first time. In the spring the papal legate had promised Charles his support for military action, both in the form of a sizeable force and very sizeable finances from Church revenues in Spain. It did not suit Charles that news of this leaked out during the Diet, when he was by no means certain of enough allies in the Empire nor even of his own army. When he first tried to reopen talks on the religious question in the spring of 1546, no one was willing to take part. The great Protestant princes did not appear at the Diet in June and July, and preparations for war were discussed openly.

Charles' position in the Empire was so weak that he had to enlist the support of various imperial princes in separate negotiations. Relations between the Habsburgs and the dukes of Bavaria had been strained for a long time. The most that Charles could now hope for, in exchange for the marriage between Duke Albrecht of Bavaria and Ferdinand's daughter Anna, was their passive co-operation in making military supplies available. He entered into agreements of service with some of the younger Protestants rulers, which clearly illustrates the weakness of his power base in the Empire. He had to overcome his fundamental disapproval of those whom he had once called 'erring, lapsed and apostate'. Among the allies he thus acquired were Duke Eric of Brunswick, the Margraves Hans and Albrecht Alcibiades of Brandenburg, and, notably, Duke Maurice of Saxony. Duke Maurice belonged to the cadet branch that governed a small region of small towns, such as Eisenach, Jena and Weimar: this region was now strategically important because on the west it bordered on the electorate of the same name. In return for accepting the resolutions of the Council of Trent and supporting the emperor's efforts 'to restore peace and justice', Duke Maurice was allowed to apply Church possessions in his domain to 'charitable purposes', and had the prospect of the lion's share of the electorate of Saxony once it was taken. The last incumbent, John Frederick, was deposed when he had been placed under the imperial ban.

In June 1546 Charles also came to an agreement with Paul III. It meant that the war against the Protestants became a crusade for which indulgences could be gained, following centuries-old custom. The fact that a number of Protestant princes joined Charles' army shows that the entire operation was based on sheer opportunism. Charles was allowed the use of Church revenues from the Low Countries and the pope himself promised troops until autumn 1547.[24] Charles declared war on Elector John Frederick of Saxony and Landgrave Philip of Hesse on 20 July 1546. He called them traitors, rebels and disturbers of the peace because they had mobilised the forces of the Schmalkaldic League to advance south against him. Now the conflict had a clearly legal aspect, which sounded very different from the crusade that the pope had announced: in a letter written to his son Philip on 8 August, Charles disclosed his real intentions:

> You will readily understand the most important reasons for my declaration of war: . . . as you know the restoration of the faith is our aim and intention, but it seemed useful to make known right from the beginning that our concern is to punish those who disobey, especially the margrave, the duke of Saxony and all those like them.'[25]

The army of the Schmalkaldic League had the advantage of being ready to fight long before that of the emperor. It was not until August that he could assemble forces from Lombardy, Naples, Spain and Germany itself. Maximilian of Egmont, count of Buren and governor of Friesland, arrived with troops from the Low Countries half way through September. Schmalkaldic units had blocked his crossing of the Rhine. Then there had been a confrontation between both forces at Ingolstadt on the Danube. Early in September the League of Schmalkalden had bombarded the imperial camp, but had not inflicted serious damage. Disagreements in the war councils of the Protestant princes led to a rapid withdrawal, and they soon lost their original advantage. Ferdinand and Maurice of Saxony, with troops from Bohemia, invaded and held large parts of the elector's lands. As the fortunes of war looked so favourable, Charles decided to continue the campaign during the winter. He bound Maurice even more closely to him by offering him not only the lands, but also the title, of the deposed Elector John Frederick.

The emperor spent the winter in southwest Germany, where he mercilessly forced Elector Frederick of the Palatinate and Duke Ulrich of Württemberg to their knees and demanded large sums of money from them in reparation for having turned against him. He allowed them both to retain their lands and titles, however, so that time-consuming military action against them would not distract him from his main purpose. In the meantime, he only seemed to meet with opposition, due to the papal Curia. On 13 January 1547 the council rejected Luther's doctrine of justification by faith, causing Charles' representative, Diego de Mendoza, to comment that this council 'under the tyranny of the [papal] legates caused more mischief than Luther. Together, the council fathers served only Rome, and individually they served only themselves.' On 22 January, Paul III added to the problems by recalling his forces from Germany, thus breaking an earlier promise. Charles fulminated to the papal nuncio that 'the pope had steered him into this difficult war, and then left him to cope with it. The "French disease" [inconstancy] is forgivable in young people, but it is intolerable in a greybeard.'[26] The cause of the pope's volte-face had apparently been the popes' old fear that Charles would become too powerful through his military successes and his influence on the council. Another reason may have been the influence of anti-Habsburg sentiment at the French court, which flared up again when it was obvious that Francis was nearing his end.

At the end of March Charles regrouped his army to advance on Saxony. John Frederick did not look very alert, and in the face of the emperor's vastly superior force of some 50,000 men he gradually retreated northwards along the east bank of the Elbe, the imperial troops on the other bank. Perhaps he had in mind a repeat of the expedition along the Marne in 1544, which ended without a fight. He probably hoped to find safety in Wittenberg, which would be difficult to besiege. While the imperial troops pressed forward, he abandoned Meissen, rashly fired the only bridge, sent his artillery on ahead, pitched his camp a few miles down-river at Mühlberg and on Sunday, 24 April 1547, gave his troops a day of rest. The emperor's army never stopped, and encouraged by the active leadership of emperor, king and duke, carried out all sorts of daring exploits early in the morning. Brave Spaniards under the command of the duke of Alva captured a bridge from the Saxons, some by swimming across the river with their swords between their teeth and chasing the defenders away. Others managed to find a ford, where in half an hour 4,000 cavalrymen with 500 bowmen mounted behind crossed to the other bank. Helped by the mist and the element of surprise, the imperial army hunted down and surrounded their enemy. Charles, Ferdinand and his son, Archduke Maximilian, remained on the field of battle till midnight. John Frederick was among those taken prisoner. The following day Charles wrote an elaborate account of the triumph to his sister Mary, 'because I know how much pleasure it will give you'.[27]

The victorious army could now take the entire electorate. Wittenberg, Luther's town, surrendered. The Catholic form of worship was re-introduced, but there was no plundering or symbolic destruction, as that might harm the position of the new elector, Maurice of Saxony. On 19 May Charles imposed the capitulation of Wittenberg on John Frederick, who abdicated the electorate in favour of Maurice but was allowed to retain some of his hereditary lands for his sons. This suited Charles, too, because it curbed Maurice's power. John Frederick and Landgrave Philip, who had by now been arrested, remained prisoners to guarantee the submission of the Schmalkaldic League. Like some triumphant emperor of antiquity, Charles took them with him. A vast amount of imperial propaganda was made out of the Schmalkaldic Wars, as had happened earlier with the battle of Pavia and the conquest of Tunis. The emperor was particularly hard on his defeated Protestant adversaries, possibly out of resentment at his own ineffectiveness in years past.

The emperor had won a battle, but certainly not the peace. A hard core of Protestant opposition remained intact in Bremen and Magdeburg. The military action and the harsh repression of the princes fed a wide opposition to the imperial government, which was perceived as tyrannical. In October 1547 imperial diplomacy succeeded in persuading all the estates to defer to the Council of Trent. Of course the Protestants had reservations about the decisions already made by the Council. It was a setback for the emperor that the Council no longer sat in Trent: the Curia had moved the venue to Bologna, outside the Holy Roman Empire, which was as unpalatable to the emperor as it was to his German subjects. The meeting was therefore adjourned indefinitely in February 1548. Charles' hopes of Church reform, which he had cherished for more than twenty years, were completely dashed.

His relations with the pope cooled even more with the murder of the pope's son, Pier Luigi Farnese, duke of Parma, in September 1547. Ferrante Gonzaga, governor of the duchy of Milan, immediately occupied Farnese's city of Piacenza in Charles' name, thus creating an atmosphere of suspicion. In the manner typical of a Renaissance pope, Paul III demanded the return of Parma and Piacenza before he would discuss the location of the council. Charles would fight a futile, expensive war for Parma, which he had to abandon in May 1552, at the very nadir of his reign.

Despite revolts in Genoa and Naples Charles' attention remained fixed on the religious question in Germany. He arranged another series of discussions between Catholic and Protestant theologians to find solutions which he hoped the Diet would enact into law. This was even less successful than all the previous discussions. In anticipation of the resolutions of the Council, the Catholics refused to accept an interim settlement because they did not want to be associated with anything that even hinted at Protestantism. So on 15 May and 30 June 1548 Charles, on his own authority, issued the 'Augsburg Interim' for the Protestants only. It contained a number of theological concessions, such as clerical marriage, the lay chalice and the perception of the mass as a peace offering and a thanksgiving. The proclamation contained nothing about the doctrine of justification, because no agreement had been reached on that subject. In consultation with the spiritual princes the emperor issued his own order for Catholics, requiring diocesan and provincial synods to start a process of internal Church reform. The wait for Rome had been too long, even for Charles.

The weakness of this legislation lay in its enforcement by local and regional governments. Protestant pamphlets decried the Interim as a diabolical trick and popery in disguise. It met with bitter resistance at every level, from courts to town council chambers to country parishes. In Saxony, Maurice adopted a middle course, with Charles' approval, which made a split in the heartland of Lutheranism possible; but he took no action against the fierce opposition in Magdeburg, which Charles had outlawed. Charles' Interim policy had its greatest success in the nearly 30 imperial towns of south Germany, where he had excluded reformist guilds from taking part in town government. The patrician oligarchies, on imperial authority, guaranteed the Catholic minority its own form of worship.

The fiasco

In spite of his impressive spread of power Charles was still unable to maintain his authority in the Empire. In February 1550 the dukes of Mecklenburg and Prussia entered into a pact to defend the Lutheran faith and what they called 'German freedom'. Maurice of Saxony soon deserted the emperor and approached the Roman king, Ferdinand, who was also king of neighbouring Bohemia. He thought that this would serve his interests better. Moreover, he felt that Charles had betrayed him by keeping his father-in-law, Philip of Hesse, prisoner when he had given his word after the battle of Mühlberg that he would be well treated if he surrendered. In May 1551 Maurice entered into a treaty with other north German princes against Charles and the 'intolerable, brutal and continual degradation from Spain' and aiming at the eventual liberation of Philip of Hesse.

In Protestant circles slogans about 'brutal servitude' and the defence of 'ancient German freedoms' were widely circulated. Charles' efforts to present his son Philip as Ferdinand's successor as Roman king stirred up bad blood, because it was seen as an extension of foreign domination. In October 1551 the Protestant princes obtained the support of Henry II of France, who had encouraged anti-Habsburg forces since his accession in 1547. He planned to take the cathedral cities of Cambrai, Metz, Toul and Verdun, which were part of the Empire, while the Protestants attacked Charles. The military campaigns went well. On their way to the Danube Maurice's troops found the gates of all the towns open to them. The Protestant form of worship was reinstated and the town magistrates replaced. They reached Innsbruck, where Charles was quartered, and forced him to make a humiliating retreat to Villach. Ferdinand remained strictly neutral, which won him the respect of, and even promises of support from, the Hungarian Protestants. He would not exert himself any more on behalf of the brother who had plunged the Empire into turmoil and who, moreover, was trying to push his own son forward as Ferdinand's successor. He negotiated between both parties and reached an agreement at Passau in August: Charles had to allow his enemies another 'Provisorium', maintaining the status quo until the next Diet, and to abandon his implementation of the Interim.

At the instigation of the new pope, Julius III, the Council met again in Trent from May 1551. German and Spanish bishops were present in greater numbers than before. After their revolt against the emperor in 1552 the German Protestants did not attend any more. They demanded independence from the pope, and that the resolutions already made against the very foundations of their doctrine be reconsidered. These were logical demands from their point of view, reflecting the developments of the last 30 years. Their rejection by the majority of the council fathers signalled the definitive failure of Charles' efforts to absorb reformation by discussion within the Church. On 24 April 1552 Julius III adjourned the Council. It would not meet again for another ten years, and then under very different circumstances.

After a delay of several years and many tussles between Charles and Ferdinand,[28] who had been estranged since the fraught discussions over the succession, the imperial Diet met in Augsburg in February 1555, under the chairmanship of Ferdinand. Charles purposely kept a low profile '*par scrupules de la religion*', fearing that the unavoidable new concessions in matters of faith would be in conflict with his conscience. The Protestant princes of Saxony, Brandenburg and Hesse prepared for the decision process by introducing the concept of a religious peace in which the religious division of the territories would be legally recognised. They insisted on the right to choose Reformation and to emigrate for reasons of belief. The transfer of Church property into Protestant hands that had taken place in 1552 was recognised; as compensation, Ferdinand pushed through the resolution that thenceforth any cleric who chose for the Reformation must relinquish his benefices in favour of a Catholic successor. As the result of Ferdinand's diplomatic yet firm actions the Religious Peace of Augsburg was promulgated on 25 September. It recognised the rights of the estates' representatives in every territory or autonomous town to decide the religious persuasion in that region. It weakened the authority that Charles had claimed for himself without being able to enforce it.

It may be seen as symbolic that it was during this meeting of the Diet that Charles, who never accepted responsibility for the resolution, decided to abdicate as Holy Roman Emperor. The messenger who brought news of this to Augsburg reached Ferdinand just an hour before he announced the Diet's resolution. Ferdinand ignored Charles' request to announce his abdication at the same time. The emperor was completely sidelined.[29]

Persecuting heretics

Reformist writings and ideas were able to spread rapidly through the Low Countries because of the open borders and the intense international commercial ties. Indeed, in the region from which Erasmus came and where he spent the greater part of his life, the prevailing religious climate had long been concentrated on the deeper meaning of religious experiences and on criticising the hypocrisy endemic to many Church institutions and practices. On the other hand the government reacted rapidly and exercised its authority immediately through legislation and control of the provincial courts. The papal bull described heresy as treason against God, for which the punishment was death or banishment for life and the confiscation of property.[30] Provincial and local governments published these edicts several times. For several years an imperial inquisitor was active in stopping the spread of reformist ideas. A letter sent to the reformer, Martin Bucer, on

4 September 1521 gives a sombre description of the situation: 'Luther is burnt every day in the Low Countries and yet it is said that he has more supporters there than anywhere else. The emperor just follows the pope.'[31]

Between June and August books were burnt in Antwerp, Ghent and Bruges. In 1521–22 a monk was pilloried in Oudenaarde, and an Augustinian prior in Antwerp was imprisoned and interrogated by a committee of five theologians and diocesan inquisitors and forced solemnly to recant. In 1523 two Augustinian monks were burnt at the stake in Brussels for their Lutheran sympathies. Various judicial bodies continued the persecution: the local aldermen's courts were the most active of these, even though at first they did not have the jurisdiction. The severe repression, and perhaps also the relatively favourable economy, hindered the spread of reformist ideas, especially those of the Anabaptists, in the Low Countries.

Charles still regularly issued edicts against heresy, and certainly whenever he visited the Low Countries, in consultation with the States General. In 1531 he observed that Luther's followers 'swarm out and multiply in our Low Countries', in spite of the threat of harsh punishment under earlier decrees, including that of 1529. The circulation of the ideas of 13 named reformers, including great historical figures such as Marsilius of Padua, John Wycliffe and Jan Hus, was strictly forbidden. Any discussion or translation of the Holy Scriptures was forbidden, except to the theologians of a renowned university. The reward for informers was increased to one half of the possessions of the convicted person up to the value of 100 pounds in groats, and then 10 per cent of the remaining amount.[32]

As early as 1530 the Confession of Augsburg had excluded the most radical reformist movement, that of the Anabaptists. In 1528 the imperial government had condemned them as heretics. In the records of the Peasants' War their rejection of temporal authority explains precisely why they were persecuted more ruthlessly than the other reformers. By 1533, 700 Anabaptists had been executed as heretics or rebels, thousands more were banished, imprisoned or forced to recant.[33] Nevertheless, the Anabaptist movement still found a large following in many towns in the Low Countries, particularly among ordinary artisans. In Münster, in Westphalia, these evangelical artisans peacefully gained control of the town in November 1532; the new town government forced the entire population to switch to the Reformation, and in the spring of 1533 even the bishop recognised the situation, conditional to the council being held. During that year the Anabaptist movement was in the ascendancy, partly under the influence of two men from the Low Countries. In the spring of 1534 these Dutchmen, Jan Matthijsz of Haarlem, and on his death Jan Beukelsz of

Leiden, emerged as leaders. They spread the apocalyptic doctrine of Melchior Hofmann, who had been imprisoned in Strasbourg the year before. Münster was the place chosen to establish God's kingdom, with a view to the end of the world, expected in 1534. The movement enjoyed wide popular support locally, partly because those who thought otherwise left or were driven out. In February the town government consisted entirely of Anabaptists. Then the town was besieged; for this the bishop received assistance from the Imperial Circles as well as from the evangelical rulers of Saxony and Hesse. Inside the city of salvation Jan Beukelsz of Leiden introduced community of possessions and of women, and unleashed a bloody terror among those who opposed him. Encouraged by his fiery preaching the people stood firm, despite all the hardships of the 15-month siege. In 1536 the three leaders were cruelly tortured to death with red hot rods, and their corpses displayed in an iron cage hanging from the town's main church.

At the end of February 1534 the central government in Brussels announced a pardon for repentant Anabaptists. Only about 15 applied. On the other hand, followers in many towns responded to calls from Münster to demonstrate, and with sword uplifted to proclaim the coming of the day of the Lord. A number of executions took place in Haarlem and Amsterdam. On 29 April the Anabaptists ventured an attack on Amsterdam which was put down by the local militia. The governor of the province of Holland, Antoine de Lalaing, count of Hoogstraten, head of the Council of Finances, member of the Council of State and *chevalier d'honneur* to the regent Margaret, was normally resident in Brussels: he made the effort of going to Amsterdam on 2 May with members of the Council of Holland, to lead in person the interrogation of the 30 people arrested. The four most stubborn were burnt at the stake on 11 May, eight who repented were executed the following day. On 10 May, 36 rebels from Kennemerland, dressed in hair shirts, bareheaded and barefoot, and carrying a wax candle for the sacrament, had to walk in the procession in which the governor and all his council and town magistrates took part. In September, the governor asked the States of Holland for a force of 1,200 men to deal with the Anabaptists and other heretics.[34]

By the turn of the year the attorney-general of Holland, on the government's orders, was watching Amsterdam carefully. The town was rapidly becoming a refuge for Anabaptists from all over the Low Countries and keeping in close touch with the 'kingdom of Zion' in Münster. The court was also secretly negotiating the possible secularisation of the rebellious cathedral city into Habsburg hands. Anabaptist groups were suppressed in Maastricht, Wezel and Leiden. Fervent adherents of the growing community in Amsterdam spread their message by walking naked through the town during the chilly night of 10–11 February 1535. Seven men were executed for this, and on 15 May two women who had also taken part in the demonstration were drowned.

The repression reached a gruesome height in the bloodbath launched by the governor of Friesland, Schenck von Tautenburg, on 7 April 1535 against several hundred Anabaptists who had taken over the cloister of Bloemkamp near Bolswaard. Anabaptist adherents planned an attack on Amsterdam on 10 May, but it ended in disaster after they had taken the town hall because of lack of co-ordination: 83 were executed. Most of those sentenced were burnt at the stake, or drowned, if they were women. The first sentences, pronounced on 14 May in the presence of the president and attorney-general of the Council of Holland, demanded that the executioner first cut out the heart of the condemned, then behead and quarter them: the limbs were then to be displayed on the city gates. For the Anabaptist bishop, Jacob of Kampen, the authorities devised an even more memorable punishment: first, wearing his mitre, he would sit on the scaffold in front of the town hall for an hour, then his tongue would be cut out, and his right hand (which he had used to baptise) and his head would be cut off. His head, with the mitre, would be stuck on a pole by the Haarlemmer gate, the rest of his body would be burnt.[35] The enactment of an ordinance against the Anabaptists applying throughout the Low Countries was the cause of a short-lived wave of repression, especially in Flanders.[36] Nevertheless, the Anabaptist movement continued to be active, with Amsterdam and Emden as meeting points for refugees from Münster and elsewhere. Menno Simons managed to rid the movement of its violence and the idea of communal possessions. The movement was spied upon, and eight Anabaptists were sent to the stake in Amsterdam; a year later 21 were banished and their property confiscated. Another 20 were arrested in 1552 for possession of pamphlets or attending Anabaptist meetings: eight of these met their death at the stake, and three who repented were put to the sword.[37]

Of course, the frequently issued regulations were far removed from the reality: this can be seen from the ordinance on the eradication of heresy of 1540. Earlier ordinances were said not to have been issued or proclaimed on time, and officials were negligent in enforcing them.

> Ordinary, simple people are threatened and misled by the false doctrines . . . the cursed, perverse sects continue to multiply and the situation goes from bad to worse. . . The sects and doctrines have not yet been weeded out and removed, but continue to flourish, and their leaders are emboldened in their wicked schemes.[38]

After that, ordinances had to be proclaimed every six months so that nobody could claim not to be aware of them. A new, much longer, list of forbidden books was published.

The topic given to participants in a festival of rhetoricians in Ghent in 1539 was 'the greatest comfort to the dying man'. Ten of the nineteen plays presented and printed were placed on the index of forbidden books because of their obviously Lutheran sympathies. Images were also censured. In 1546 the emperor was forced to conclude that 'the decrees were not observed as they should have been and as was necessary'. Printers found any number of ways to publish translations of the Bible, schoolteachers used bad books in their lessons. This resulted in a new approach, and the emperor produced a list of works that were permitted.[39] Nevertheless, in 1545 a printer was beheaded in Antwerp for spreading Lutheran texts.

A number of plays of Flemish rhetoricians levelled criticism at the clergy, the inquisition and papal indulgences. Apostle plays breathed an evangelical spirit and paraphrased Bible texts. In Antwerp, the *Souterliedekens*, rhyming versions of the psalms set to profane music, underwent several printings. The works of some rhetoricians in Ghent were forbidden or the rhetoricians themselves were banished. The poets of *Schriftuurlijke Liedekens*, songs inspired by the Scriptures and reprinted several times after 1554, were prosecuted. Yet rhetoricians and street singers were cautious and seldom turned radically against the old orthodoxy. Printers, painters and dramatists, working for profit, played up a question that interested everybody. The government fought a hard battle to keep the minds of its subjects purely for itself and the Catholic Church. In 1552 the magistrates of Bruges even forbade the singing of songs and ballads in public squares.[40]

Regent Mary of Hungary was given a report on 1 January 1555 dealing with the negligence of officers of justice in Lille, Antwerp and along the Flemish coast:

> Few people can be found who are willing to turn the heretical offenders over to the courts and speak the truth under oath. This makes the heretics confident that they will not be punished unless they make a confession or are denounced by two positive witnesses for the same crime. Therefore they make sure not to show their venom ... There are even cases where criminal proceedings are not brought, not even in order to find their accomplices.

A battle for jurisdiction raged between imperial, papal and episcopal inquisitions, the Privy Council – the highest court for the administration of justice in the Low Countries – and local aldermen. Members of the provincial courts did not entirely trust the orthodoxy of local aldermen and often encountered a defensive attitude. The regent and her council intervened in some cases but usually, by appealing to their own common law and privileges, the local authorities were not only able to protect their own competency but also increasingly to soften the repression through passive resistance. The central government also protected the sheriffs from the interference of the episcopal courts.

Research into the number of judicial proceedings taken in the southern Low Countries between 1520 and 1555, on the basis of the remaining, but incomplete, sources shows that at least 1,473 people were prosecuted, and at least 169 of them executed. An extrapolation of that data to the entire population points to between 4,000 and 8,000 people being persecuted for their religious beliefs in that part of the XVII Provinces during the reign of Charles V. This is less than one half of one per cent of the total population. After 1540 the repression clearly increased, in the number of both prosecutions and executions. In the large cities, the ideal breeding ground for reformers, the number of public executions nearly tripled, while it doubled in relation to the number of prosecutions, from 15.5 per cent to 30 per cent. Other sentences included fines and the confiscation of property. The repression struck in waves, depending on the informers on certain groups and the activities of particular prosecutors. The increases were especially noticeable from 1542 to 1545, and again after 1551, but other years remained calm.[41] The peaks coincided with the years of particularly high taxation and economic problems, which would have caused worry and unrest among the people. Most victims came from the large towns, especially Antwerp, and were found among the artisans and trades people: they were most sensitive to new cultural trends and most affected by fluctuations in the economy.

The reformist body of thought was accepted in the German lands and the Low Countries much sooner than in Italy. There, the apparatus of government seemed only partly willing, and certainly not at all able, to enforce any far-reaching discipline over the hearts and minds of the people. Reformist ideas were widely propagated in the duchy of Milan from about 1540. In 1538 Charles had forbidden the circulation of 'tainted books' from Switzerland, but nine years later still felt compelled to instruct his governor, Ferrante Gonzaga, to act rigorously. In 1547 images of saints were taken from the churches and destroyed.[42] The introduction of the inquisition in Naples in the same year caused a popular uprising, which was directed more towards the increase of the government's powers than towards restrictions put on religious freedom. The uprising was crushed immediately, thanks to the urban nobility who 'fraternised with the people during the day and in the evenings sought the company of the viceroy'. But the inquisition was never established firmly there.[43]

Powerful machinery for repression existed in Spain, but the struggle against reformation was only a marginal phenomenon. The Spanish Inquisition was established during the last Christian offensive against the Jews and Moors of Granada. *Conversos,* mostly converted Jews, were also among the main victims of religious persecution. The *cortes* of Valencia was particularly concerned with the disputes of competence between the inquisition and the secular courts, and more with Muslim dissenters than Protestants.[44] Its attention was focused on the persecution of Jews and Muslims. During the whole of the sixteenth century the inquisition in Toledo proceeded against no more than 59 people suspected of Lutheranism. The inquisitor acquitted 40 who renounced their (Lutheran) faith, apparently spontaneously.[45]

For many years after their first contact with Charles, the *cortes* of the various kingdoms were emphatically opposed to the breaches made by the inquisition in the sense of justice. They were particularly offended by the secret trials, new forms of torture, imprisonment of the accused for many years without any clear indictment, and the confiscation of the *conversos'* estates. The kings considered the inquisition an extremely useful instrument of power and defended it from all attacks. In 1518 a serious conflict arose between the *cortes* of Aragon and the young Charles. In exchange for a tax levy Charles had agreed their request to curb the power of the inquisition, then immediately asked the pope for dispensation for breaking this promise. It led to the arrest by the inquisition of Juan Prat, notary to the *cortes*, who had correctly recorded the agreement. After two years, the poor man was freed by order of the pope, but the inquisition continued to follow its own untroubled path. During the conflict Charles had informed the representatives: 'You may rest assured that we would agree to lose a part of our lands and kingdoms rather than to allow something to take place there that is contrary to God's honour and the authority of the Holy Office'.[46]

The activities of the Spanish inquisition were clearly aimed at converted Jews and Muslims; the penetration of the Reformation in the land was far less visible. In 1525 it started persecuting the *alumbrados*, a mystical movement similar to many already seen across Europe. In a small number of cases sentences were passed against them, fines and the renunciation of 'heresies' imposed. Several members of Charles' retinue, especially those who had travelled with him in Germany and the Low Countries, were familiar with the ideas of Erasmus and Luther. They, too, were exposed to the suspicions of the inquisition, although until 1558 fewer than 50 cases of Lutheranism were involved. A number of preachers at Charles' court suffered for this. In 1533 the inquisition of Seville arrested Alonso de Virués: in 1537 he was forced to recant his alleged Erasmian 'heresies' and sentenced to be shut up in a monastery and forbidden to preach for three years. This was too much for Charles. He persuaded the pope to annul the sanction and four years later Virués was appointed bishop of the Canary Islands. In 1552, Juan Gil, the bishop of Tortosa and a protégé of Charles, was accused of heresy, dismissed from his position and forced to recant ten theses. Scholarly humanists with foreign connections were under strong suspicion.

In 1552 the inquisition in Seville confiscated 450 printed Bibles and ordered the public burning of heretical books. The interrogation of 747 suspects in Toledo from 1540 to 1550 revealed that barely 40 per cent of them were able to recite the Our Father, Hail Mary, the Creed, Salve Regina or the Ten Commandments in Castilian. Opposition to the inquisition was strong in Italy, the Low Countries, Aragon and Catalonia because it contravened local privileges and fostered a general atmosphere of suspicion and mistrust. The inquisition took firm root in Castile, on the other hand, partly through the collaboration of local elites whose members were included in its activities as lay judges.

The soul of the Indian

In 1493 Pope Alexander VI granted the Catholic kings, Charles' Spanish grandparents, control over the recently discovered, and yet-to-be discovered, lands in what we now call America. At the same time they were asked to make good Christians of the inhabitants. The *Requerimiento*, a short text formulated at the Spanish court in 1514 to be read to the native population, attempted to explain that they were now privileged to be the subjects of the king of Castile, if they surrendered to him and converted to Christianity.[47] The text of the *Requerimiento* was written after the Dominicans had criticised the exploitation of the Caribbean island of Hispaniola. The message began with an explanation of how God had created the world and had passed His earthly power on to Peter, who had been succeeded by the popes. One of these popes had given the continent and the islands over the ocean to the Catholic kings in Spain. Their representative then called upon the natives to recognise the Church as the highest universal authority and, in the Church's name, the pope and his representative, His Majesty. The clergy had to be allowed to spread the only true faith freely.

> His majesty, and I, acting in his name, will receive you and leave your wives and children free and without any form of slavery . . . and we shall not force you to become Christians. If you do not do so, however, I shall take action against you with God's help, and fight you everywhere, and subject you to the yoke and obedience to the Church and His Majesty. I shall take your wives

and children and enslave them, and I shall confiscate your possessions. I shall cause you all the ills and harm that a ruler can cause his vassals who do not obey him or do not accept him. I solemnly declare the blame for the death and damage that will follow will be apportioned to you, and not to His Majesty or to me, nor to the gentlemen who accompany me.

It is doubtful that the natives could have understood such a speech; that apart, it is absolutely absurd as a justification for Spanish domination, because it takes the acceptance of the superiority of Christianity for granted. Rejection of this would lead straight to violent and total subjection, for which the blame was placed entirely and solely on the natives. Muslim rulers gave Christian communities the status of *dhimmi*, and conquered Muslims in Iberia had the status of *aljamas*; similarly, Spanish law allowed those Indians who had submitted the right to govern their own communities in accordance with their own customs, and to pass their property on to each other. The long, intense contact between Jews, Muslims and Christians on the Iberian peninsula helps to explain this curious borrowing of the ceremony of conquest and the conditions of submission.[48]

In ordinances of 1520 Cortés referred to the spiritual conquest of the Indians as the legitimate main purpose of his war. The Aztec practices of cannibalism and human sacrifice were used as arguments by the Spaniards to justify their own actions. The reality was that the colonisers ousted the native aristocracy and divided up the land to support themselves. They created a sort of territorial exploitation, the *encomienda*, with the Indians as tied labourers, or even slaves. In Spain the practice provoked heated discussion, but in the colonies the systematic exploitation of the resources continued unchecked. In 1524 Cortés published a decree in which the Indians were allocated as hereditary property to the new landowners provided that these landowners spent enough time on their estates. Cortés used the state of war and economic necessity as arguments to counter the view of some Spanish theologians that the Indians must be free to become good Christians. The distance made it difficult for the Spanish crown to regularise the situation. In 1532 the *Audiencia* of 'New Spain' also informed the king that the Indians were so warlike that it was essential to use force, not only to ensure the safety of the Spaniards but also to spread the faith.[49]

The court, on the other hand, was bombarded with accounts of the shocking treatment meted out to the natives. A former colonist, the Dominican Bartolomé de las Casas, was among those who described the situation. The royal ordinance of 1526 contained pages and pages listing all sorts of abuses. It stressed the duty of all conquistadors to explain to the Indians, by means of interpreters, the motives of the Spaniards for coming to their land, viz. to free them (the Indians) from their bad ways and to bring them the salvation of the true faith. It was the duty of the clergy to explain the rudiments of Christianity to the Indians and to protect them from abuse. Colonists would lose their rights if they were in breach of this ordinance. In 1530 Charles expressly stipulated:

> that nobody should dare enslave an Indian, either in war or in peacetime, nor keep an Indian as a slave on the pretext that he was acquired in a just war, repurchase, purchase or exchange, nor under any other claim or pretext, not even the Indians whom the original inhabitants of the islands and of the mainland consider to be their slaves.[50]

The 'New Laws', enacted by the king in 1542, prohibited every *encomienda* of the Indians and placed them directly under the protection of the crown. The reality in the colonies was already so far removed from the humanitarian ideas of de las Casas and his followers that the colonists rebelled, and this article had to be revoked in 1545. In 1537 de las Casas began an experiment in Tuzutlan, using purely peaceful methods to guide the rough mountain folk to the true faith: the experiment was a miserable failure and de las Casas resigned as bishop of Chiapa in Guatemala. Under pressure from the opposition to the 'New Laws' Charles passed an order, in April 1550, forbidding any new conquests until a committee of theologians and advisors had found a just way of carrying them out. In the next, famous Dispute of Valladolid, de las Casas won an intellectual victory over the advocates of the fundamental inequality. A second round of talks a year later failed to produce unanimous proposals for new legislation. Merciless exploitation had already wrought far-reaching results.[51]

Christendom divided

Charles never stopped stressing to friend and foe alike that, as Holy Roman Emperor, he was the 'protector of all Christendom'.[52] It was a task he took extremely seriously; so seriously indeed, that the moral dilemma in which he found himself after the Religious Peace made by the Diet in 1555 decided him to announce his desire to abdicate. The next emperor, Ferdinand, would not rule over the universal 'Roman' empire because the hereditary lands in Italy and the Low Countries were destined for Philip. Worse still, not all his subjects would be adherents of the Catholic Church. The unity of Christendom, for which Charles had striven all his life, ended with him.

The Reformation had indeed given him an unprecedented challenge. Never before had a heretical doctrine spread through Europe so rapidly – the result of printing techniques and fervent preaching. Charles had to accept the break from the Catholic Church of Christian III of Denmark and Henry VIII, once his aunt's husband and an almost indispensable ally. Political interests forced Charles to override dynastic and religious scruples. He had even greater difficulty in accepting the apostasy of a growing number of princes and free cities in the German Empire, anticipating the territorialisation of religious choice that was eventually recognised in 1555. A German Emperor simply did not have the resources to follow an independent policy against the wishes of a number of important princes. It was not only the Protestants who rejected Charles' authority. Most Catholics did so too, including many – notably the dukes of Bavaria – whose attitude was decided purely by their dynastic rivalry with the Habsburgs.

In Germany, the centuries-old structures of power prevented Charles from imposing his ideas about the Church and faith. He was unable to impose them in the colonies, because it was materially impossible to assert his authority when it was contrary to the direct interests of the colonists. Was he any more successful in the Low Countries where both these restraints were felt less? The various reformist movements were certainly attractive, but harsh, widespread repression followed immediately. The repression was not enough, however, to stop the Reformation from spreading further. At the end of Charles' reign there were more Protestants in the Low Countries than ever, and their number would continue to grow vigorously.

Linking religious matters to politics made it difficult to solve problems in either area. The huge differences in the earlier history of each region made a universal policy not only impossible but even detrimental to all concerned. Institutional reforms within the Church which Charles considered justified and even desirable never came about, because they were connected through the Roman emperorship to a complex range of political discrepancies on regional, imperial and continental levels. If political conflicts blocked any solution to Church problems, then religious tensions weighed heavy on political relationships.

We are forced to the conclusion that Charles' vision of the Catholic Church and the emperorship as the two fundamental pillars of Christendom, whose unity should be as unassailable as their mutual cooperation, could function in Spain, perhaps even in the Italian territories, but never in the German Empire or the Low Countries. When Adrian of Utrecht was elected pope in 1522 Charles wrote to his former teacher and advisor:

> With the papacy in your hands and the Empire in mine I think that great things can be wrought through our unanimous actions. The love and obedience I bear you are no less than that of a good son towards his father. With such a mentality you have no reason to fear that in the nature of things I could do otherwise.[53]

In little more than a year Adrian was dead, however, and relations with his successors were much more difficult. Clement VII and Paul III found the balance of power in Italy and Europe more important than matters of faith. They would rather see Charles having to deal with the Protestants than that they should feel dependent on him as ruler of the world. In the relationship between emperor and pope it was the former who adhered strictly to orthodoxy and Church authority, while the pope found a few apostates in northern Germany less awful than a supreme emperor. It was difficult to remain confident with such a reversal of roles.

Despite all this Charles remained unswerving in his efforts to bring about internal Church reform by means of a general council. After the Council of Trent, which had opened in December 1545, had been adjourned for the second time by Julius III on 24 April 1552, in the spring of 1554 Charles declared in his instructions to the Diet:

> As far as the general council is concerned, it is well known and an undeniable fact that there is no way or method in existence, or which may be invented, of eradicating all the heresies, misunderstandings, doubts or struggles in the faith, which is more suitable, organised and certain to arrive at a full and justified settlement, than holding a general council. And so all the estates have been in agreement with us, in all seriousness and good faith, at all the Diets that have been held during our reign.[54]

For nearly 30 years all his hopes for a solution to the religious problems had been centred on a general council. When this actually came about, however, the method no longer worked, because the positions of the parties had drifted too far apart. Throughout all those years, despite an uneasy conscience, Charles had made temporary compromises with his Protestant adversaries in order to cope with a more urgent matter – the defence of Christendom against the Turks. He had not seen that the Protestants interpreted every provisional concession made as a step closer to their objective, nor that these concessions had been in place for so long that they were seen as an irrevocable achievement. Right until the end Charles and his advisors underestimated the seriousness of the religious differences and the determination of the reformers. He found it unacceptable that the oft-repeated temporary agreements of tolerance should have developed into a reality that could not be altered.

Could the emperor have acted differently? First of all, we should remember that as a result of the vast area over which he ruled and his vulnerability to consistent, powerful and sometimes even co-ordinated attacks from both France and the Ottoman Empire, he was confronted with unparalleled problems of government. Nowadays, we would say that the 'span of control' of his empire exceeded not only his own resources but also those of every ruler of his time. The unceasing external military pressure, combined with the disintegrating legitimacy of his authority as a result of the Reformation, posed insoluble problems for him. But in 1545 the two great external threats disappeared: he had signed the Peace of Crépy with France in 1544 and reached a truce with Sulaimān. He was at last free to tackle the religious problems.

The problems remained insoluble because Charles clung obstinately to the unity and universality of *Sacerdotium et Imperium*, Church and Empire, not in one person but in the persons of Pope and Emperor. Ferdinand, his successor, solved the problem in 1555 by no longer tying the emperorship to Rome – he would not be crowned by the pope – nor imposing the religion of the emperor on all his subjects. Charles did not have the flexibility shown by his brother. Differences in education, experience, character, surroundings and insight will have played a part in this. It is clear that what Ferdinand did – in 1555 he emphasised to the Protestant estates that he 'also had a conscience and a sense of honour'[55] – was indeed conceivable at that time and in that environment. Charles could have acted differently, less rigidly, and thereby have saved himself and his subjects a great deal of suffering.

Could the ultimate difference in the positions of Charles and Ferdinand be traced back merely to divergent visions, or were Charles and his advisors guilty of errors of judgement? In this connection let us consider three questions.

1. Was it wise to continue to ask consecutive popes, for fully 20 years, to summon a general council, and to link all Germany's problems to it? In the 'political testament' that Charles and his chief advisor, Nicholas Perrenot de Granvelle, drew up for his son Philip at the height of his power in 1548, he said: 'You already know how the present pope, Paul III, has treated me, and especially how ill he honoured his agreements during the last war'.[56] Clement VII had earlier disappointed Charles just as deeply, partly by his stubborn refusal to call a council. Charles and his advisors should have understood better the internal-Church and international-political reasons that caused a general council to be so long delayed. They did not realise that other possible options – a German synod was discussed as early as 1524 – could have prevented the situation in which the long delay damaged the credibility and, in the long term, the effectiveness of a council as a solution. In the end the emperor and the Diet prescribed certain institutional reforms for the Catholic Church in Germany in 1548. It could have happened much earlier, and that would have made a difference.

2. Did the emperor and his advisors have a sufficient understanding of the reformation movement itself? In 1521 the young emperor returned to

Spain optimistic, in the belief that the Edict of Worms and the decrees in the Low Countries would put an end to the heresies he so execrated. For ten years he remained uninvolved in the matter, occupied as he was with domestic problems in Spain, the war with France and supremacy in Italy. Because events were allowed to take their course in the Empire for ten years, even when it was perfectly clear that the Edict of Worms was not being observed, the Reformation gained considerable ground. It gave structure to the formulation of the demands of the rebellious peasants. But even the incredible violence of that movement failed to waken the Spanish court, which was under the spell of the triumph at Pavia.

Not only should the court have been better informed, it should also have questioned the motives for the massive support for the Reformation. It is known that Charles personally felt little for theological issues. This meant that he regularly left those matters to *ad hoc* committees and was thus at the mercy of the disagreements of their members. It also helps if we realise that Charles could only think about religion in very authoritarian terms: anyone who overstepped the official rules violated both the divine and worldly majesty and deserved the appropriate punishment. Above all, if the court had been slightly more sensitive to religious feelings, it should have realised that each year of tolerance made it increasingly difficult to reverse the events: the systematic secularisation of Church property and income, the introduction of new practices and ideas. From the moment in 1530 when Charles started to combine official censure with unofficial tolerance, he himself intensified the lack of clarity and the legal uncertainties, thus feeding the hope that the reforms would be recognised. It should have been realised then that ten years of real progress could not be reversed by legislation. Above all, the imperial court should have appreciated that it was impossible to leave an essential policy – which the religious question most certainly was - in the twilight zone for 30 years and at the same time to adhere to a rigid standard.

3. Did it make much difference what religious policy was followed at the level of emperor, Diet and government? The emperor's failure certainly shows his lack of authority, but does it mean that his actions had no impact at all? In the German Empire in particular, the religious question decided the agenda of every Diet under Charles, and the Diet was the most important political platform. In the Low Countries it was only in the last years of his reign that local government showed any political sensitivity on that point. The political debate should not make us lose sight of the victims of the policy of repression: many thousands of Charles' subjects were persecuted, punished, robbed, tortured or murdered for reasons of religion. Such repression must have slowed the spread of the Reformation.

Moreover, the government's inflexibility contributed to the growing alienation from the obvious needs of large parts of the population, which in turn seriously damaged the functioning of the political system as a whole. Charles' religious policy took an extraordinarily heavy toll. He was no exception in his time. His Spanish forebears and other monarchs were no less harsh in their treatment of dissentients, such as the Spanish Jews and Muslims. The reformers did not show much tolerance either. Or was this just a reaction to the violence surrounding them? What is certain is that Charles' policy of repression was in keeping with the exclusivist views of medieval popes and princes. His failure seems to show that society, especially in the towns, had evolved to a point where differences were accepted.

Notes:

1. P. Fredericq, *Corpus Documentorum Inquisitionis haereticae pravitatis Neerlandicae*, I (Ghent, 1889), nos 424, 431, 435; IV (Ghent, 1900), nos 31, 32, 42.
2. *Deutsche Reichstagsakten unter Kaiser Karl V.*, Vol. 2: *Reichstag zu Worms 1521*, ed. A. Wrede (Gotha, 1896), 466–70; A. Kohler, ed., *Quellen zur Geschichte Karls V.* (Darmstadt, 1990), 70–1.
3. M. Brecht, *Martin Luther*, 3 vols (Stuttgart, 1981–87), especially I, 413–53.
4. *Deutsche Reichstagsakten*, 2, no. 82, 594–6, translation in Kohler, *Quellen*, 74–5; H. Rabe, 'Karl V. und die deutschen Protestanten. Wege, Ziele und Grenzen der kaiserlichen Religionspolitik', in H. Rabe, ed., *Karl V. Politik und politisches System* (Konstanz, 1996), 321–2.
5. *Deutsche Reichstagsakten*, 2, 653–8; Kohler, *Quellen*, 76–7.
6. A. Grundmann, 'Die Beschwerden der deutschen Nation auf den Reichstagen der Reformation. Erläuterung und Begründung der Sonder-edition', in H. Lutz and A. Kohler, eds, *Aus der Arbeit an den Reichstagen unter Kaiser Karl V.* (Göttingen, 1986), 69–129, for this passage: 69–76.
7. Grundmann, *op.cit.*, 84–90.
8. *Deutsche Reichstagsakten*, 2, 153–6, 203; Kohler, *Quellen*, 71–3, 75–6.
9. C. Roll, *Das zweite Reichsregiment*, 20–1.
10. Rabe, 'Karl V. und die deutschen Protestanten', 323–4.
11. Kohler, *Quellen*, 146–56, quotation on 147; Kohler, *Karl V.*, 198–208.
12. Kohler, *Karl V.*, 208–18.
13. Grundmann, *op.cit.*, 95–105.
14. Rabe, *op.cit.*, 327–30.
15. R. Aulinger, 'Die Verhandlungen zum Nürnberger Anstand 1531/32 in der Vorgeschichte des Augsburger Religionsfriedens', in Lutz and Kohler, *Aus der Arbeit*, 204, 220.
16. Kohler, *Karl V.*, 220–1.
17. *Ibid.*, 197–204; *Deutsche Reichstagsakten*, Vol. 10. *Der Reichstag in Regensburg und die Verhandlungen über einen Friedstand mit den Protestanten in Schweinfurt und Nürnberg 1532*, ed. R. Aulinger (Göttingen, 1992).
18. Kohler, *Karl V.*, 222–3.
19. Brandi, *Kaiser Karl V.*, II, 278.

20. *Ibid.*, 280.
21. A. P. Luttenberger, *Glaubenseinheit und Reichsfriede. Konzeptionen und Wege konfessionsneutraler Reichspolitik 1530–1552. Kurpfalz, Jülich, Neubrandenburg* (Göttingen, 1982), 93–150.
22. Aulinger, *op.cit.*, 204–6; Rabe, *op.cit.*, 333; Kohler, *Karl V.*, 261–72.
23. Kohler, *Quellen*, 324–5.
24. Kohler, *Karl V.*, 299 onwards.
25. Fernandez Alvarez, *Corpus documental*, II, 490.
26. Brandi, *Kaiser Karl V.*, I, 486–7.
27. Kohler, *Quellen*, 370–3; Kohler, *Karl V.*, 307–19.
28. See the comprehensive instructions and further letters from Charles to Ferdinand: Kohler, *Quellen*, 433–65.
29. Kohler, *Karl V.*, 345–50; Rabe, 'Karl V. und die deutschen Protestanten', 337–45.
30. Fernandez Alvarez, *Corpus documental*, IV, nos 32 and 42.
31. J. V. Pollet, *Martin Bucer: Etudes sur les relations de Bucer avec les Pays-Bas, l'Electorat de Cologne et l'Allemagne du Nord* (Leiden, 1985), I, 12.
32. A. Goosens, *Les inquisitions modernes dans les Pays-Bas méridionaux (1520–1633)*, Vol. II (Brussels, 1998), 76–82.
33. Rabe, *Reich und Glaubensspaltung*, 233–6.
34. A. Mellink, *Amsterdam en de wederdopers* (Nijmegen, 1978), 30–6; M. Baelde, *De collaterale raden onder Karel V en Filips II, 1531–1578* (Brussels, 1965), 271.
35. Mellink, *op.cit.*, 39–72.
36. Goosens, *Inquisitions*, 102–4.
37. Mellink, *op.cit.*, 95–104; L. G. Jansma, *Melchiorieten, Munstersen en Batenburgers* (Buitenpost, 1977).
38. Fernandez Alvarez, *Corpus documental*, IV, 224–9.
39. *Ibid.*, V, 307–12.
40. J. Decavele, *De dageraad van de reformatie in Vlaanderen, 1520–1565* (Brussels, 1975), I, 193–230.
41. Goosens, *Les Inquisitions*, II, 89 (quotation on p. 103), 95–107, 188–92.
42. Chabod, *Lo Stato e la vita religiosa a Milano nell'epoca di Carlo V* (Turin, 1971), 331–56.
43. R. Villari, *La rivolta antispagnola a Napoli* (Rome, 1976), 34–5.
44. R. Garcia Carcel, *Herejía y sociedad en el siglo XVI: la Inquisición a Valencia, 1530–1609* (Barcelona, 1981), 21.
45. C. Wagner, 'L'Inquisition de Tolède face au protestantisme au XVIe siècle', *Revue d'Histoire et de Philosophie religieuses*, 74 (1994), 166–69.
46. H. Kamen, *The Spanish Inquisition* (New Haven and London, 1998), 75–81; for the following paragraph: 86–92, 112, 263.
47. The texts: S. A. Zavala, *Las instituciones jurídicas en la conquista de America* (Mexico, 1971), 213–17.
48. P. Seed, *Ceremonies of Possession in Europe's Conquest of the New World, 1492–1640* (Cambridge, 1995), 69–99.
49. S. A. Zavala, *La encomienda indiana* (Mexico, 1973), 40–9; L. Hanke, *La lucha por la justicia en la conquista de America* (Madrid, 1988), 194.
50. Hanke, *La lucha*, 295–6; T. Todorov, *La Conquête de l'Amérique* (Paris, 1982), 167.

51. Zavala, *La encomienda*, 80–89; Hanke, *La lucha*, 190, 203–8.
52. P. Rassow, *Die Kaiser-Idee Karls V: dargestellt an der Politik der Jahre 1528–1540* (Berlin, 1932), 401–5.
53. Kohler, *Quellen*, 97; K.Lanz., *Correspondenz des Kaisers Karl V.*, I (Leipzig, 1844), 58.
54. Kohler, *Quellen*, 437.
55. Kohler, *Karl V.*, 348.
56. Fernandez Alvarez, *Corpus documental*, II, 575–7.

5

Charles' political system

Imperial politics exerted a profound influence on the internal relationships in all of Charles' territories. In the first place his subjects were immediately aware if their sovereign was in the land or elsewhere. Castile and Germany were particularly sensitive in this respect. When he left a country Charles always appointed regents, and in those lands where his absences were protracted he appointed viceroys, stadholders or governors; yet he always ran the show himself. He placed such restrictions on his deputies that any important decisions, especially those relating to appointments,[1] had to be laid before the emperor. This inevitably resulted in lengthy correspondence, embassies and slow decision-making. Because of the difficulty of access to their ruler all his subjects felt that they were a link in a much larger whole.

This awareness was strengthened by other circumstances: the emperor's decisions were guided by a complex range of factors extending far beyond the borders of each individual territory. His subjects had difficulty in accepting that their interests were subordinated, postponed or even prejudiced for the sake of higher dynastic concerns. They were often the victim of attacks, raids or blockades resulting from conflicts which in their view did not concern them directly but which somehow stemmed from their ruler's tangled, continent-wide interests. Charles' subjects in the Low Countries were anxious to maintain peaceful relations with France, England, Denmark and Guelders, but they were repeatedly drawn into war with them against their will as a result of the changing dynastic coalitions.[2] For many years the people of Italy had to put up with attacks by the armies and fleets of France, Switzerland, Germany, Spain and Turkey, even though they had never wanted to quarrel with these countries. Their peninsula had become the board on which the major powers played out their rivalries, setting out their pawns for the game.

A more serious problem was that Charles also expected financial and material support from his subjects for his military expeditions in distant lands. The representative bodies in all his territories fiercely resisted the use of their taxes outside their borders. Constantly pressed for money, the government entered into complicated credit arrangements with international bankers who furnished money when necessary, assured of receiving income from taxes elsewhere and of a substantial commission, of course. The Fuggers, who supplied 64 per cent of the more than 850,000 guilders which in 1519 procured the electors' votes for Charles, were in 1525 granted the rents from the Spanish military orders for a period of three years.[3] In time his subjects had to foot the bill for the emperor's foreign wars and, in addition, to pay the costs of the banks' transactions. The net result was felt in steadily increasing taxation.

So an enormous administrative problem faced the emperor: his subjects felt that his government was more distant, more complicated, slower and less effective that that of the previous, native-born, rulers, and his activities obliged them to cope with his enemies and the increasing pressure of his taxes. The administrative answer to this came in the form of the rapid expansion of state machinery. At the same time it is noticeable that only a very light structure was created at the level of Charles' authority. In the middle of the 1520s his grand chancellor, Mercurino di Gattinara, considered strengthening the Council of State to be the overall body governing the entire empire. The Council did not have any German members; it consisted originally of Burgundians and Netherlanders, but in a short time became part of the Castilian administration.[4] The expansion of government institutions thus actually served to strengthen the unique character of each of the individual territories and not that of the dynastic state.

The absent prince

The common factor in all the different lands was their link with the same ruler. Some lands, too, were part of the Holy Roman Empire, but in most cases this was an extremely theoretical construction. Apart from some common principles relating to the royal dignity, the conditions for the exercise of power were very different in all the principalities. Paying homage and mutual oath-taking were held to be cornerstones of the relationship between the ruler and his subjects. In the event of his prolonged absence a ruler preferred to appoint a close relative as his deputy, or possibly a high nobleman and a council of regents.

When Charles succeeded in Spain in 1516–17 the situation there was already extremely delicate. In his will, Ferdinand of Aragon had appointed the 80-year-old Cardinal Cisneros as regent of Castile and his own illegitimate son, Ferdinand, archbishop of Zaragoza, as regent of Aragon. For many years relations between the towns and high nobility in both kingdoms had been uneasy. The fact that it was two years before Charles appeared in his new lands, and in the meantime issued any number of rather undiplomatic orders from Brussels, only helped to increase the tension. In addition, there was the question of whether the high-handed proclamation of himself as king in Brussels on 13 March 1516 – even though jointly with his mother – did not ignore her rights. Although the Royal Council recognised Joanna's inability to govern, opponents could still make use of her, as indeed happened during the revolt of the *comuneros* in 1520.[5]

When Charles hurriedly left Spain on 20 May 1520 to accept the German crown, he left his tutor, Adrian of Utrecht, by now a cardinal, as regent. In doing this he broke a solemn promise made to the *cortes*, that he would not give any more government posts to foreigners. In a speech in March of that year, which clearly shows the hand of Gattinara, he had explained in detail to the *cortes* the reasons for this departure.

> I have not taken up this great task for my own pleasure. I would have been content with the Spanish Empire with the Balearics, Sardinia, the kingdom of Sicily, a large part of Italy, Germany and France and with that other gold-bearing world. . . . But there has been a fatal exigency concerning matters which force me to set sail. This decision had to be made out of respect for the faith whose enemies have become so powerful that the peace of the commonwealth, the honour of Spain and the prosperity of my kingdoms can no longer tolerate such a threat. Their continued existence can only be assured if I unite Spain to Germany and add the title of Caesar to that of King of Spain.[6]

It soon became clear that the well-meaning Cardinal Adrian, now left as regent in Spain, was unable to deal with the tensions, which before long turned into revolt. In September two important Spanish noblemen, Admiral Enriquez and the commander-in-chief, Velasco, were appointed to assist him restore law and order.

In April 1529, when Charles again left Spain after a stay of seven years, to be crowned Holy Roman Emperor by the pope, he asked Isabella of Portugal, whom he had married in Seville on 10 March 1526, to undertake the regency. As early as 1520 the *cortes* of Castile, anxious as they were for the continuity of the dynasty and the permanent residence in Spain of a member of the royal house, had recommended this lady to him. They urged him to enter into marriage with this 'exceptional person, the most beautiful princess Isabella of Portugal, a faithful friend to our people and to all Castilians, who speaks Castilian as we do'.[7] The fact that Isabella was the daughter of Charles' aunt, Mary of Aragon, and thus his first cousin, seemed to be no hindrance at all, even though a marriage within the fourth degree of kinship was contrary to Church law. Charles' departure for Italy was actually postponed until the considerable dowry (including revenues from the Moluccas) had arrived from Portugal, enabling him at last to equip himself with the desired magnificence.

Empress Isabella proved very adept at ruling the Spanish kingdoms in her consort's name. In 1528 she governed Castile while Charles was away in Aragon and Valencia. During his four-year absence in Italy, Germany and the Low Countries from 1529 to 1533, he sent her lengthy official letters every week, and as his regent she sent him a number of documents. Nothing personal can be found in his letters to Isabella. Perhaps the private correspondence, if it existed, was kept apart from the official and has not survived. Some of Isabella's private letters have come down to us: they reveal her deep concern for her husband's undertakings, his honour and reputation, her anxiety for his health – she had processions held and prayers said throughout Spain – and above all, her fervent, increasingly expressed hope for his speedy return to his Spanish possessions. Isabella enjoyed the emperor's complete trust but even she, like the other regents, viceroys and governors, could not grant pardons or appoint officials or administrators in the major towns. A state council consisting of two archbishops and two high noblemen assisted her in her task.[8]

The fact that Charles was 25 before he could decide upon a wife illustrates how insecure he was during the 1520s. As a young boy he had been betrothed to French and English princesses, for the sake of the alliances. Early in the 1520s he was still hesitating between Mary Tudor, Henry VIII's daughter, born in 1516, and Isabella, whom the Castilian *cortes* had so warmly recommended to him. She was just three years younger than he, but the political situation was unclear until, during the captivity of Francis I, relations with England cooled. In October 1525, when Charles was negotiating Francis' release and his marriage to Isabella, the support of England seemed a less important consideration than settling the Iberian kingdoms and a large Portuguese dowry. The members of the *cortes* were aware that Charles was putting the continuity of his dynasty at risk by waiting so long before taking steps to arrange a marriage and ensure legitimate issue.

From a political point of view, Isabella's early death in 1539 deprived Charles of his alter ego who could take his place in Castile. When he left Spain later that year to suppress the rebellion in Ghent, he had to leave his 12-year-old son, Philip, with a regency council of Spanish dignitaries. In 1543 Charles left Spain and did not return until after his abdication in 1556. During that time Philip was again regent, and when he went north from 1548 to 1551, Charles' daughter Mary and her consort, Maximilian of Austria, took his place; then Philip was regent again, and after 1554 Charles' youngest daughter, Joanna. The lack of experience of these youthful regents placed a heavy burden on their advisors, who took the opportunity to extend their own power and build up their own networks.

The emperor's family

From the moment that he was proclaimed king of Spain it took Charles eleven years to provide himself with an heir. There was no reason to doubt his ability to procreate, nor his taste for the female sex. At the beginning of his Joyous Entry in Valladolid in the autumn of 1517 he naturally met Germaine de Foix, the 29-year-old widow of King Ferdinand. Her residence was situated opposite the royal palace and a covered wooden bridge was built between the two buildings to enable them to visit each other discreetly. Laurent Vital, the chronicler from the Low Countries who witnessed this episode, refers to the king's infatuation and the lovers making frequent use of the bridge, but he does not mention the lady's name. Germaine de Foix accompanied the king to Barcelona, presumably not only to acquaint him with the administrative customs of the kingdom of Aragon. In 1519 she was given in marriage to Margrave Hans of Brandenburg-Küstrin, but she went on to live as the wife of Duke Fernando of Calabria, whom the king honoured with the attractive post of viceroy of Valencia. Germaine died there in October 1536. The proof of her relationship with Charles has recently been discovered in her testament in which she wills her 'best necklace with 133 fat pearls to the illustrious doña Isabella, infanta of Castile, daughter of his Majesty the Emperor, my lord and son, and this because of the great love and affection which we bear towards his Highness'.

The widower, Fernando of Calabria, confirmed in a letter to the empress that this bequest had been to the 'illustrious infanta, doña Isabella, your daughter', when her only daughters were named Mary and Joanna. So a half-sister was brought up at court with them who was both Charles' daughter and aunt. At present it is not known if this infanta played any role in public life.[9]

We know of three more children born to the young, unmarried emperor in this period. A relationship during the siege of Tournai in the autumn of 1521 with Joanna van der Gheynst, the daughter of a tapestry weaver, resulted in the birth of Margaret, who was brought up in Brussels, close to the regent Margaret. Her mother was given an annuity and married to Johan van den Dijcke, an official in the Chamber of Accounts in Brussels. Charles deployed his daughter when she was still very young to improve his relations with Italy. Under the terms of his agreement with Clement VII he promised her at seven years of age to Clement's nephew, Alexander de Medici, who had to be reinstated to power in Florence. On 29 February 1536 Charles watched the wedding of the barely 14-year-old Margaret to the man who was notorious for his vile excesses. In the following year

Alexander was killed by the Florentine opposition, led by his brother. Two years and one pope later, Margaret had another husband, this time the grandson of Pope Paul III, who in the summer of 1538 had done his utmost to restore peace between France and the Habsburgs. When Ottavio Farnese, later the duke of Parma, stood before the altar with her in November 1538, he was only 13. Margaret and her son Alexander would later be of great service to Philip II, she as regent in the Low Countries and he as a talented military commander.

Not all of Charles' natural children were brought up at one of his courts. A certain doña Juana, born in 1522 or 1523, died at a convent in Avila in 1530. Her mother complained there about the lack of interest shown by Juana's imperial father. A stay in Flanders inspired the emperor to a relationship with a beautiful Italian widow, Orsolina de la Peña, which also resulted in the birth of a daughter. Orsolina was persuaded by her brothers to return to Rome, and on the journey, accompanied by a lady-in-waiting, she gave birth to Tadea in Bologna. Tadea grew up in a convent near Perugia. When Charles was in Bologna in 1530, and again in 1532–33, he summoned and received Tadea. Soon afterwards, her angry uncles removed her from the convent to marry her off, although she was barely ten years old. After that she opted for convent life. Charles does not appear to have evaded his responsibilities in any of these cases. When possible, he used his natural children for his political ends, as his Burgundian forebears had done. This was particularly true of the famous don Juan, born in Regensburg on Charles' birthday, 24 February 1547. The mother, Barbara Blomberg, was 21 or 22 and the daughter of a girdle-maker. In his will dated 1554, Charles recognised this son, who grew up in Valladolid at the court of his half-sister, the regent Joanna, together with his contemporaries Carlos, the son of prince Philip and thus a nephew of don Juan, and his cousin Alexander Farnese.[10]

We know nothing directly about Charles' amorous adventures during the thirteen years of his marriage, although sometimes we come across discreet references to them. His former confessor, Loaysa, writing from Rome in June 1530, urged him not to let himself be led astray by 'your wicked sensuality'. In 1531 he found it necessary to explain to his brother that he had not appointed Egmont's young widow to their sister Mary's household for reasons that he would understand on the basis of previous conversations. 'I am not yet such a bad husband', he added.[11]

The freedom allowed to men in noble circles was inconceivable for women. Empress Isabella considered that her primary function was to bear children. Philip was born in 1527, Mary in 1528. Isabella suffered so greatly from her husband's lengthy absences that her courtiers became increasingly aware of it. The birth and death of their third child, Ferdinand, in 1530–31 occurred in Charles' absence; he received the sad tidings with stoicism. Their second daughter, Joanna, was born during the siege of Tunis – an event which was probably more important in Charles' view. Isabella began to show signs of depression at this time. In October 1537 she gave birth to Juan, who died soon afterwards, and she herself died in childbirth on 1 May 1539. Only then did Charles appear to be really moved by her fate.

After a period of retreat in a monastery Charles decided not to marry again. He asked his sister Mary to send him her portrait of Isabella, because that was the best likeness of her. When the portrait arrived he wrote a letter in his own hand expressing his disappointment that the likeness was not what he had imagined.[12] Charles had other portraits of Isabella painted – Titian was one of the artists – which he took with him on all his journeys, until his final stay at Yuste. As father of only one legitimate son, his decision not to remarry was politically risky and deprived him of more dynastic trump cards. Does it then show sincere conjugal fidelity?

Still, Charles was very distant from his motherless children. He subjected the girls to a life of seclusion that was incomprehensible even to his contemporaries. Philip, on the other hand, a young widower in 1545, could satisfy his fancy among the Portuguese ladies-in-waiting. As head of the family, Charles was authoritarian, cool and manipulative with the female members of the dynasty: their own feelings must always yield to the Habsburg interests as Charles saw them. At the age of 17 he forced his sister Eleanor to break off her romance with the count palatine Frederick, with whom she had grown up at the Burgundian court since 1513. In anticipation of their departure to Spain from Middelburg in the summer of 1517, Frederick paid court to Eleanor. Charles took from her a letter written by Frederick, apparently not the first. In it he swore to *'ma mie'* that he only wanted to be hers and she his.[13] Eleanor was destined to become the third wife of 50-year-old Manuel I of Portugal, who died in 1521. In 1530 she had to leave her daughter, Mary, behind in Portugal when, after a four-year betrothal and a bout of depression caused by the outbreak of war, she finally married Francis I to seal his peace with Charles. No children were born out of this marriage, possibly because of Francis' obvious preference for other ladies, possibly also because of his venereal disease. After his death Eleanor went to live with her sister Mary in Brussels, and returned to Spain with her and Charles in 1556. At Eleanor's dogged insistence, her daughter Mary, '*La Abandonada*', reluctantly agreed to see her in the border town of Badajoz in January 1558, a month before her death. Mary never married; in 1553 she was nominated as a second Portuguese bride for her cousin,

Crown Prince Philip, but preference was eventually given to Mary Tudor. Neither mother nor daughter had much happiness in their lives, which were sacrificed to dynastic interests.[14]

Charles' other sisters were also married for strategic reasons, mostly arranged by their grandfather Maximilian: Isabella in Denmark – the story of her short, unhappy life has already been told – and Mary in Hungary – her marriage seems to have been loving and lively, but it ended early on the battlefield of Mohács and she remained childless. Following the example of her aunt Margaret she resolutely chose to remain a widow, and thus achieved greater freedom. She was regent of the Low Countries for 25 years, a position she could exercise with a reasonable degree of independence. Charles' youngest sister, Catherine, who could only be released from the company of her mentally disturbed mother by means of a ruse, was the only sister to enjoy a long and peaceful marriage: her husband was John III of Portugal. Their two children, John and Mary Manuela, were married to Charles' children, Joanna and Philip, in a double wedding arrangement. This was the second generation in which first cousins were married.

It was an increasingly systematic policy of the Habsburgs to strengthen their dynastic unity through double marriages and marriages within the fourth degree of kinship. In three cases they even used both strategies together. The marriage in 1496–97 of the Spanish and Habsburg heirs with the other's sister had led to the union of the two dynasties, a method that would be repeated in succeeding generations. Emperor Maximilian also arranged the treaty by which the double marriage would later take place between his grandchildren Ferdinand and Mary and the Hungarian royal children. This was how Hungary, Bohemia and Moravia came into Habsburg hands.

The double union of cousins took place on two occasions between the royal houses of Spain and Portugal, and once between Charles' children and those of his brother Ferdinand. In 1525 John III of Portugal married Charles' youngest sister Catherine; later in the year it became a double marriage union when Charles decided to marry John's sister Isabella. The Catholic kings Ferdinand and Isabella were the grandparents of all four of these marriage partners. In the next generation the exercise was repeated when Charles' children married the two children born to their aunt Catherine's marriage. Charles' three legitimate children each married a cousin; Philip married a cousin twice, because his fourth, 22-year-younger wife was Anna of Austria, the granddaughter of his uncle, the German Emperor Ferdinand. This marriage would eventually produce Philip's successor, Philip III. Carlos, his son by his first wife, whose weak constitution and cruel, arrogant behaviour had alarmed Charles in 1556, died in prison in 1568, having been arrested on his father's orders. The mental disturbance of his great grandmother Joanna the Mad was probably not the only explanation for this drama: the boy was the product of two generations of inbreeding. During their negotiations of 1550–51 Charles and Ferdinand had agreed in principle to the double marriage of their respective heirs with their cousins. Charles' daughter Mary married Ferdinand's eldest son Maximilian in 1548: the second marriage took place 20 years later. It seemed to be an obsession with the Habsburgs.

It is quite clear that this policy of family marriages brought dynastic advantages. It enabled Philip II to become king of Portugal. Moreover, all the female Habsburgs could be used to consolidate alliances. As head of the dynasty Charles had at his disposal the 15 children of Ferdinand, as well as the children of his sisters Isabella and Catherine, to compensate for his own shortage of legitimate offspring. Having been passed over by her cousin Philip, Eleanor's abandoned Portuguese daughter refused to make herself available for another union. Her great aunt, Mary of Hungary, had made a similar choice. Ferdinand's daughters became marriage partners for Duke William of Jülich-Cleves after his submission in 1543, and the dukes of Mantua and Ferrara. Charles was noticeably saddened by the death of the young son of his dead sister Isabella and the deposed king Christian II of Denmark. The boy had then lived with Charles. Charles said in his handwritten letter of condolence to the boy's two sisters that he had had great expectations of him.[15] An undertone of political practicality, perhaps? There is no record of Charles showing any emotion at the death a year earlier of his own baby son, Ferdinand, whom he had never known. He was able to make use of the young Danish princesses in his system of alliances. At the age of 12 Dorothea was married to the count palatine Frederick, who was over 50 – the same count whom Charles had denied his sister Eleanor in 1517. In 1533 Charles wanted to send Dorothea's 11-year-old sister Christina to Francesco Sforza, the 38-year-old duke of Milan, so that their marriage could be consummated immediately; the regent Mary, who had looked after the children after Margaret had first taken care of them, was outraged at the suggestion. She reminded her brother of the statutory minimum age of 12 years and of the risks to the girl's health, but Charles coolly brushed aside her arguments as fodder for lawyers and ordered her departure, for Milan was still of strategic importance. Mary managed to postpone things until 1534; Sforza died in the following year and Christina once again became the subject of diverse marriage plans. In 1541 she celebrated her wedding to the future duke of Lorraine.

The dynasty was the most important binding agent of the Habsburg empire. This makes the almost obsessive preoccupation of its chief members with marriage understandable. Marriage alliances had been a main concern of aristocratic families for centuries, each at its own level. Double marriages were a familiar tactic used to consolidate possessions. Seen in this light, it becomes obvious why conjugal relations did not have a primarily emotional significance and extramarital adventures were amply tolerated, for men in royal circles at any rate. Compared to Emperor Maximilian, Charles did not have many illegitimate children, and as far as marital fidelity was concerned he was far more correct than his contemporaries Francis I and Henry VIII. He showed little affection for his children, not even on the death of his wife in childbirth or of his son's wife six years later. What amazes the present-day observer is the systematic infringement of the Church's ban on marriage within the fourth degree of kinship, and the fact that young girls were often forced into marriage with unattractive, much older men. It reveals a fundamental disdain for women that Mary of Hungary opposed remarkably vigorously. Charles seems to have been totally indifferent to the risks to the physical and mental health, or even the life, of the young brides, even when his own daughter Margaret was involved. In the early stages this attitude helped to make the dynasty great, but later it proved to be its undoing, mentally and physically. Charles should have realised that.

Servants of the emperor

Charles considered his aunt Margaret his first servant. When he went to Spain in 1517 she remained in the Low Countries with a regency council; after 1519 she was recognised as regent and governor. She had been married to the crown princes of France and Spain, then to the duke of Savoy. On the strength of her wide range of personal contacts and her royal status she was inclined to take initiatives in international politics, which often caused friction with the councillors or with her nephew.[16] Yet in 1529 he gave her a free hand to negotiate the Treaty of Cambrai with her sister-in-law Louisa of Savoy, the mother of the French king. Initially, from 1521–22, he treated his brother Ferdinand on the same footing as his deputy in the German Empire, assisted by the *Reichsregiment*. The young prince's lack of experience and pressure from the Diet forced him to keep a low profile then. By the middle of 1524 the desire to appoint a Roman king was being voiced in Germany because,

> the emperor or Roman king [Charles] is young and has little experience of the relationships within Germany, so that we are not governed by the will, desire and wisdom of our emperor but by his advisors, who often come from

foreign lands, at least the most prominent among them, and who are not familiar with the customs, good and bad, of the German nation as those who were born here are. For this and other reasons we consider that the emperor is responsible for many kingdoms, lands and patrimonial domains, which will severely hamper him in governing the German lands; he will be able to stay in Germany little or not at all, so that matters will be left to drift along and will lead to the decline of the Empire rather than to its increase.[17]

This analysis, made by Charles' first secretary and member of the German court council, Jean Hannart, found support in the opposition movements then active in the German Empire and which were in part justified by the Reformation. In 1522 and 1523 the knights of the Upper Rhine region made fruitless attempts to strengthen their position *vis-à-vis* the princes; in the following years, the peasants broke out in massive revolt in south and central Germany, leaving no less than 75,000 victims.[18] In the meantime the Reformation was gaining ground in the north. The imperial court paid little attention to these dramatic events and had no control over them. The death of his brother-in-law, Louis, in 1526 brought Ferdinand the royal crown of Bohemia, and the following year that of Hungary, and with them the personal status he desired. Constitutionally, Charles could not fulfil the wish to have a Roman king elected until he himself could pass the Roman crown on after he had been crowned Emperor. It was not until 1529 that Clement VII's attitude made this a real possibility. At Epiphany 1531 the crown of Germany devolved upon Ferdinand, on the express condition that Charles would have the final power of decision. The Fuggers' gold encouraged the electors to be accommodating in this election too. The understanding between the two brothers was successful until 1550–51, when the question of the succession caused a breach of trust.

No such conflict threatened Mary of Hungary, who in 1531 succeeded her aunt as regent of the Low Countries. She already possessed the title of queen, had no issue to protect, and could give the appearance of submissiveness towards her brother that was expected of her as a woman. Her superior intelligence and diplomatic skills enabled her to present matters in such a way that the emperor accepted her views and gradually gave her a freer hand than he had ever allowed her aunt. In October 1538 – after many joint banquets, dances and hunting parties – Mary signed a treaty of cooperation with Francis I in Compiègne. Her sex was only a hindrance when war was concerned because there the military leaders refused to accept her involvement.[19]

When Eleanor was queen of France, she was of course loyal and obedient to her consort, Francis I. However, she could pass on information to Charles about relationships at the French court and could sometimes act as mediator. Her intervention was decisive in arranging the meeting between the two monarchs at Aigues-Mortes in July 1538 where, after two years of hostilities, a truce was agreed.[20]

The monarch or his deputy was the centre of power in his territory. Charles never built an architecturally impressive, permanent residence – in marked contrast to Francis I and Henry VIII, both of whom were indefatigable castle-builders. However, in 1526 he did designate the choir of the cathedral in Granada to be a family mausoleum and had it enlarged in Renaissance style. The remains of his father, Philip the Handsome, were brought there from Tordesillas in 1525, his consort Isabella was interred there in 1539, and in 1546 his sons Juan and Ferdinand, who had died so young, and his first daughter-in-law, Mary Manuela. The idea of building a Renaissance palace next to the Palace of the Nasriden in the Alhambra must have originated from about the same time, 1526 or 1527. Work on this started in 1533 and continued intermittently until 1637, but it was never finished. The roof had still to be completed in the twentieth century. Neither the emperor nor his son ever actually lived there, and from the outset that can never have been the intention. The aim was to plant a symbol of the power of the Christian emperor and peacemaker in the heart of Andalusia, the Moorish kingdom that had been conquered in 1492.[21]

Charles was an itinerant ruler in the medieval tradition: he never invested much in his places of residence, even the house at Yuste where he spent the last months of his life, for his stays were always short. The Castilian monarchs had chosen Valladolid as their capital and had residences in a number of other towns including Tordesillas, Toledo, Alcalá de Henares, Ocaña and Madrid. The court that surrounded Charles was not based on the Spanish model, however, but on the Burgundian, simply because of how it came into being, for it was an offshoot of the Burgundian court in the Low Countries.

In the Burgundian tradition the court was made up of a group of counsellor-chamberlains (*conseillers-chambellans*) and other noblemen who were close to the ruler and advised and assisted him. In this way the ruler bound the most important nobles from his own country and from friendly circles to him personally. This created ties, because the nobles could approach the monarch easily and obtain all sorts of favours from him. Conversely, the monarch had a certain hold over the nobles whom he could set to work in his own interests, and on whom – by means of appointments, gifts and marriages – he could depend in the complex areas of power.

A number of specific areas of care at the royal court had grown into honorary positions that the nobles filled ceremoniously and symbolically. Among them were the table services for offering bread, pouring wine and carving meat and the supervision of the stables; squires, *ecuyers*, were appointed to these four sectors. Sometimes a separate group of noblemen was responsible for serving in the royal bedchamber. Very precise rules of access were laid down, under which ordinary courtiers, *gentilhommes*, were allowed no further than the antechamber while gentlemen-in-waiting and stewards were permitted to enter the second chamber. In the palace in Brussels these rules corresponded with the physical layout of the rooms. The court was a strictly hierarchical and tightly organised symbolic microcosm, where everybody had his appointed place and had to behave in a manner befitting it.

The table ceremonies, with their ritual placing and order of precedence, formed a daily opportunity for a theatrical exhibition of the relationships between the ruler and his most important servants. Beneath this upper layer of nobles, dozens of members of the royal household were responsible for the spiritual, physical and material comforts. The consort, the queen mother and minor children had separate households, simpler versions of the king's model.

A list of Charles' household was drawn up shortly before he left for Spain in June 1517. It contained a total of 473 people, 265 of whom were servants. At the higher levels there were seven stewards, 54 counsellor-chamberlains, and more than 30 squires for each of the four sectors; finally, 16 pages were listed, referring to young noblemen from the retinue of courtiers. Together with the senior courtier, Henry III of Nassau, the lord chamberlain, this retinue included 208 noble courtiers. Not all were required to be in attendance at the same time: there was a quarterly or half-yearly duty roster, which meant that the court was in fact less than half this size. For every day of actual service counsellor-chamberlains and stewards received an allowance of 48 *patards*, the squires 24 and their pages 12. 12 *patards* was then twice the daily wage of a master craftsman in Ghent or Brussels; in addition, these court servants were well fed and housed.

The court that followed Charles to Spain had the same structure, but was smaller. As many as 322 names appear on a pay sheet dating from 1523-24, but the counsellor-chamberlains were reduced to a group of eight and the squires to 82. If we look at the court that remained in Mechelen with Margaret, and which had a similar structure, we find that of the 473 members in 1517 there were now 155 left. The head of her court bore the title of knight of honour. In 1524 the position was occupied by Antoine de Lalaing, count of Hoogstraten, knight in the Order of the Golden Fleece, governor of Holland, Zeeland and (from 1528) Utrecht, head of the Council of Finances, in short one of the most influential noblemen in the Low Countries. With a view to the establishment of an independent court for Philip, who would deputise for him in Spain and, in the course of time, succeed him, Charles had a description made of the arrangements and ceremonials in 1545. In this way the Burgundian pattern was repeated and extended in the Spanish royal households. After his return to Spain in 1522 Charles systematically introduced Spanish noblemen into his court. By 1535 this consisted of 473 persons (not counting his bodyguards), the majority of whom were Spanish nobles.[22]

The budget for the ordinary expenses of the kingdom of Castile in 1544 gives us some idea of the importance of the diverse households in this part of the empire, at a time when Charles was campaigning in Champagne. Two-thirds of the Castilian budget was earmarked for the army and navy and one-quarter for the royal households: Charles' household consumed 69 per cent of that quarter. When looking at these figures we should remember that a considerable part of total state expenditure was covered by loans and by other lands. Nevertheless the figures show the great importance of the court as an institution which felt the influence of noblemen and officials from all corners of the empire.[23]

The regents in the Low Countries kept substantial households; other viceroys and governors copied the Burgundian model but had to be satisfied with less splendour.

Over the centuries diverse administrative bodies and organs of state had grown up out of the court through functional differentiation. The most important of these was the Court Council, originally an assembly of the most important counsellor-chamberlains. At some time the judicial and financial functions had split off into separate bodies, which in the Low Countries were known respectively as the Council Chamber and the Chamber of Accounts. Between 1435 and 1445 a high court of justice, which in time became known as the Great Council, was formed in the Burgundian Low Countries. In 1504 it settled permanently in Mechelen. The Court Council, the small group of political advisors that was also known as the Privy Council, was ambulant, accompanying the ruler on his

Table 5.1 Budget of ordinary expenditure, Castile 1544

HOUSEHOLDS	DUCATS
Charles	250,000
Queen Joanna	38,000
Prince Philip	32,000
Princess Mary Manuela	22,000
Princesses Mary and Joanna	20,000
GOVERNMENT	98,000
DIPLOMACY	50,000
ARMY	508,865
NAVY	455,500
Total	1,474,365

continual moves. The financial administration remained a problem for a time, but when Margaret had been formally reappointed regent in 1519, a Council of Finances was established under the chairmanship of Antoine de Lalaing who held the seal and had the power of signature, provided he kept the regent fully informed.[24]

As emperor, Maximilian also had a Court Council consisting of four bishops and three other officials. The position of chancellor devolved on the archbishop-elector of Mainz, assisted by a vice-chancellor of the Empire. They were still in function at the Diet of Worms in 1521, but after that the German Court Council lost all significance: the Diet had appointed a *Reichsregiment,* with members from its own circle, to look after matters of state. Whereas advisors and officials from the Low Countries accompanied Charles to Spain, no Germans did.[25] Apparently the German dignitaries did not conceive of moving beyond the frontiers of their prestigious Empire in order to govern it. This was a major reason for the lack of information about, and neglect of, German affairs at the Spanish court. Another contributory cause was, of course, the considerable differences in language and culture; they would end in Charles' inability to control German problems after 1530, and finally in the break-up of the Habsburg empire after his abdication.

The fierce revolt of the *comuneros* in 1520–22 was aimed at the corruption of the Council of Castile. On his return to Castile in July 1522 Charles found a country where the taxes, which had been agreed in 1520 after lengthy secret negotiations, had not been collected, while a debt of 57 million maravedis (375 maravedis = 1 ducat) to the Fuggers was still outstanding. Administrative reform was urgent. The Royal Council and the *Consejo de la Suprema y General Inquisición,* both lightly structured institutions established under the Catholic kings, had remained intact until then. The *Consejo* dated from 1480, its primary function being the persecution of false Christians, Muslims and Jews throughout Spain. The Royal Council was actually the crown council of Castile and consisted of 12 *letrados,* university-trained lawyers from noble families, presided over by a prelate.

During the early years in Spain, the young Charles depended mainly on his confidants from the Low Countries: Adrian of Utrecht, cardinal of Tortosa, whom he appointed grand inquisitor in 1517, William of Croy-Chièvres his chief lord-in-waiting, and Jean le Sauvage (the Flemish lawyer, Jan de Wilde) his grand chancellor, who was succeeded on his death in 1518 by the Piedmontese Mercurino di Gattinara, a close associate of Margaret and former president of the parliament of Dole.

For the administrative restructuring in Spain these advisors followed the model developed in the Low Countries. In 1523 a *Consejo de la Hacienda* was established to manage finances. It consisted of three advisors, a treasurer, a secretary and a clerk. For foreign policy a Council of State was formed, made up of several high noblemen with experience of diplomacy and war, such as the former ambassador to France, Nicholas Perrenot, lord of Granvelle, and the military commander, Fadrique Alvarez de Toledo, duke of Alva. Other influential members included Cardinal Tavera, the archbishop of Toledo, Juan de Zuñiga, tutor to Crown Prince Philip, and minister of state Francisco de los Cobos, who was also head of the *Consejo de la Hacienda*. It is a sign of his exceptional influence that this civil servant was able to penetrate this most important of government bodies. Until 1526 members from the Low Countries and Franche-Comté still dominated in the Council of State. Apart from the grand inquisitors Tavera and Fernando de Valdés and the president of the Royal Council, not many Castilians were appointed to the Council of State because it was feared that they would allow national interests to prevail above those of the *imperium*. In principle, the emperor himself presided at the meetings of the Council of State: all the other councils had their own president. Under Charles, these councils did not, in fact, form strictly separate institutions with clearly defined powers and constitution, but consulted regularly and informally with the most important advisors.[26]

The less important councils were for 'India', presided over by Charles' confessor, Garcia de Loaysa, general of the Dominican Order and the Council for the Military Orders. The Council for the Crown of Aragon functioned under the guidance of the viceroy with the kingdom's own institutions, as also happened in the kingdoms of Naples and Sicily, the duchy of Milan (which came under the emperor's direct rule in 1535) and, of course, in the Low Countries. On his visit to the Low Countries in 1531 the emperor restructured the central governing councils along the same lines as in Spain. The immediate reason for this was the death of the regent Margaret on 30 November 1530. Under a decree of 1 October 1531, the new regent, Mary, Charles' sister and former queen of Hungary, would govern the Low Countries together with three administrative councils: the Council of State, presided over by Mary herself acting in her brother's name, the Privy Council, which was responsible for domestic government, legislation and administrative justice, and the Council of Finances. Local noblemen and bureaucrats served on these councils. For the Council of State, which was now more important than the former Court or Privy Council, the members were two prelates, Erard de la Marck, bishop of Liège, and Jan Carondelet, archbishop of Palermo, and ten members from old noble families who were also members of the Order of the Golden Fleece: Adolphe of Burgundy, lord of Beveren, Philip and Anthony of Croy,

Floris of Egmont, count of Buren, John of Glymes, lord of Bergen op Zoom, Antoine de Lalaing, count of Hoogstraten, Philip de Lannoy, lord of Molenbaix, Jacques of Luxembourg, count of Gavere, as well as Jean Hannart, viscount of Liedekerke, and Jan van Marnix as secretary.[27]

The similarity to the constitution of Castile is striking. At the same time, the limitations of centralisation are evident: in every region, local administrators ran the show, applying the laws and customs of the land and looking after their own interests. Although the structure showed a degree of homogeneity in some aspects, it was still extremely complicated and diverse in practice. The German Empire was not integrated at all and the Italian territories largely pursued their own course. Nevertheless, the attempt to get some grip on this immense empire through a tight organisation is impressive. Behind the councils were entire networks of chancelleries, registries and secretariats, hundreds of small offices full of officials and clerks.[28] In the provinces governors and stadholders worked with a small household, chancellery, judicial councils and treasury, at first following the instructions of the viceroy or regent. Local officers of justice and receivers worked under them. In Castile this bureaucratic paraphernalia, together with the rapidly growing permanent and special diplomatic representation accounted for some 10 per cent of the budget for ordinary state expenditure in 1544. The machinery of state was clearly expanding.

The mastermind behind all this was Mercurino di Gattinara, grand chancellor from 1518 until his death in 1530. It was Gattinara who was able to guide the council meetings with his clearly reasoned advice and powers of persuasion, especially after the death of William of Croy-Chièvres in 1521. He gave shape to the idea of a universal monarchy that the emperorship would have awarded to Charles.[29] An astute lawyer, it was he who formulated the diplomatic notes and the texts of treaties. To the Spanish advisors he continually defended the necessity of pacifying Italy under the hegemony of Charles. Thanks to his negotiations, Genoa, and most importantly Andrea Doria, chose the side of the emperor in 1528. His policies were crowned with Charles' coronation in Bologna in 1530. During the 1520s Gattinara's grand ideas and clear analyses moulded the still politically immature emperor into the independent ruler of the 1530s. This late maturity became evident when, after Gattinara's death at Innsbruck on 5 June, Charles did not appoint a successor. The linchpin of his policy of imperial unity was now lost. He was replaced by two secretaries of state who were extremely competent, but restricted in their powers: de los Cobos for the Spanish and Italian lands, and Granvelle for the Low Countries and Germany. In practice the vice-chancellorship of Germany was subordinate to Granvelle. Two Luxembourg lawyers, Matthias Held (1531–41) and Jean

Naves (1541–50) – men from the Low Countries again – were appointed to this position. The abolition of the post of grand chancellor in 1530 meant the disappearance of one of the few elements that embodied the unity of Charles' empire.

The network

It was not the institutions that linked the various parts of Charles' political system, but a small group of people. These were his confidants, high nobles, prelates and burghers and members of the lower nobility who through a university education and faithful service had risen in the world. Charles was still an itinerant ruler, unlike his son Philip, who scarcely left Madrid or the Escorial after 1559. Charles hoped that, being on the spot, he would be able to carry out the tasks of government most effectively, by being in direct touch with people in responsible positions and with his subjects. His presence, and the brilliance of his court, fulfilled a binding and legitimising function, which should not be underestimated. His subjects insisted upon it.

The travelling emperor was an enormously complicating factor in internal and external communications: the outside world had to be constantly informed of his movements, and masses of documents had to travel with him so that decisions could be properly made. This was inconvenient as well as risky. In 1541 a number of ships of Charles' invasion fleet sank off the coast of Algiers, taking a considerable part of his archives down with them. There was no longer an ambulant council-near-the-ruler, as there had been in the times of the dukes of Burgundy, so that when the monarch moved only a small number of confidants and specialist representatives from the particular region were available to advise on policy decisions.

The complex system was increasingly supported by two instruments: the exchange of letters and the embassies. Archives in Vienna, Simancas, Brussels and elsewhere still hold more than 120,000 letters written to and by the emperor and his regents and most important advisors. Some of these letters have survived in their original form, others as drafts, while yet others were registered by the recipient; in a number of cases we have different versions of the same letter. They contain the actual stream of information, questions, advice, decisions and orders that enabled the composite monarchy to achieve its unity of action. The regents and chief advisors in the diverse states formed the mainstay of this correspondence, of which the surviving copies alone point to an average of 8.5 letters sent per day during the 40-year reign.[30]

Thanks to the postal system, a letter from Brussels to Toledo took no more than 12 or 14 days in peacetime and during the summer; in the winter, or in times of war, it was more like a month. The same period of time was necessary for an overland letter from south Germany or one coming through the harbours of Genoa, Barcelona, Santander or Bilbao. Sometimes two or three copies of the same letter were sent via different routes to overcome the uncertainties of the journey.

To ensure privacy a large number of letters were sent in code. This also helped to counteract leaks in the chancelleries, especially when official appointments were concerned. Charles and his regents generally wrote about such matters in their own hand, or added a paragraph that was not for other readers' eyes. There are very few personal remarks in Charles' letters, even when he is writing to his brother or sister. Mary, on the other hand, was often open, witty and personal. She sketches mercilessly the ignorance of certain advisors and commanders. She wrote freely of her and Charles' passion for hunting, for she saw it as her task to support her earnest brother in every way and to make his life more bearable. 'The more important the business of a ruler, the more essential it is that he has a jester. Since I cannot carry out my task in person, I must do it by letter.'[31]

External relations were entrusted to ambassadors. Members of the different state councils served on temporary missions, as did secretaries on occasion.[32] Charles kept resident ambassadors in the lands of some of the major powers, such as France, England, Rome and Venice. Spaniards were sent to the Italian posts: Lope and Diego Hurtado de Mendoza were often used as ambassadors. Of the 11 ambassadors resident in England, two were Spanish prelates who were there at the time of Catherine of Aragon, the rest were from the Low Countries. One Brabantine, three Flemings and six *Comtois* were sent to France, obviously because of their mastery of the language. Most ambassadors had received a university education, half of them had a degree in law, which was undoubtedly useful during negotiations over treaties. In most cases they ended their career in the Council of State; many were members of the Privy Council before their embassy. Other prominent members of these councils were also frequently sent on diplomatic missions. Cornelis de Schepper, for example, was appointed to the Council of State, after being sent on a mission to France, 'because of the good services he has rendered me over many years . . . on embassies and journeys and in other matters, especially recently in France, and he is experienced in affairs of state and knows many languages'.

Three Flemish councillors were among Charles' most important advisors and diplomats: Louis of Flanders, lord of Praat, an illegitimate descendant of count Louis of Male and Duke Philip the Good of Burgundy; Louis of Schore, a lawyer who in 1540 became president of both the Council of

State and the Privy Council, and was thus a key figure in the central government in Brussels; and Cornelis de Schepper, already mentioned, who served as commissioner of the imperial fleet in 1536, 1544 and 1550–55. The scholarly Frisian Viglius, Aytta van Zwichem, succeeded him in 1549 and undertook important missions in Guelders and the German Empire.[33]

Charles' chief ministers exhibited remarkable loyalty and professionalism. Their university education undoubtedly contributed to this. Many of them came from the bourgeoisie or were members of the minor nobility, so that a promotion to the highest ranks of government represented an important social advance. They owed their position entirely to the emperor and his regents. They were dependent on his good will in obtaining a dormant noble title, for example, or a higher position. Perhaps Charles really did appreciate the quality of his close officials, but he also depended heavily on the recommendations of his regents. The fact that so many of his officials were from Franche-Comté was a direct result of the efforts of Margaret, dowager of Savoy and countess of Bresse and Burgundy. These *Comtois* included Gorrevod, Carondelet, de Plaine and Granvelle, who filled the highest official positions, the last three of them father and son together, and Carondelet with a nephew too. The university and parliament of Dole were important centres of jurisprudence, but it is striking that so many *Comtois* followed Margaret to the Low Countries, and thence travelled to Spain where there were opportunities for promotion which their own small country could not offer. Gattinara himself was also promoted through his service to Margaret. A university education, experience and the ability to adapt to different environments were essential ingredients of their success.

Their success can also be explained by the relationship of trust between the officials. Someone like the Castilian Secretary of State, Francisco de los Cobos, built up an extensive network of contacts for whom he provided jobs in exchange for faithful service. One of the most prominent of these was his first secretary, Alfonso de Valdés, who was responsible for writing Charles' defence after the Sack of Rome. When de los Cobos died in 1547 Fernando de Valdés exchanged his position as president of the Royal Council of Castile for that of inquisitor general, making him the most powerful of patrons.[34] In the Low Countries Viglius owed much to the protection of Louis of Praat. Patronage was particularly important for academics of relatively modest origins. The great noble families, of which the Croy family was undoubtedly the greatest, had less need of such patronage for they had the advantage of family connections and fortune. They had no difficulty in being appointed governors and commanders or to important positions in the Church or the Council of State: these positions were, after all, reserved for people of their rank. The location of their estates and titles often enabled them to play a role in different provinces, and even to opt for another prince. The advancement of more obedient lawyers weakened their traditional positions of power.

Even at the highest level Charles reaped remarkable successes in winning the personal loyalty of opponents. In 1523 his agents won the services of Charles de Bourbon, the *connétable* of France, the highest commander and one of the greatest princes in the realm. His switch to Charles' side considerably weakened Francis I.[35] No less spectacular was the about-turn of Andrea Doria, the great Genoese admiral in the service of the French, whose withdrawal from Naples in 1528 cost the French their conquest of that kingdom. Doria remained Charles' mainstay in the Mediterranean. Just as a good personal relationship developed between him and Charles, so a true friendship grew between Charles and his contemporary Federigo Gonzaga, marquis of Mantua, whom Charles made duke. His stable of Arab thoroughbreds fascinated Charles, besides being of military importance to him. Federigo introduced Charles to the Venetian painter Titian, who immortalised him on canvas. In 1535 Charles appointed his brother Ferrante viceroy of Sicily, in 1546 governor of Milan. In 1543 Ferrante led the imperial army against Guelders.

Charles' political system was based on the unconditional devotion of members of his dynasty, the loyalty of the great noble families and a professional bureaucracy. The question was whether a network of good personal contacts with obedient, capable officials and flexible noblemen was enough to keep a vast empire together.

Notes:

1. For the regents in the Low Countries, see Gorter-van Royen, *Maria van Hongarije*, 129–61.
2. For dangers at sea, see Sicking, *Zeemacht en onmacht*, 106–46.
3. Fernandez Alvarez, *Carlos V, el César y el Hombre*, 109–10.
4. F. Walser, *Die spanischen Zentralbehörden und der Staatsrat Karl V.* (Göttingen, 1959), 231–67; J. M. Headley, 'Germany, the Empire and *Monarchia* in the Thought and Policy of Gattinara', in H. Lutz and E. Müller-Luckner, eds, *Das römisch-deutsche Reich im politischen System Karls V.* (Munich and Vienna, 1982), 22–3.
5. Haliczer, *Comuneros*, 69–86.
6. Headley, 'Germany', 19.
7. Haliczer, *Comuneros*, 158–79.
8. Fernandez Alvarez, *Corpus documental*, II, up to no. CLXV; idem, *Carlos V, el César*, 403–6, 459–62; M. J. Rodriguez Salgado, 'Charles V and the Dynasty' in H. Soly, ed., *Charles V* (Antwerp, 1999), 69–72.

9. Fernandez Alvarez, *Carlos V, el César*, 97–9, 114.
10. Kohler, *Karl V.*, 85–9; J. Martinez Millán, 'Familia real y grupos políticos: la princesa doña Juana de Austria (1535–1573), in *idem*, ed., *La corte de Felipe II* (Madrid, 1994), 84.
11. Gorter-van Royen, *Maria van Hongarije*, 127.
12. H. Stratenwerth, 'Aktenkundliche Aspekte der politischen Kommunikation im Regierungssystem Karls V.', in H. Rabe, ed., *Karl V. Politik und Politisches System* (Konstanz, 1996), 66.
13. Brandi, *Kaiser Karl V.*, I, 67–8; II, 90.
14. G. Dorren, 'Plichtsgetrouw tegen wil en dank', in B. van den Boogert, J. Kerkhoff and A. M. Koldeweij, eds, *Maria van Hongarije, 1505–1558: Koningin tussen keizers en kunstenaars* (Zwolle, 1993), 210–3.
15. Stratenwerth, 'Aktenkundliche Aspekte', 66.
16. Gorter-van Royen, *Maria van Hongarije*, 136–42.
17. Headley, 'Germany', 26, 31.
18. Rabe, *Reich und Glaubensspaltung*, 190–204.
19. Gorter-van Royen, *Maria van Hongarije*, 145–58, 247–50, 264–71, 297.
20. Knecht, *Renaissance Warrior*, 386–9.
21. R. Wohlfeil, 'Kriegsheld oder Friedensfürst? Eine Studie zum Bildprogramm des Palastes Karls V. in der Alhambra zu Granada', in C. Roll *et al.*, eds, *Recht und Reich im Zeitalter der Reformation. Festschrift für Horst Rabe* (Frankfurt am Main, 1996), 57–96, especially 63–72.
22. L. P. Gachard and C. Piot, *Collection des voyages des souverains des Pays-Bas*, II (Brussels, 1881), 389–96; M.-A. Delen, *Hof en hofcultuur rondom Willem van Oranje* (PhD thesis at the University of Leiden, 2001), ch.1; C. J. de Carlos Morales, 'La evolución de la Casa de Borgoña y su Hispanisación', in J. Martinez Millán, ed., *La Corte de Carlos V* (Madrid 2000), vol. 1, 231–4, vol. 2, 67–77.
23. Fernandez Alvarez, *Carlos V, el César*, 193.
24. Gorter-van Royen, *Maria van Hongarije*, 137.
25. Kohler, *Karl V.*, 129.
26. Fernandez Alvarez, *Carlos V, el César*, 199–218; Kohler, *Karl V.*, 117–36; J. A. Escudero, 'El gobierno de Carlos V hasta la muerte de Gattinara. Canciller, consejos y secretarios', in B. J. García García, ed., *El Imperio de Carlos V: Procesos de* (Madrid, 2000), 83–96, especially 88–93.
27. M. Baelde, *De collaterale raden onder Karel V en Filips II, 1531–1578* (Brussels, 1965), 17–31; Gorter-van Royen, *Maria van Hongarije*, 142–61.
28. Model studies of these officials: J. Houssiau, *Les secrétaires du Conseil Privé sous Charles Quint et Philippe II, c.1531–c.1567* (Brussels, 1998); J. Martinez Millán, *Instituciones y elites de poder* (Madrid, 1992); J. A. Escudero, *Los secretarios de estado y del despacho*, 4 vols (Madrid, 1969).
29. J. M. Headley, *The Emperor and his Chancellor* (Cambridge, 1983).
30. H. Rabe and H. Stratenwerth, 'Die politische Korrespondenz Kaiser Karls V. Beiträge zu ihrer wissenschaftlichen Erschliessung', in Rabe, *Karl V. Politik und Politisches System*, 12–20.
31. Gorter-van Royen, *Maria van Hongarije*, 194–5, 264–71, 297–8; Stratenwerth, 'Aktenkundliche Aspekte', 64–8.
32. J. Houssiau, *Les Secrétaires*, 238–42; *idem*, 'Missions diplomatiques des Pays

Bas outre Manche au XVIe siècle: contribution à l'histoire des relations internationales et à l'histoire des institutions', *Publication du Centre européen d'études bourguignonnes*, 35 (1995), 199–212.
33. Baelde, *Collaterale Raden*, 306–10, 324–7; M. Lunitz, 'Die ständigen Gesandten Karls V. in Frankreich – zur Strukturwandel des Gesandtschaftswesens im 16. Jahrhundert', in Rabe, *Karl V. Politik und Politisches System*, 119–22; Fernandez Alvarez, *Carlos V, el César*, 209, 246; Sicking, *Zeemacht en onmacht*, sub De Schepper.
34. Martinez Millán, 'Familia real y grupos políticos', 80–1; H. Keniston, *Francisco de los Cobos, secretario de Carlos V* (Madrid, 1980).
35. Knecht, *Renaissance Warrior*, 200–15.

6
The cost of the Empire

Objectives

A deep chasm yawned between Charles' political ideals and the reality. From the very beginning to the bitter end of his reign he declared that he strove for peace between the Christian monarchs. Under his leadership and that of the pope these monarchs should fight the enemies of Christendom: the Protestant heretics and the Muslims who besieged it from without. Charles never came to lead the other monarchs in a crusade, even though in every peace treaty he exacted promises from Francis I to that end. The Peace of Crépy, of 18 September 1544, contained precise stipulations as to the size of the force that the king would bring against the Turks. Next day the king was forced to make the following statement:

> We and the emperor have in mind first and foremost our duty to God and the recovery of the perfect unity of our holy faith and religion, and the end of the abuses which have regrettably enabled new and damnable sects to appear in different places and to spread. In our name and at the request of our dear brother the emperor, our representatives have agreed in that treaty [of Crépy] that henceforth we shall assist him in the subjection [of the sects] and the reform [of the abuses].[1]

Yet Charles was at war for 23 of the 41 years of his reign, 16 of them against France. Francis' successor, Henry II, immediately protested against the Peace of Crépy and quickly allied himself with the German Protestants against Charles. Peace came only when France was exhausted by the long years of war: from 1515 to 1520, 1529 to 1536, 1538 to 1541 and in 1545–46. When everything was at last quiet on that front Charles felt that he had to move against the Turks and Moors.

In September 1532 a very large German army, led by Frederick, the count palatine, defeated the Turkish rearguard which had in vain laid siege to the fortress of Güns in Lower Austria. In the summer of 1535 Charles personally led a campaign against the Barbary bases in and near Tunis, and in the autumn of 1541 he outfitted a mighty fleet against Algiers, whither admiral Barbarossa had withdrawn. Apart from a number of confrontations between the imperial and Turkish fleets in the Aegean, Adriatic and Mediterranean seas, these campaigns had to pass for Charles' crusades. With the same logic, Charles made use of the peace with France and the truce with Sulaimān to prepare a great expedition against the German Protestants. Did Charles indeed fail to pursue his real objectives, let alone achieve them, because the so-called 'most Christian' kings of France allowed their own strategic concerns to take priority over their duties as defenders of the faith? This was the explanation Charles gave on his abdication in 1555 (to the members of the States General of the Low Countries) for his continual wars, while he himself would have wished for nothing more than peace.

If Charles found it unacceptable that his great rivals formed alliances with the Turks and German Protestants, then his own strategic concerns are also open to question. As long as his grand chancellor, Gattinara, was alive the priorities were perfectly clear: Charles must gain hegemony in Italy in order to fulfil his mission as universal monarch and protector of the Church and Christendom. One of the conditions to which Charles agreed in the long-drawn-out (June 1529–May 1530) negotiations on his imperial coronation with Clement VII, was the reinstatement of the pope's decadent nephew, Alexander de Medici, to power in Florence: Alexander's loyalty would be assured by his marriage to Margaret, a natural daughter of the emperor. Charles supplied him with both financial and military aid to subdue Florence, which had rebelled against the rule of the Medici family. Despite lengthy insistence, Charles was unable to persuade the pope to call a general council and give authoritative answers to the dogmatic and organisational challenges posed by the reformers. The Reformation remained Charles' problem. Like his successor, this pope was more interested in political calculations. In his tenacious pursuit of internal Church reform and his defence of Christendom in its entirety, Charles was actually more Catholic than the popes of his time. They looked on the German Protestants as a problem that was not their concern but that did offer some strategic advantage in their efforts to stop the emperor from gaining hegemony over Europe.

The tragedy of a viceroy

The emperor remained in Bologna for several months in 1529–30, negotiating with the pope. His viceroy in Naples, Philibert of Chalon, was entrusted with the task of taking Florence for Alexander de Medici, one of Charles' sacrifices for his imperial coronation. His task was to implement the strategic agreement forged between emperor and pope. Who was this

Philibert of Chalon, whom Charles called 'my cousin', and who was very frank with Charles in long letters written in his own hand, yet signed himself 'your most humble and most obedient servant and subject'?

His father, John of Chalon (1443-1502), was prince of the small sovereign principality of Orange, and was among the most important vassals of the duke of Burgundy.[2] The family's patrimony extended into both the dukedom and the free imperial county of Franche-Comté. His marriage to Joanna de Bourbon, a sister-in-law of Charles the Bold, made him a close relation of the dynasty and this is why Emperor Charles called him cousin. John of Chalon was equally exposed to French influences. The changing fortunes of the principalities of Burgundy left their marks on the Chalon family. In March 1477 John had chosen the side of Mary of Burgundy in her struggle against the surprise attack by the French. To this he was indebted for his appointment in 1478 as stadholder of Franche-Comté – not a peaceful possession in view of the constant French attacks. Louis XI confiscated his property and John was forced to retreat to the Low Countries. The transfer of the free imperial county as a dowry for Margaret of Austria, who was married to the dauphin in 1482, meant that John's property was returned to him, but also that he was drawn into the French camp. On occasions he mediated between the royal houses. The strategic situation of their lands and the size of their fortune made the Chalon family a much sought after ally for both sides.

The ties with the Burgundian Habsburg house were strengthened in 1516 when John's son, Philibert, was admitted to the Order of the Golden Fleece at the age of 14. He was commander of an ordnance corps and, in his turn, was made stadholder of Franche-Comté, now in the name of countess Margaret of Austria. In 1515, Philibert's sister, Claudia, married Henry III of Nassau, a member of a prominent family that had served the house of Burgundy faithfully for generations. This marriage joined the fortunes of the princes of Orange to that of the counts of Nassau. Henry's uncle, Engelbrecht, had become a knight of the Golden Fleece in 1473, when he was 22; in 1483 he was made stadholder of Luxembourg, in 1487 stadholder of Flanders, and was twice governor-general of the Low Countries under archduke Philip the Handsome. Henry received the chain of the Golden Fleece in 1505, when he was also 22. In 1510 he was appointed to the Council of Finances, in 1515 to the Privy Council and the governorships of Holland, Zeeland and Guelders. In 1521 he was given the title of first gentleman of the bedchamber, thus becoming one of Charles' most important advisors, but it was as military commander that he made his mark. Réné of Chalon, the son of Henry and Claudia, became a knight of the Golden Fleece in 1540, also aged 22; the following year he was made stadholder of Holland, Zeeland and Utrecht, and in 1543 of Guelders too. He died childless one year later, of cannon wounds received at the siege of Saint-Dizier. The property of the Chalon family, including the principality of Orange, passed to his cousin, William of Nassau, who was born in 1533. Towards the end of his reign, Charles grew fond of this William, who had been brought up at the court of Mary of Hungary. In 1559 he too became a knight of the Golden Fleece and soon afterwards stadholder of Holland, etc. The loyalty shown by the great noble families over generations facilitated their appointment to positions of importance at an early age.

This was true, too, of Philibert of Chalon, who had been a useful commander for Charles in Italy and in 1528 was rewarded with the particularly important position of viceroy of Naples. The siege of Florence, with which he was entrusted, was no sinecure, however: it dragged on from October 1529 to August 1530. This could have been anticipated, for the city had for many centuries been protected by very long ramparts. A selection from Charles' extensive correspondence with Philibert gives us amazing insight into the state of affairs in the field.

Philibert had been given orders for *'l'emprise de Florence avec ceste la de Ferrare'*. Nothing came of the conquest of Ferrara. In the second half of September 1529 he went north from Naples and could report the capture of Cortona and Reggio, some distance from his target. Then, he wrote enthusiastically on 23 September, 'I have no more opposition except Florence'.[3] Yet on 18 September he had already expressed some misgivings:

> Sire, you know that I have written on a number of occasions about the dire financial problems of the army. I am the most desperate man in the world for having to trouble you so often, but so that matters do not end other than you would wish, I must inform you of what I feel these people will do if their pay is delayed any longer. The Italians will desert to the enemy who will buy them, which is what they are keen to do. The Germans will mutiny and leave, at the very least. The light and heavy Spanish cavalry will refuse to obey any orders at all.

A month later nothing much had changed. Philibert wrote from his camp before Florence, 'I cannot think of any remedy, if neither you nor the pope send me money or if Florence does not yield'. On 25 October Clement appears to have promised 10,000 *scudi* to pay the Spanish, who had missed their last pay; in five days' time the entire army would have to be paid again, and where was the money to come from?

> If you are resolved to take this town I think that you will not succeed with the small force I have here; believe me, I should have to remain here for ten years to see the end [of the undertaking]. If you want the town you must send ten or twelve thousand men immediately to lay the siege on the other side of the

river, together with a good artillery crew, which you could find in Bologna. In my view, the Germans who, it is said, do not accomplish anything, and the Spaniards, could then put a rapid end to this siege. Without that help, and without money, you should not expect a successful outcome, for there are as many inside the city as we are here outside. I have stayed close by the wall of San Dammiate and cannot see how we can do more to take the town than we are doing now by extending our trenches and bulwarks.

Sire, you have now heard everything, and will answer as you think fit. I can only make every effort to carry out your wishes. But I beg you, whatever your decision, to remember that I do not have any money at all, and without money it is impossible to maintain this army any longer.

Philibert sent a list of the expenses with this letter. On 30 October he had heard from the emperor's envoy that the siege must be continued; now Philibert sounds resigned:

In any event I shall do what I can, but I think that it will not be much. Sire, I fear greatly that you will regret this long delay. May God will otherwise, but without money I see your army on the verge of mutiny.

The Germans said that they had served their agreed term and would themselves send a delegation to the emperor to find out for sure whether they would be paid.

The Spaniards are after me every day and ask if I can work miracles so that they can live without food, saying that they cannot eat if they have no money and that I have not told you this. They are so dissatisfied, and with such good reason, that I can only tell them that I am expecting money from you any day now. As you know, I haven't a penny, and nothing to borrow against should this end badly. I beg you not to blame the person who would grieve the most, should it be so. If God does not work a miracle and provide you with money I think a general mutiny is almost a certainty. I am the unhappiest man in the world that I must trouble you so often with this urgent matter, but it is my duty, both for your service and my honour. . . . Please send your answer by this same messenger, even it is just to do something useful towards ensuring that it is not I who lost this good army without a fight. If you will, relieve me of this command and give it to another who can do what I must do without money, I beg you. At least, spread a rumour that your troops and artillery are on the way from Bologna, with money; that too could work wonders.

A good week later, 8 November, Philibert returned more insistently to the subject of increasing the artillery:

Of the 10 cannon I have here four are broken, and I think the same is true of those that came from Siena for they have never fired more than two or three salvos. Then I still have four from the pope, so you can imagine what I can achieve with those. It would be excellent if you could manage to provide some from Bologna or Genoa. If there are none there, I believe that if you were to

> ask the duke of Ferrara to lend you some, he would not refuse.... There are a number of places in this town where artillery would be of great use.

Charles generally sent his answers through envoys. Nevertheless, on 12 November, he urged his 'cousin' in a letter to 'send news often'. Charles had managed to placate the captains and they promised to remain in his service until 15 December at least. And the duke of Ferrara agreed to lend six cannon. On 30 November Philibert asked for three or four thousand foot soldiers that could plunder castles in the vicinity and thus supply the army with food. A week later, after a visit to the emperor, Philibert was forced to ask for another 8,000 *scudi* to pay the Germans and to send reinforcements from Naples. There was a shortage of powder for the arquebus and cannon. The duke of Ferrara had to be reminded of his pledge to provide six cannon.

> From my information from inside the town it seems that they are resolved to wait and see what fate brings. Therefore, if you will, you will have to use some force so that they will feel the pain and the shame and you will enjoy the honour.... Believe me, Sire, the artillery will bring them [the Florentines] to their senses.

By 15 December finances were a pressing problem again; the pope had pledged 60,000 *scudi* for November, but there was still no sign of the money.

> I am the most amazed man in the world, for the entire army will ask me for what I have promised. I beg you, Sire, send it quickly, for on my word of honour if that money is not here within four or five days, it will be a total disaster. There is no doubt that all the nationalities in our camp will mutiny. I shall have to flee, otherwise they will hack me to pieces because of the promises I made them on your orders.

On 20 December he reported a successful skirmish with the Florentines, but also that the sentries who had not been paid for two months were threatening to leave. 30,000 *scudi* were made available on 28 December but this amounted to only half of what was needed per month. Not everybody could be satisfied, while 'the rest of the army is very hard pressed and has borne as much as it can'. The Florentines repaired the damage to their fortifications day and night, the pope had to be reminded of his promise of 4,000 men and 2,000 minelayers. His master builder would also be useful for the possible construction of a new bridge over the Arno. Charles' answer on 3 January 1530 was very understanding. Pressure on the pope produced another 10,000 *scudi*, although he had promised 60,000 for each of the months of November, December and January. The emperor had no money either. The Genoese were too late with their payments, he was hoping for contributions from Flanders, Venice, Milan and Naples. They were waiting for Genoese merchants to supply credit. The promised foot-soldiers had been delayed because they had not been paid and the road was bad. The pope would do his best to supply the promised troops.

> I beg you, cousin, to make the best of things. What you write about the two months [pay] that was still due to the army when you were here [in Bologna], I truly thought that this only applied to a few units. As time goes on people will have to do as best they can.

Comforting words, maybe, but no tangible support for an army that had to get through the winter after a siege that had already dragged on for three and a half months. Reinforcements trickled in by degrees, but the same problems remained. On 10 March Philibert complained that he only had enough ammunition for one day, 45 shots per cannon. He would try to buy some in all the neighbouring towns but still asked the emperor to provide some as soon as possible, to ask the dukes of Ferrara and Urbino for some and to have Andrea Doria send some from Genoa. In one letter he even asked for ammunition to be sent by boat.

> If we were even able to make a breach we could not keep it open, because of the shortage of munition. If you will, remind the pope that the Spaniards and Italians are due to be paid on 12 March. I have received nothing from him, he has not a penny for an ordinary mortal. I have managed to borrow a little from three or four captains.

By 18 March, Philibert was once again on the brink of despair. Of the 2,000 minelayers promised by the pope, no more than 400 had turned up. And pay day had passed without any sign of the money.

> Sire, I do not know what I can do for these people, for our need is so great that everything is in short supply. The Italians have only been paid 2,000 *scudi*, and the Spaniards nothing at all. The Spanish are desperate, and believe me, Sire, they have every reason to be. Almost all of them have gone from the camp, I think only about 200 are left. They say they are going to get food wherever they can find it. I think they will plunder their way from town to town. The Germans are on the point of looting everything in the vicinity. If you do not take action this army will disintegrate and do the very worst you can imagine. Please give a swift answer to the bearer of this message so that we can at least arrange to save the cannon if you are unable to help; even that would be impossible, I think, if they all mutiny. . . . I believe the pope is making a fool of you and me. He is quite wrong if he thinks that Florence can be taken in four months because its inhabitants are hungry. They still have grain supplies and with the dried meat they are resolved to stand firm until their last crust. . . . But it is impossible to keep an army as large as this alive on promises.

Charles' answer came three days later from Bologna: the pope was doing what he could to pay the troops. Philibert reacted immediately, complaining that the captains had abandoned their companies en masse, preferring to stay in some court or other. The emperor himself would have to order them to complete their service. Many foot soldiers had died of the hardships.

> For me to be certain that the pope would keep his word, he would already be here [in Florence] and we would not be in this mess. I am really afraid that he will not send me the money in time. That was why I was content to let the troops fend for themselves in the neighbourhood of Siena, under orders to behave honourably, of course. If you will, let me know whether it is certain the 20,000 *scudi* promised by the pope will be available at the end of the month. If that money comes too late, even just a little, it would be better to keep the mutiny at a distance, because here the mutineers would encourage all the others.

On 25 March 500 mutinous Spaniards had left the camp, but they returned later. The problems continued until July. Then they demanded six months' pay and threatened to go to Pisa and avenge themselves on its inhabitants. The other soldiers would make no attempt to stop them. On 7 July Philibert begged Charles, who was now in Augsburg, to pardon the mutineers, because

> the poor devils have already suffered enough in their purses, they have nothing and are dying of hunger. If you will, have pity on them and on all the soldiers in this camp, I beg you. . . . And the Germans say they want to leave, even if they were paid, because of the plague that has brought so much death.

Indeed, Philibert's Spanish bookkeeper had died of the plague and two of his assistants were sick, so that the overall financial picture was missing. Yet there were signs that since the implementation of the peace between Charles and Francis I – confirmed by the return of the latter's two sons and his marriage to Eleanor – the people of Florence were losing heart. On 1 August Charles sent his instructions for the surrender of the town: effectively, the house of Medici was to be restored to government, '*bon debvoir et prudent office*', as soon as possible, and plundering, '*saccagement et extreme ruyne et desolation*', was to be avoided at all costs. The troops, therefore, had to remain outside the town and disband in an orderly fashion, and were to be given decent expenses for their return home. Philibert did not live to see the crowning of all his efforts nor the emperor's reward for his outstanding, loyal services. He died on 3 August from wounds received in one of the last skirmishes of the operation. The Republic of Florence surrendered on 12 August 1530. Charles made the Medicis archdukes, which was what it was all about. In 1537 Alexander de Medici was murdered by the opposition.

Strategy, resources, choices

Philibert of Chalon may have come to a tragic end: his sometimes passionate pleas to the emperor clearly testify to his sincere compassion for the foot soldiers who languished through a whole winter and suffered a plague epidemic during the summer thanks to the negligence of the financial management of pope and emperor. He had no pity at all for the people of Florence who, in his view, deserved all they got because they dared to resist the emperor. Yet the thousands of inhabitants of Florence, the pearl of Humanism, suffered just as much from the hunger and hardships of the siege. What was the point of it all? The restoration of a monarchic government in the city-republic for the benefit of a cousin of the pope, and thus for the pope himself. The pope's most important quid pro quo was his opting for an alliance with the emperor against the French – a choice long-since made out of opportunistic motives – and his readiness to invest Charles as king of Naples and to crown him emperor. A *realpolitik* choice and two symbolic deeds. Charles failed in his efforts to persuade Clement to summon a council with a view to Church reformation, even after a new round of negotiations in 1532–33. If Charles' arrangement with Clement for the recovery of Florence was questionable, his failure to use it to achieve his main aim as protector of the Church adds a very bitter taste to the 11-month siege.

The correspondence quoted above makes it clear that, even as the object of the exercise was dubious, a lot remained to be desired as far as strategy and resources were concerned. Clearly, the decision was made to take Florence at any cost, but without any idea of the resources needed. If Philibert thought in September 1529 that, after Florence, he could take Ferrara, then things turned out very differently. Beginning a siege so late in the year shows that an early success was expected, because commanders are normally anxious to avoid wintering in the open. It would seem that the besiegers did not have enough information about the city's defences, its food supplies and the morale of the people. They were faced with a very large town with a long circumference. From Philibert's letters it is clear that he had to wait until spring – six months – for the arrival of technically-trained minelayers who were competent to get close to the fortifications and undermine them. Still it was not this, but the exhaustion and demoralisation of its inhabitants, that finally caused the town to surrender. Philibert had to wait for months for reliable cannon and for reinforcements, and there was a constant shortage of gunpowder. It was the logistics of the operation that failed, apparently the result of insufficient information and preparation.

It is astonishing to read that all these logistical details were repeated on an average of once a week in the lengthy correspondence between the viceroy and his emperor. Was this the level at which soldiers' pay and the purchase of powder should be discussed, with the accounts enclosed? Charles' answers show that, even in personal conversations, some with the pope, he was very concerned with this sort of detail and that he agonised over finding money to make up the constant shortages. The organisation of the *imperium* was clearly not yet specialised enough to respond to the heavy demands created by the massive military operations. All the problems, large and small, came to rest on the emperor's shoulders.

Both sides stuck to their plans. The beleaguered city gave way first, its food supplies exhausted, stricken by epidemic, the hopes of French support faded. The besieging army also had its weaknesses but, objectively seen, the mutinies and plundering actually helped the attackers because they impoverished the surrounding countryside, thus further endangering the town's supplies. The tenacity of both sides, the strength of Florence's defence and, finally, the enormous size and endurance of the imperial and papal army made this the longest siege of Charles' reign. Withdrawal would have meant an unprecedented loss of face for both emperor and pope. The longer the siege continued the worse the situation became, so they staked everything on it. Clearly they had far greater resources than the isolated town.

This is why the continuing financial problems of the attackers are so baffling. The pope honoured his commitments only partially and after long delays, although the siege seemed to be chiefly in his own interest. The problems of payments occurred during the early months of the siege so they cannot be blamed on depleted reserves, but rather on insufficient organisation for the objective. The incompetence on Charles' side is equally baffling: improvisation, getting what one could where one could, too late, finally borrowing from the Genoese bankers. In the long run it was the taxpayers of Naples and the pope's subjects who had to bear the brunt of this venture of purely dynastic prestige.

On the other hand it must be remembered that it has always been difficult to foresee the progress, length and cost of war. Contemporaries were not much more successful at such prognostications. During the sixteenth century war was considered the prerogative of princes. Even when the representative bodies of their subjects – either through discussion about the allocation of taxation or in principle – demanded some say in their involvement in wars, the princes retained the exclusive right to declare and end war. Their subjects were always left to pick up the bill. Charles himself made this very clear in a speech to his Council in 1528: 'It is not fitting for a prince to think of money when he is occupied with heroic deeds: in matters of honour the people must commit their persons and their fortunes'.[4] This implies that the prince himself must decide which heroic deeds deserve his complete dedication, and the fortunes of his subjects are implicitly presented as being part of his. We are only familiar with this text through a chronicler, but even if the original version had a more delicate nuance, it expresses a view that is in keeping with Charles' actions.

A prince's honour is beyond price. Florence, too, was all about Charles' honour, as Philibert of Chalon said. The consequences of such a viewpoint were felt constantly during the performance of these heroic undertakings. Financial resources had to be raked together from various sources, usually much too late; failure to pay the soldiers was a regular phenomenon, as were their resulting raids made at the cost of the innocent local populace. After their astonishing victory at Pavia in 1525, some poorly paid imperial troops remained marauding in Italy. The League of Cognac, struck in May 1526 between pope Clement VII, Francis I, Venice and the unfortunate duke of Milan, launched another offensive against the imperial positions.[5] Writing no more than ten years after the events, the dismissed Florentine statesman, Luigi Guicciardini, noted in his history of the Sack of Rome that this had been a risky enterprise, badly advised and lacking unanimously determined targets and the necessary financial means.[6] The loss of the Milanese citadel for Sforza was, in his opinion, the fault of the pope's chief general, wrong evaluations by the duke of Urbino and his all too slow response to the attack by Charles de Bourbon.[7] By his unwillingness – due to personal interests – to join the core of the League's army in Tuscany, he left the field to the imperial troops which, according to the reliable Spanish chronicler Santa Cruz, consisted of German, Italian, Spanish and Swiss companies, numbering up to about 45,000 men.[8] But these troops, too, suffered from delayed pay, unclear missions and antagonism between their generals.[9] Guicciardini considered Clement VII responsible for the lack of defence of Rome, as he had disbanded his army immediately after making a truce with Charles of Lannoy, viceroy of Naples, in September 1526.

A similar criticism was expressed by his fellow countryman, Francesco Vettori, who was removed from his political offices in Florence after 1527 and wrote his *Brief History of Italy* before 1529. The pope lacked both captains and money to conduct a war but he became involved in an action to recapture Siena, while in Rome itself he had to fly before the Colonna attack on 19 April 1526, plundering the holy city and even its churches.[10] The pope's changing sides made him unreliable as an ally and suspect as an enemy. In the meantime he left Rome undefended while he spent his money elsewhere. It was mainly the failures in the execution of the policy, even if it was changing, that made the situation so uncertain, writes

Guicciardini.[11] Such weaknesses on both sides led to the disastrous Sack of Rome: Bourbon could no longer restrain his captains from moving against Rome since the pope did not keep his promise to pay them, and instead had excommunicated them altogether. Both armies were badly organised, lacked coherent leadership and suffered from their pay being delayed. In 1527 Clement VII's failure to make the promised payments to the imperial troops had driven the starving force to attack Rome. Three years later the lessons learnt from the Sack of Rome made Charles ensure that his troops would not enter Florence under any circumstances, any excuse would be used to buy their departure. The city had to be handed over to the Medici ruler in good condition.

Politics and organisation, rather than the size or equipment of the armies, seem to have been the dominant factors in the evolution of the military situation in Italy. The debate on the chronology and the nature of the so-called 'Military Revolution' focuses on the effects of the tremendous increase in the size of the armies and the growing power of the field artillery. Charles V commanded about 55,000 men and 150 guns during his siege of Metz in 1552. Although this may have constituted the largest and best-equipped army in Europe since the decline of the Roman Empire it was unable to take the city, whose new fortifications proved able to withstand the bombardment. The cost of the armies, as well as of the construction of the defence systems, rose so sharply that even France and the Habsburg Empire could build only a limited number of fortresses of the new Italian type: even then, the competition exhausted both states financially in the 1550s.[12] The new military techniques raised huge logistic and organisational problems for the political leaders. The question arises of whether the political apparatus was able to bear the executive functions required for an adequate implementation of the technical novelties. Indeed, the sources presented above appear to show that the political rigidity overshadowed the potentials so decisively that the notion of 'Military Revolution' seems rather inappropriate for the two major confrontations in Italy from 1526 to 1530, the very period during which Charles' hegemony over Italy was established and the first new systems of defence were developed.

A clear division in the way Charles conducted his wars can be seen half way through his reign. During the first 20 years his commanders led the operations; he was occasionally to be found at a safe distance from the scene of battle, as in 1521 when he followed the siege of Tournai from Oudenaarde, in the charming company of Joanna van der Gheynst. There was a radical change in 1535 with his expedition to Tunis where he put himself at the head of what was termed a crusade. After that, he campaigned almost every year, leading all the major military operations himself: in 1536 in Provence, against Ghent in 1540 and Algiers in 1541. In 1543 he left Spain to go to Guelders, although Ferrante Gonzaga was his commander-in-chief. In spite of attacks of gout, Charles led his army from Guelders, through Hainault, to France where, in November, he took the citadel of the cathedral town of Cambrai, which belonged to the German Empire. The onset of winter and his exhausted finances forced him to withdraw. In 1544 he commanded the six-week siege of Saint-Dizier and the long march along the Marne in person, and in 1546–47 he led the war against the German Protestants. In the autumn of 1552, together with the duke of Alva, he led an enormous army from south Germany to Metz, despite severe physical and emotional pain. 'I shall at least do all that is possible on my part, even at risk to my person, if it is suitable and rational.'[13]

His presence raised the morale of the troops, but any failure – as at Metz – was an immediate threat to his honour. The besieged inhabitants immediately let him know that he would get no further, 'No further than Metz', an allusion to his device. Moreover, was it wise to spend so much of his time on long, risky military operations while urgent political discussions were delayed? For Charles, the choice of leading his military operations himself seems to have been dictated by his awesome sense of duty, his missionary instincts and his innate feeling of honour. For these he sacrificed his personal comfort, for his physical ailments caused him much pain on all his moves and in all his encampments. Moreover, he sacrificed a lot of administrative power through his obsession with certain conflicts, which he tried to solve by personal involvement. Because of his lengthy presence at, and preoccupation with, one hotbed of problems after another, he lost sight of the problems in the other parts of his empire.

The emperor's personal effort began with the crossing to Tunis, where he gained much prestige from his struggle against the Moors. For many years, the south Italian coast had suffered under the Turkish attacks and the Spaniards were troubled by raids from north Africa. At the turn of the century the Spanish kings had gained footholds – Oran, for instance – in north Africa. The propaganda for Charles' crusade fitted in with the idea of the *reconquista* of Spain, which had not fully achieved its aim at Gibraltar. In 1534, Barbarossa, the Berber commander, spurred on by Sultan Sulaimān, had seized upon the death of the king of Tunis, who was a vassal of the Spanish king, as an opportunity to take that city. From there he would be able to control the western passage past Sicily. With the support of the *cortes*, Pope Paul III, Portugal, Genoa and other regions of Italy, Charles mustered a fleet of 400 ships with which he crossed to the bay of Tunis in June. The siege and capture of the port of La Goleta took little more than a month. The army then advanced on Tunis, which was nearby. The summer heat and the shortage of drinking water caused sickness among the soldiers but, thanks to a revolt by the Christians inside the city, Tunis was taken in mid-August. Barbarossa retreated to Algiers, weakened but by no means defeated. Charles decided to move back to Sicily because of exhaustion and heavy losses among his troops and in view of the distance to Algiers and the approaching end of the sailing season. He installed a vassal king in Tunis.

Charles' historiographers and visual artists presented the conquest of Tunis as one of his great triumphs. It was only half-successful, a second voyage would have to follow. Charles could only go ahead with the second expedition in the autumn of 1541, after dealing with the renewed outbreak of war with France and commitments in the Low Countries and the Empire. It is odd, in view of the excuse of the sailing season used in 1535, that in 1541 Charles stubbornly insisted on braving the autumn storms. The expedition was planned to take place earlier in the year, but Charles had been delayed by delicate negotiations in the Diet and discussions with the pope. Perhaps he considered any more delay a sign of weakness. Despite warnings, the fleet set sail and reached the turbulent waters off the coast of Algiers on 21 October. Two nights later, before disembarkation had been completed, 150 ships sank during a storm, taking men, supplies, munition and a large part of the imperial archive to the bottom. Charles retreated immediately. In both expeditions the expediency of the timing – the height of summer and then the autumn – was questionable. The losses to their own ranks were considerable while military success was only tangible in the first expedition. The emperor never thought to question the pros and cons, his strategy was weak in both expeditions. He gave little thought to finances nor to the lives of a few thousand Christians.

At the end of July 1536 Charles marched into Provence in response to Francis' invasions of the Low Countries, Savoy and Piedmont. In the north his stadholders, especially Henry of Nassau, put up a determinedly fierce resistance. Was it a wise choice to march through Provence rather than to go at once to the aid of his brother-in-law, duke Charles III of Savoy or to defend Piedmont? What was the point of this attack on French territory? The most it would achieve was to force the French to stretch their forces over two fronts. Charles de Bourbon had tried it without any success twelve years earlier, but he was by now long dead, and his claims to the region with him. The French used the scorched earth policy, which imposed a heavy toll on their own people but created enormous difficulties for the imperial army. After just one month, 7,000 or 8,000 deaths from starvation and dysentery had been reported.[14] By the middle of September Charles was in retreat, without having achieved anything. It was for this that he had postponed his second expedition to Algiers.

The course of the war in 1542–44 was very surprising. Just as he had done in 1536, Francis I made use of Charles' exhaustion and absence following the Algerian expedition to follow time-honoured fashion and launch attacks on two fronts, Luxembourg and Perpignan. The response had been seen earlier, too: a joint invasion, by the English from Calais and by the imperial troops from the north-east, with Paris as the objective. The number of troops mobilised was enormous. During the summer of 1544 English and imperial troops were in control of the region and took a few towns, but they made slow progress. The sieges of Boulogne and Saint-Dizier delayed the attacking armies for two months and six weeks respectively. After that, their finances and the morale of the troops were practically exhausted. The French army avoided open battle and took advantage of the exhaustion. In early September Charles began to negotiate, without even waiting for his ally, Henry VIII.

What was now the connection between this remarkable show of strength and reasonably co-ordinated efforts and the separate peace? Charles relinquished all the conquests that he had made in France during the most recent campaign and was even prepared to give up the dukedom of Milan to Francis' younger son, Charles, if he married either his own daughter, Mary, or Ferdinand's daughter, Anna, whichever the emperor should decide during the following four months. All that Charles required of Francis was that, 'as befits the most Christian king', he should take part in the struggle against the Turks with a well-defined number of men; that he should join in reformation of the Church in a general council, and that he should cease to co-operate with the German Protestants. Of these demands, only the council was realised in December 1545, and that was not very successful. All in all, the results of a war on such a large scale were very meagre.

The Austrian historian, Alfred Kohler, in a modification of Karl Brandi, does not see a 'grand plan' behind Charles' actions after 1543, but up till 1547, a coherent reaction to events.[15] First of all he eliminated the problem of Guelders, an ally of both France and the Protestants, which threatened his rear from the north-east. Then he turned his attention to France. It was never his intention to conquer France, as he had already written to Ferdinand in 1530: 'I see neither opportunity nor reason to conquer France. Even if I had just one part of it, it would cost me a century of war'.[16]

This attitude would explain the ease with which he gave up his own conquests in Champagne as well as his casual breach of the coalition with Henry VIII. In spite of repeated agreements with Henry, Charles never really sought for one moment a joint conquest of France. This was abundantly clear after the battle of Pavia in 1525. After Henry's break with Rome there was even less reason to trust him. What really continued to interest Charles was to have France on his side in the religious questions: only after 1544 could he confidently embark upon phase three of his 'grand strategy', the long-contemplated and much-delayed punitive expedition against the German Protestants. In a fourth step this would then lead to the convening of a general council and the reformation of the Church – for which Charles had striven for twenty years.

With a clear superiority in the number of troops, Charles' military activities against the German Protestants in 1546–47 met with success. This success was very nearly thrown away through political mistakes. The early failure of the council blocked his escape from the German religious question. There seems to have been a total lack of direction in his reaction to the new developments. In 1551 his former allies entered into a pact against Charles that swiftly received the support of Henry II of France. The nadir of Charles' military operations was reached in 1552 when rebellious Protestants even drove him out of Innsbruck in the Habsburg lands and forced him to make concessions in the Treaty of Passau. In Italy he lost a long-drawn out war for Parma and Siena rebelled. The Turkish fleet had a number of victories in the Tyrrhenian Sea. Henry II took the cathedral cities of Metz, Verdun and Toul in Lorraine. In spite of the skilful leadership of the duke of Alva, Charles' army of 55,000 failed to retake Metz in the autumn after a long siege. To reinforce his army, Charles even persuaded his former Protestant enemy, the peace-breaker Albrecht Alcibiades of Brandenburg, to join him, which raised questions about his regard for the peace of the Empire. Charles returned to Brussels with a heavy heart, and his spirited sister Mary deputised for him for several months.

One can ask if any of these enormous expeditions brought any lasting success. They certainly inflicted vast financial, human and material losses. The emperor was increasingly portrayed as a *miles Christi*, a soldier of Christ, as Titian had immortalised him after the battle of Mühlberg. However, Charles found himself more and more in the grip of the resistance that his imperial policy provoked among the French and Turks and that his religious policy incited against him in the Empire. The coalition, or even the coincidence, of both counter movements shook his entire political system.

Money, money and money again

Traditionally a monarch had two sources of money: ordinary and extraordinary income. The first consisted mainly of the revenues from what were known as his crown domains and, in addition to the income from the estates belonging to the monarch's patrimony, included administrative rights such as income from tolls, the exploitation of mines, mintage and the administration of justice. Extraordinary income came from subsidies agreed by negotiation with the regional representative bodies. Charles tried to increase every form of income in order to solve his constant financial problems. He was fortunate in that his revenues from America increased fourteenfold between 1516 and 1555, growing by leaps and bounds after 1536.[17] There was a lot of give and take in the negotiations with the representatives of the various estates in the attempts to raise more extraordinary income.

During Charles' reign there was very little central taxation in the German Empire; taxes were raised in the individual principalities. Because of the Turkish threat, after 1526 more resources gradually became available centrally, but in most cases the principalities remained in control and preferred to provide troops rather than money. This was the subject of tremendous negotiation in the Diet, notably by the Protestant princes, who systematically demanded greater religious freedom in return for their military efforts. In the main it was the hereditary Habsburg lands, Bohemia and Moravia that bore the heaviest burden for the defence of the Empire, simply because they were in the greatest danger. A total of just 4.3 million guilders was collected at the imperial level, approximately 2.2 million Castilian ducats.[18]

In the Naples parliament the representatives – under pressure from the Turkish fleet – were willing to approve ever higher taxes, even when it was clear that a large part of them were used to finance the emperor's wars elsewhere. On 27 September 1538 the Habsburg fleet, under the command of Andrea Doria, retreated ignominiously from the Turkish galleys near Preveza, on the Greek coast south of Corfu. The fortifications along the Neapolitan and Sicilian coastlines were strengthened and the construction of hundreds of watchtowers commenced. The enormous undertaking would take several years to complete, swallow up money, and still not prevent the Ottoman admiral Barbarossa from taking Nice in 1543 and wintering in Toulon.[19] In the course of Charles' reign the average amount of the *donativi* in the kingdom of Naples increased by one half, from 205,000 ducats per annum from 1528–37, to 311,000 in 1538–47 and 300,000 in 1548–56.[20] The kingdoms of Naples and Sicily, on Charles' orders, made massive contributions to the defence of, or the conduct of the war in, Lombardy, Piedmont, Germany and the Low Countries. This first happened in 1537 and was to continue on a large scale in the 1540s and 1550s through the mediation of the bankers of Genoa, Augsburg and

Antwerp.[21] Castile had paid over some 100,000 ducats for the war around Milan as early as 1522. These subsidies were repeated during the war years of 1536–38, and between 1551 and 1555 more than two million ducats streamed in the same direction from the revenues out of the Americas. The transfer of 22 million guilders from the Castilian treasury to the Low Countries in 1551–56 to help finance the war against France was one of the causes of the enormous deficit in Castile, but the phenomenon was common.

The evolution of the *servicios* showed a similarly substantial increase in the kingdom of Castile. These *servicios* were the extraordinary taxes that the *cortes* approved and shared over the towns and individuals liable to tax. In the period 1537–54 they amounted to an average of 311,581 ducats per year,[22] 37 per cent more than in the preceding 16 years and 56 per cent more than during the period 1510–17. The great leaps to continuously higher amounts took place in 1530–31, 1538 and 1549. During the last six years of Charles' reign the Castilians paid more than twice as much as they had during the initial period. In addition to these taxes, there were the ordinary crown revenues. Firstly, the *alcabala*, an indirect tax of Moorish origin, amounting to 10 per cent of all transactions of money or goods; then the *tercias*, a direct levy of 10 per cent on all income received from agriculture and crafts in Church domains, 2/9 of which the pope then handed to the crown; various excise duties such as that on the export of Castilian wool, silk from Granada and on revenues from the colonies, notably the *quinto real* of 20 per cent on precious metals from the Americas. From 1516–20 until 1551–55 income from the *alcabalas* and the *tercias* rose by 14 per cent, far less than that from the *servicios*. The reason for this was that in most towns, and from 1536 throughout the entire kingdom for a period of ten years, the *servicios* were farmed out and thus remained under the level of economic growth. As time went on, an ever larger share of the *servicios* had to be used for the repayment of *asientos* and loans, struck mainly with the bankers from Augsburg and Genoa, but increasingly also with Castilian merchants.[23]

Total revenues of the Castilian crown quadrupled from 1522 to 1560, from one million to four million ducats. The *alcabala* represented from 40 per cent to 45 per cent of this, the *servicios* some 20 per cent – although this percentage gradually increased. Since the *servicios* were levied on the non-privileged in the towns and country, it was these people who bore the increase in the state's revenues. In addition, the crown received an appreciable part of its income from its stewardship of the extensive possessions of the Military Orders. These were dependent on papal favour, and thus on good relations between the pope and emperor.

The taxes and wars were undoubtedly harder on the people of Lombardy than on any other part of Charles' empire. One historian says they were 'squeezed to the very marrow'. The monthly levy, the *mensuale*, jumped from 12,000 to 25,000 ducats in 1547, of which 10 per cent could not be collected because the people were simply unable to pay. In Lombardy, as in the Low Countries, the government introduced the sale of rents and positions and the assignment of sources of income to financiers. This caused the ordinary income to fall drastically. In 1545, 1550 and 1551 all government income had already been spent or assigned before the year began. Considerable additional financial resources from Naples, Sicily and, most of all, Castile, failed to prevent the Spanish troops in Lombardy from mutinying and plundering the towns and villages because their wages were long overdue.[24]

In the Low Countries tax levies were far more capricious. In 1531–34, a period of peace and moderate taxation, total state revenues in the Low Countries averaged 864,000 Carolus guilders, more than 400,000 ducats per year. The taxes permitted by the towns and assemblies of the States in the Low Countries did not grow at a steady rate, but with marked ups and downs, caused by the large military operations in each region. So in the war years of 1521, 1522, 1537, 1544 and 1545 the province of Flanders produced sums amounting to twice, thrice or even ten times the taxes paid shortly before or afterwards. Tax receipts in Flanders do not show a simple upward line, but two plateaux, one at the beginning and the other at the end of Charles' reign: they represented twice the receipts of the intervening years. During the peak years the agreed taxes rose to between 500,000 and 600,000 guilders, and in 1545–46 to 1.2 million guilders, some 566,000 ducats.[25] Similarly, the conquest of Utrecht in 1528 led to net tax revenues of 373,000 guilders in the county of Holland, a dramatic increase from the level of about 60,000 per year which had been normal before; during the war years 1542–44 they rose to an average of 243,000 guilders, and in 1552–53 they flew up first to 266,000 and then to 506,000 guilders.[26]

The major difference from Castile and Naples, for example, lay in the strong urban basis of taxation in the Low Countries. While only one tenth of the population of Castile lived in towns, in Brabant, Flanders and Holland at least one third did. Abrupt increases in tax revenues could only be realised here because a considerable part of them was financed by loans in the form of annuities. The representative bodies, composed mainly of delegates from the towns, were persuaded to provide surety for the government by floating public loans in which the inhabitants of other towns could invest their money. Those who had capital thus enjoyed a high return (6.25 per cent) at the expense of the ordinary taxpayer. Naturally enough such loans had a snowball effect on local finances, which only slowed with the death of those people who lived off their annuity income. In 1531 the interest burden of these loans accounted for 21 per cent of the taxes permitted in Brabant and 28 per cent in Holland. In this way, the county of Holland had built up a mountain of debt of 1.2 million guilders during 1552–60, the years of very high taxation, and Flanders and Brabant more than 2 million each. The accumulated burden of debt was an important factor in the financial crisis of the 1560s.[27]

The government was naturally constantly looking for new means of obtaining the money that was needed so urgently for the wars to be fought on one or other front. Traditional revenues from the princely demesne – the property and princely rights such as mintage, tolls, fines and confiscations – served firstly as collateral for the loans taken out with the bankers in Antwerp, Augsburg and Genoa. In normal years, 1534 and 1551 for example, the whole domain of the Low Countries was good for 20 to 25 per cent of revenues, while the rest came from taxes. In times of war and financial deficit, 1535–38 for example, parts of the demesne had to be alienated, causing its income to fall and driving the taxes even higher, so that the contribution from the demesne was no more than 13 per cent. In 1545, a year of particularly high taxation, the demesne's share fell to barely five 5 per cent. Yet monetary yields, in the form of grain prices and ground leases, doubled between 1505 and 1550, causing the revenue from the properties to rise.[28]

Even at the beginning of Charles' reign financiers were not satisfied with the emperor's guarantees and demanded the personal guarantees of his officials. At a later stage credit would only be extended in exchange for the agreement of the collectors of the taxes to whom the loan was assigned. By the 1540s even that was not enough, for the financiers required the promises of the assemblies of the States that had approved the taxes. The mechanism of the state debt brought various advantages to the wealthy classes who served in the assemblies of the States. First, they succeeded largely, and in Holland completely, in ensuring that commercial capital was untaxed and that commerce was affected only temporarily and to a limited extent. Secondly, the loans were generally given by members of a town government and people of substance, who cleared a nice profit. This meant that the interests of the local elite were closely tied to the fortunes of the state. Thirdly, those representatives of the towns and States acquired more and more control over the collection of taxes, and after 1543 they had a growing say in how the taxes were allotted. Fourthly, 38 per cent of these loans were paid for by the townspeople through excise duties and special taxes on the consumption of beer and wine; this was a markedly retrogressive device, which laid a relatively heavier burden on the lower income groups. The remainder was realised by a levy of 10 per cent on real estate, ground leases and interest, of which the yield in Holland increased by 111 per cent between 1543 and 1558.[29]

Only private credit could supply the crown with the desired resources everywhere and rapidly, but it had a price. Charles' war against the German Protestants was financed by 3.7 million *scudi* on credit, to be paid in Spain, and another 750,000 obtained in the Low Countries. On the other hand, the fines imposed on the vanquished brought him at most 800,000 *scudi*, and he also confiscated their artillery.[30] Charles' debts to the bankers of Antwerp increased from 700,000 ducats in 1538 to 1.9 million in 1554. During the last years of his reign the floating debt shot up from 650,000 ducats in 1543 to 3.5 million in 1556 and doubled the consolidated debt. The short-term credit was mainly the province of German bankers – the Fuggers and Welsers – until 1535. After that, the Genoese – Grimaldi, Spinola, Gentile and Centurione – the Antwerp firms of Schetz and Gaspar Ducci (originally from Pistoia), and from 1551 the Castilians too, supplied enormous sums of money – as much as 3.6 million ducats in 1552. In those years, Charles and his sister Mary had put pressure on his son Philip, who was now regent in Spain, to cash bills of exchange for Antwerp and Genoa.[31] As the financial problems increased so did the interest that bankers demanded on *asientos*, the short-term loans with all sorts of repayment guarantees, through allocated sources of income such as the silver imported from America. In 1521–32 Charles still paid 17.6 per cent interest, 21.3 per cent in 1533–42, 27.9 per cent in 1543–51 and 48.8 per cent in the extreme years of 1552–56. For *juros*, long-term credit with guarantees, the interest was less than 10 per cent. In 1522 36.6 per cent of the ordinary revenues of Castile went to the repayment of the *juros*; in 1543, 65.4 per cent.

Major financiers such as the Fugger and Welser families of Augsburg preferred to assign the repayment of their loans to the expected crown revenues in Castile, which did not have to be approved by the *cortes*. Above all, the leasing of the *maestrazgos* – the king's income in his capacity as grand master of the three military orders – the levy for the crusade and the revenues from the American colonies were tapped as security for the loans. In 1551–55 the three types of income brought in an average of 844,245, 650,000 and 416,000 ducats per year, while the loans had accumulated to 28 million ducats.[32] It is a well known fact that this reckless debt led to the government suspending its interest payments, first in Milan in 1546 and 1554, and in all the Habsburg territories in 1557, along with the compulsory conversion of *asientos* into *juros* at 5 per cent.[33]

The seemingly unlimited credit facilities led the two warring parties, France and Habsburg, into financial disaster. At first, more and quicker money appeared to produce a tactical advantage; but when the enemy had access to the same resources, credit came to mean nothing more than multiplying and postponing the costs of war. The enormous demand for government credit caused a fundamental disruption of the financial markets; commercial credit became scarce and economic growth slowed. In 1552 regent Mary of Habsburg wrote to the emperor that 'the market in Antwerp is completely drained of money'; it led to a crisis in the market in the following years. Any rational consideration of costs and expenses was not a criterion adopted by the state, and the extravagant rates of interest sucked all the capital into loans to the government. As long as the interest was paid off, the mass of ordinary taxpayers paid for the excessive profits made by the wealthy lenders. In the 1550s, when the government was no longer able to do this, it lost the support of the middle class.

The first half of the sixteenth century was generally a period of population increase and economic growth in western Europe. In Castile the supply of money increased by 272 per cent, partly due to the influx of American silver. In the Low Countries the price of grain and ground leases doubled. In a number of regions this led to a drastic fall in the purchasing power of wage-earners. Artisans in Ghent saw their purchasing power drop by half. The loss could only be compensated by increased labour, including that of women and children. The picture varied from region to region, depending on the state of its economic development. In Antwerp, the heart of the world economy, the purchasing power of the artisans improved slightly. If we set these facts alongside the above-mentioned figures for taxes, then we are forced to conclude that the tax burden became considerably heavier, certainly after about 1540. The purchasing power of the workers remained intact only in the core areas such as the region round Antwerp, but 50 miles away it was halved, while taxes doubled. The quadrupling of the revenues for the crown of Castile was insufficiently covered by the growth of the money supply. At the end of his reign the emperor's war policy forced taxation and government debt to a much higher level than the economic growth could support. Massive poverty, a slowdown in economic growth and a freeze on state finances were the direct results of this.

Discussion and repression

As the financial problems grew so the negotiations with the representative bodies became more frequent and more difficult. In Spain these bodies were the *cortes* of Castile and the three kingdoms under the crown of Aragon, in south Italy the parliaments of each kingdom, in Germany the Diet, and in the Low Countries the States General and the Provincial States. The princes and their advisors were not really keen on such assemblies where they were always confronted with long lists of grievances against their rule, opposition to requests for money and attempts by the worthy representatives to obtain some personal advantage, perhaps in exchange for their vote. Charles wrote to his sister Mary, with whom he was most frank and open, about his discussions with the *cortes* of the crown of Aragon at Monzón in 1537; as ruler he had to endure much unpleasantness and make pretences for the sake of his cause: 'Take now the present *cortes* of Aragon, which I heartily wish to the devil!' In 1542 Mary expressed herself in similar terms in reference to her negotiations with the States and the individual towns: 'Doing business with these people was enough to drive one mad.' In Flanders the previous year she had seen no other possibility for getting her way than 'by giving in to the demands of the three great towns, as usual'.[34] Throughout his reign Charles only met with the *cortes* of Castile eight times, and just four with that of Aragon,[35] but he presided over the Diet, whose assemblies could go on for months, six times; Ferdinand presided over the Diet four times, under the emperor's mandate. After 1517 Charles appeared occasionally in the States General of the Low Countries, in 1531 and 1540. On the last occasion his advisor, Louis of Schore, delivered a lengthy speech about the policies followed, and naturally ended with a request for a higher fiscal contribution. In the coastal regions the deliberations of the principal cities were considerably more frequent and influential than the formal and broadly-attended assemblies of the States.

From the beginning of his reign Charles was faced with rebellions. All ended in a formal submission and punishment, but this does not mean that they totally failed in their aims, nor that their supporters were dreadfully suppressed. Charles was involved most directly with the revolt of the *comuneros* and *germanias* in Spain, from 1516 to 1523. In the German Empire the territorial princes bore the brunt of the Peasants' War of 1524–26 and Charles did not intervene at all; when local rebellions occurred in the Low Countries or Naples it was the regent or viceroy who used his military strength to restore order.

In Spain the urban elites were traditionally heavily dependent on the crown, which appointed and supported the *regidores* and *corregidores*. In the years preceding Charles' accession the king's administration had been increasingly weakened through the erosion of rights and incomes, to the advantage of the high nobility. They maintained their own private armies, which could be used to persuade over-zealous officials to think differently. The towns complained to the royal councils about all sorts of abuses, but never received satisfaction because of the rampant corruption. The first assemblies of the *cortes* over which Charles presided in 1518 and 1520 gave full vent to their grievances. The opposition to the aristocracy was expressed there in the shape of demands aimed at the crown, which was also a target of criticism. As yet, the crown was too weak to curb the nobility. In 1520 the government urged the towns to send representatives with the power to approve new taxes, but the magistracies demanded indigenous crown officials, that tax money be kept in the kingdom, the assurance of an heir, and restoration of the farming out of taxation. By judiciously handing out gifts and offices to the representatives present the government was still able to secure the tax it wanted.

Meanwhile Toledo was in open revolt and the clergy preached against the king. When the representative from Segovia returned home, he had to pay for his corrupt willingness to please: a seething mob assaulted him and hanged him by his feet. A revolutionary *junta* took over control of the town. In addition to the town council, its members included canons from the cathedral chapter and representatives of the parishes, and therefore of the workers. Troops sent by Charles' regent, Cardinal Adrian of Utrecht, proved unable to turn the tide of events and after wandering around for a number of months they were chased off in disarray by a militia from Salamanca, Toledo and Toro. On 30 July these towns joined Segovia to form a *junta* with its seat in Avila, with the intention of restoring order throughout the kingdom.

The towns did not hand over any more taxes to the crown because they felt they could administer them better themselves. A government attempt to strengthen its military position by taking the artillery depot in Medina del Campo ended in complete disaster. The royal troops met with fierce resistance from the local populace, inflicted a lot of damage and behaved, according to the town government, 'more cruelly than the Turks', but still had to retreat without the prize. This gave the rebels a second wind and they took Tordesillas, where Charles' mother Joanna lived; flattered by all the attention, she listened to their humble requests. In the capital Valladolid, news of the destruction of Medina led to a riot and forced the conservative members of the town council to flee.

The *junta* was now based in Tordesillas and linked 13 towns. It consisted of delegates from the town governments that had attracted a broad social basis in their local *juntas*, and in many cases enjoyed the active support of the clergy, professors and students. The representatives from the towns' wards came from less elevated circles than did the traditional town governments; it was not entirely clear whether they had the support of another organisation, such as a crafts guild. This explains the ease with which they were excluded from power after the rebellion. From September to the beginning of December 1520 the *junta* of Tordesillas was able to represent the kingdom itself and managed to defend the monarchy better than the royal officials. The *junta* abolished the Council of Castile, much hated because it was so corrupt, and made every effort to govern well on finance and justice. The fact that the town magistracies had initiated the uprising explains why they had no difficulty in undertaking the administrative tasks at the level of the entire kingdom. They built upon a long tradition of urban alliances and their experience of all that had gone wrong in the past. The *junta* had access to increasingly ample resources and the numbers of its supporters grew, even among the peasants who started to rebel against their masters at the end of August. This of course provoked a reaction from the aristocracy, who deployed their mercenaries. On 5 December Tordesillas was retaken from the *comuneros* and queen Joanna was rescued from rebel hands. Yet the royalist camp fell apart at once. The *junta* settled in Valladolid, the capital; members of government institutions had scattered and sought safety elsewhere.

Gradually cracks appeared in the remarkable coalition supporting the *comuneros*. In the towns the movement was radicalised, causing the more conservative elements, such as members of cathedral chapters, to withdraw. The support given to the peasants' uprising was a divisive element, and in the towns the claims of the common people was a growing source of irritation to the old elites. On 9 September 1520 Charles added two important Spanish noblemen, admiral Enriquez and commander Velasco, to cardinal Adrian's government. In April 1521 their armies succeeded in defeating the *comuneros*. The leaders of the *comuneros* lacked unity and professionalism and their cavalry was small. Hundreds of members of the town militias were killed at the battle of Villalar. Toledo, which had provided the largest number of fighting men, resisted valiantly until February 1522. In Valencia the radicalisation was aimed specifically at the urban oligarchies and, on the part of the peasants, against their lords' administration of justice. In 1523 the crown managed to suppress the movement there as well.[36]

When Charles reappeared in Castile on 16 July 1522 the rebellion had been largely put down, but his authority had been severely damaged and his administration was in confusion. The resistance may have been defeated but it was by no means broken, and this prompted an extreme inclination towards reconcilation. In 1523 the *cortes* won agreement to a fundamental reformation of state finances and the royal councils, the replacement of four members of the Council of Castile and the settlement of their complaints before the end of the session. In 1525 and 1527 they achieved the formation of a permanent deputation that would monitor the enforcement of resolutions of the *cortes*.[37] Changes were thus introduced in the functioning of the *cortes* and the government which were in line with the *comuneros*' demands.

In all the regions under Charles' control the pressure from the central government was felt profoundly in its ever more urgent fiscal demands, to which the subjects' representatives were unable to put up effective opposition. Their willingness to accommodate can be explained in part by the strengthening of the might of the central authority in each individual territory. The considerable political, social and material advantages acquired by the representatives individually, and as a group, in the course of negotiations must have played a large part too. It was a part of the policy of Charles' government whenever the opportunity arose – after the subjugation of the revolt in Spain, for example – so to alter the constitution of the towns that the political voice of the craft guilds was silenced. In 1525 Margaret, the regent of the Low Countries, prohibited all assemblies of guild deans, jurors and 'wicked men' in 's-Hertogenbosch. Charles congratulated her in 1528 because 'you have issued a new ordinance on behaviour in Brussels and taken power out of the hands of the people, of which I certainly approve'. In the same year the craft guilds in Utrecht also lost their political role because they had regularly sided with the duke of Guelders against their bishop. The government immediately decided to build a citadel and establish a garrison there, in order to maintain control over the town and the bishopric. The States of Holland even proved willing to approve an extraordinary tax of 80,000 pounds (of 40 Flemish groats) to build the Vredenburg (in Utrecht) because peace on their eastern borders was in their own interest, and also because they were promised that brewing outside the towns would be prohibited. Solidarity between the towns and provinces was still too weak to offer any resistance to the central government.

When the representatives of Holland, in exchange for approving special taxes, demanded that steps be taken to protect merchant shipping and fishing or opposed new taxes on commerce, they were acting in the interests not only of their province in general but also of their close relatives. The protection of their interests was even more exclusive in 1530 when they won from the emperor an edict banning industries outside the limits of the towns. Representatives from the larger towns blatantly made use of their position to further their own ends, sometimes to obtain tax advantages, for example.

On the other hand, the central government gradually acquired more authoritarian features too. In 1549 when the delegates from Holland tied various conditions to their approval for paying for improvements to shipping safety with an exceptional levy on the wine trade, as the other provinces had already done, Regent Mary threatened that they ran the risk of 'incurring His Majesty's displeasure' by delaying. The stadholder of Holland quickly chose a few other noble delegates who 'would happily concur with His Majesty's request'. Amsterdam continued to plead for relief for the expenses its merchants would incur, 'that commerce would not be driven out of the land', but had to give way in the end.[38]

In 1536 the magistracy of Ghent, after consulting with the 'Broad Council', which was controlled by the masters of the craft guilds, refused to contribute an extra tax towards the defence of the land against the French invaders. The government considered this illegal. The conflict escalated in the local tradition of rebellion, with displays of lese-majesty. Because Ghent was the foremost town in Flanders, and the second most important in the Low Countries, the government thought that the crushing of the rebellion should serve as an example. In 1540 Charles came specially from Spain for this solemn occasion. The magistrates of the rebellious town were subjected to a symbolic humiliation: with nooses round their necks – as rebels they deserved to be hanged – and in their undershirts, they were forced to beg for mercy. At the suggestion of his advisor, Louis of Schore, Charles so altered the town's charter that the guilds lost all their political influence and the rank of guild-master was opened to all newcomers. A citadel was built and garrisoned in the most symbolic place in Ghent, the centuries-old Benedictine abbey of Saint Bavo.[39]

Similarly, in 1548, Charles used the opportunity of his victory over the Protestants to remove the guilds' representatives from the governing councils of nearly 30 imperial towns in south Germany. He did not trust the people and preferred to negotiate with the oligarchies, which he could influence easily in return for small favours. In addition to divergent religions his government tried to eradicate certain popular customs through laws and repression. In 1551 the German Protestants accused him of replacing their 'ancient freedoms' with 'brutal slavery'; the *comuneros* reproached him in 1520 for treating his subjects as slaves. This confrontation was exacerbated by the use of the art of printing, the new and as yet uncontrollable mass medium.

In the early years of his reign Charles had passed strict legislation in the Low Countries against the reformers and their publications. He regularly gave orders, and certainly during each journey that he made to the region and in consultation with the States General and other bodies, for the publication of edicts against heresy. In 1531 he observed that Luther's followers 'swarm out and multiply in our Low Countries', in spite of the heavy penalties threatened. The view that the emperor and his advisors took of his subjects is characterised by the publication on the same day of an important decree covering a whole range of subjects, which, in his eyes, were all connected to public order. Once again, it dealt in the first place with heresy, and then with a great variety of subjects such as vagrancy, begging and poor relief, fairs, marriage and baptism, clothing regulations, public drunkenness, alehouses, blasphemy, bankruptcy, monopolies, reformation of the coinage, horse trading, etc. The emperor and the Diet had published a similar *Polizeiordnung* in the previous year. It is clear that the emperor was keen that the behaviour of his subjects should be strictly regulated: feasts were not allowed to last for more than a day, wedding feasts no more than a day and a half.[40] An attempt was obviously being made to introduce identical legislation in the Empire and the Low Countries, as had been done with religion.

In 1540 and 1546 the emperor was again forced to conclude that 'the ordinances were not obeyed as well as they should be and as was necessary'; printers found ways of publishing translations of the Bible, schoolmasters used bad books for teaching. Now another approach was tried: a list of permitted texts was published.[41]

Charles would have wanted peace among all Christians and the defence of the Catholic Church as the themes of his reign; because of the policies he followed, however, his reign ended in more warfare, higher taxation, decreasing prosperity and growing repression.

Notes:

1. Kohler, *Quellen*, 308–17.
2. H. Cools, *Mannen met macht. Edellieden en de moderne staat in de Bourgondisch-Habsburgse landen (1475–1530)* (Zutphen, 2001), 185–6.
3. I was able to consult copies of the letters in the University Library of Konstanz, thanks to the systematic collection made by Professor Horst Rabe and his colleagues, who were particularly kind in allowing me access to their treasure-house. The original letters are in Vienna, Haus- Hof- und Staatsarchiv, PA Belgien, nos 68/3, ff 40–77, 69/2, ff 49–56 and no. 69/4, ff 1–61.
4. Kohler, *Quellen*, 137.
5. Fernandez Alvarez, *Carlos V, el César y el Hombre*, 364-367; A.Kohler, *Karl V*, 184–6 ; G. Parker, 'The Political World of Charles V', in H. Soly, ed., *Charles V (1500–1558) and his Times* (Antwerp, 1999), 149.
6. Luigi Guicciardini, *Il Sacco di Roma, narrazioni di contemporanei*, ed. C. Milanesi (Florence, 1876), 19–25.
7. Guicciardini, *Il Sacco*, 38–47.
8. Fernandez Alvarez, *Carlos V, el César*, 366.
9. Guicciardini, *Il Sacco*, 75–85.

10. Francesco Vettori, *Sommario della storia d'Italia*, in E.Niccolini, ed., *Scritti storici e politici* (Bari, 1972), 135–246, especially 227–38.
11. Guicciardini, *Il Sacco*, 124.
12. G. Parker, 'The Political World of Charles V', 175, 216; G.Parker, *The Grand Strategy of Philip II*, 111–14.
13. Fernandez Alvarez, *Corpus documental*, III, 479.
14. Knecht, *Renaissance Warrior*, 334–8.
15. Kohler, *Karl V*, 277.
16. Kohler, *Quellen*, 148.
17. Fernandez Alvarez, *Carlos V, el César*, 196.
18. W. Schulze, 'The Emergence and Consolidation of the "Tax State". The Sixteenth Century', in Bonney, *Economic Systems*, 269. In order to make comparisons simpler, in this paragraph I have converted the amounts into Castilian ducats. The Castilian ducat was approximately equivalent to one Italian *scudo*, 2 Rhine guilders and 2.1 Carolus guilders in the Low Countries.
19. Braudel, *Mediterranean*, II, 850–1, 904–7.
20. My own calculations, based on D'Agostino, *Parlamento e società*, 218–301; compare with G. Felloni, 'Economie, finances et monnaie dans les possessions italiennes de Charles V', *L'escarcelle de Charles V*, 236–50.
21. F. Chabod, *Lo stato e la vita religiosa a Milano nell'epoca di Carlo V*, 126–8.
22. They were expressed in *maravedis*; 375 maravedis were equal to one ducat. J. M. Carretero Zamora, 'Fiscalidad Parlamentara y Deuda Imperial', in García García, *Imperio de Carlos V*, 160–2.
23. Carretero Zamora, 174–80.
24. Chabod, *Lo stato*, 109–20; Felloni, 'Economie, finances et monnaie', 250–4.
25. Maddens, *De beden in het graafschap Vlaanderen tijdens de regering van keizer Karel V (1515–1550)* (Kortrijk-Heule, 1978), 426–8; my own calculations, published in 'Finances publiques et inégalité sociale dans les Pays-Bas aux XIVe–XVIe siècles', in J.-Ph. Genet and M. Le Mené, eds, *Genèse de l'état moderne: prélèvement et redistribution* (Paris, 1987), 86.
26. J. D. Tracy, 'The taxation system in the county of Holland during the reigns of Charles V and Philip II, 1519–1566, *Economisch- en Sociaal-Historisch Jaarboek*, 48 (1985), 109.
27. J. D. Tracy, *A Financial Revolution in the Habsburg Netherlands. Renten and Renteniers in the County of Holland, 1515–1565* (Berkeley, 1985), 139–92; idem, 'The taxation system', 83–4, 94–6; K. J. W. Verhofstad, *De regeering van de Nederlanden in de jaren 1555–1559* (Nijmegen, 1937), 101.
28. W. Blockmans, 'The Low Countries in the Middle Ages', in R. Bonney, ed., *The Rise of the Fiscal State in Europe* (Oxford, 1999), 281–308.
29. J. D. Tracy, 'The taxation system', 85–91; idem, *Holland under Habsburg Rule, 1506–1566. The Formation of a Body Politic* (Berkeley, 1990), 115–46.
30. G. Parker, 'The Political World of Charles V', in Soly, *Charles V*, 193.
31. Chabod, *Lo stato*, 130–4.
32. J. D. Tracy, 'Charles V, his Bankers, and their Demands', in Jan Denolf and Barbara Simons, eds, *(Re)Constructing the Past: Proceedings of the Colloquium on History and Legitimisation* (Brussels, 2000), 119–43.
33. G. Muto, 'The Spanish System: Centre and Periphery', in Bonney, *Economic Systems and State Finance*, 249–55.

34. Stratenwerth, 'Aktenkundliche Aspekte', 66; Gorter-van Royen, *Maria*, 238, 270.
35. Fernandez Alvarez, *Carlos V, el César*, discusses the meetings *passim*.
36. J. Valdeon Baruque, 'The Monarchic State and Resistance in Spain', in P. Blickle, ed., *Resistance, Representation and Community* (Oxford, 1997), 72–6, 94–7, 103–7; R. García Carcel, *Las germanias de Valencia* (Barcelona, 1981).
37. Haliczer, *Comuneros*, 208–23.
38. Adriaen van der Goes, *Register van de saecken van den Lande van Hollandt 1544–1549* (The Hague, 1554), 624–46.
39. W. Blockmans, 'The Emperor's Subjects', in Soly, *Charles V*, 269–71.
40. *Recueil des Ordonnances des Pays-Bas*, III (Brussels, 1902), 262, 265ff.
41. *Ibid.*, V, 307–12.

7
The image in balance

The creation of a classical hero

Charles' first journey to Italy in 1529 marked a break in his reign: his coronation as emperor confirmed his hegemony in Italy as much as it did his universal role as protector of Christianity and the Catholic Church. From then on the emperor impressed his own views on governmental policies more emphatically. At the same time his personal appearance underwent a metamorphosis: the long-haired, beardless German youth we see in all the pictures before 1529 followed the advice of his grand chancellor Gattinara, and on the way to his triumphant journey through Italy recreated himself as the incarnation of a Roman emperor. In 1528 his court chaplain, the Franciscan Antonio de Guevara, had written a biography of Marcus Aurelius, whom he recommended as an example for Charles to follow.

In Italy the enthusiasm for classical forms and languages was at its peak. In 1507 Pope Julius III had placed a magnificent ancient marble statue of Hercules and Telephos at the entrance to the courtyard in the Vatican, a few days after it had been unearthed in Rome's Campo dei Fiori. The bronze equestrian statue of Marcus Aurelius that stood opposite the church of St. John Lateran was copied several times, sometimes for members of the Gonzaga family, the marquises of Mantua.[1] In order to make a positive impression in such an environment Charles was forced to follow the Italian fashion.

Charles' cultural background was clearly rooted in the last flowering of the world of chivalry at the court of Burgundy. He celebrated his Joyous Entry into Valladolid in 1517 with a tournament, much to the consternation of the Castilians. In order 'to show the Spaniards how brave these gentlemen are', scions of the great families of Croy, Lannoy and Luxembourg appeared, flanked by thirty magnificently apparelled knights, 'each like a Saint George'.[2] As late as 1540 Charles ordered a Castilian translation of the allegorical romance of chivalry, *Le Chevalier délibéré*, written by Oliver de la Marche, chronicler to the court of Burgundy. During the reception for Crown Prince Philip in 1549 the regent Mary had the guests at her castle of Binche take part in a spectacular entertainment inspired by a chivalric romance. The old culture had evidently not yet lost its charm for the courtiers.

Charles did not consider the world of chivalry purely as fiction and amusement, as his attachment to the princely code of honour shows. It compelled him to respect the safe-conduct he gave to Martin Luther, even after he had been sentenced by the Diet in 1521, and to treat his rival Francis I with all honour while he was his prisoner. He burst out in anger at Francis' 'cowardice and treachery' when he broke the promises made in January 1526 in the Treaty of Madrid. Like a true knight, Charles challenged him to a duel, a challenge he was to repeat on two later occasions. His rival, although taller and more powerfully built, was unwilling to become involved in such dangerous reminders of a bygone age.

Francis I took a much more lively interest than Charles in the cultural currents of his day. He had a new wing built on the Louvre and commissioned the building of the magnificent Renaissance palaces of Chambord and Fontainebleau. Following the Italian custom he had an art gallery built in these palaces where he insisted on showing his guests around himself and lecturing them on the exhibits. He was patron to a number of artists and scholars, founded the *Collège Royal* and was interested in learning for its own sake.[3]

There is no trace of such cultural leanings in Charles as a young man. The portraits we have of him from that period were the work of the court painters of the regent Margaret, Conrad Meit and Bernard van Orley, or of the court painters of Emperor Maximilian, such as Hans Weiditz. Van Orley made the first portrait study in which the new look can be seen; the portrait by Jan Cornelsz Vermeyen is the first in that style that has survived.[4]

Triumphal arches modelled on those of the Via Sacra in Rome, where the ancient Roman triumphs took place, greeted Charles on his arrival in Genoa on 12 August 1529. In the harbour, a copy of the single arch of Titus on the Forum Romanum had been constructed and decorated with the two-headed eagle that was the symbol of the imperial domination of the world. The cathedral was embellished with a copy of the arch of Septimius Severus with its three archways, crowned by Lady Justice.[5] These Genoese triumphal arches were the first in a whole series of copies made on the models of antiquity, and seen, for example, in 1535–36 during Charles' entries from Palermo to Lucca as conqueror of the Turks, and in 1549 in the towns of the Low Countries during his joint tour with Philip for the latter's inauguration as his successor.

The *moment suprême*, of course, was the imperial coronation at Bologna on 24 February 1530, Charles' birthday. In the tradition of the Western empire that Charlemagne had restored in 800, Charles had been crowned king of the Langobards two days before. The grandeur of these events was immediately reproduced, thanks to the propagandist activities of the regent Margaret, in a series of 24 woodcuts with commentaries, which was published in Antwerp after a design by Robert Péril. Nicholas Hogenberg later made a series of 40 copper engravings based on these woodcuts, with only a short description in Latin. From the prints we can see that the procession passed under four Renaissance-style triumphal arches on its way from San Petronio's cathedral to the church of San Domenico. There were two baldequins: one protected the holy relics and was carried by 12 Roman patricians led by 12 prelates of the Holy See carrying torches. The other was held above the anointed heads of the universal rulers, Clement VII and, on his left, the emperor. This arrangement denied Charles that extra honour that Paul III would accord him at his entry into Rome in 1536, the place of honour at the right hand. The early enmity, the deep humiliation of his captivity and the Sack of Rome apparently still rankled with Clement, as this subtle symbolism made apparent.

The two rulers were preceded by groups spreading their banners in display and by four princes of the empire, each bearing a symbol of the imperial insignia: sceptre, sword, imperial orb; the empty hands of the fourth prince on the return journey showed that the emperor was wearing his crown. They were immediately followed by the emperor's principal chamberlain, Count Henry III of Nassau, and the pope's secretary and personal physician. In front of this group rode the herald, of whom the commentary said,

> The herald called Burgundy had two bags hanging from his saddle, filled with newly-minted gold and silver coins. On one side of the coins was the effigy of the Holy Majesty and the inscription *Carolus Quintus Imperator Augustus*, and on the other the two pillars and *Plus Oultre*. During the procession to and from the cathedral the herald used both hands to scatter the coins in all directions to the people in the street, crying out 'largesse, largesse', and the people shouted loudly back, '*imperio, imperio*', for the empire, long live the Catholic Emperor Charles.

The coins were an ancient way of proclaiming the generosity of the victor, but also a mass medium through which the new emperor could make himself known. The coronation attracted large numbers of Italian artists to the imperial court in the hope of obtaining commissions. The most famous among them was Parmigianino, of whose work the contemporary painter and art critic, Giorgio Vasari, said that it much pleased the emperor. 'He made a very large oil painting in which Fame placed a crown of laurels on Caesar's head while a boy resembling the young Hercules presented him with the world.'[6]

In about 1530 a tapestry commissioned by Charles' brother-in-law, John III of Portugal, was woven to a design by Bernard van Orley or his workshop. It was entitled *Hercules Carries the Heavenly Spheres*.[7] The glorification of the emperor, associated with Hercules and his labours, was now taking place on an increasingly large scale.

The appeal of the new artistic style of the Renaissance lay in its form; its reference to classical antiquity fitted exceptionally well into the symbolism of the universal imperial role which those close to Charles propagated as fully as possible. The emblems and device of the emperor appeared everywhere on public buildings, such as the Bisagra gate in Toledo, the rood screen in the cathedral there and in the church at Vianen in the Netherlands, where Charles visited the Brederode family in 1540. The chimney piece in the offices of the *Vrije* (the free rural district) in Bruges shows the emperor and his dynasty carved in wood, in the town hall in Kampen in sandstone, while that of the town hall in Kortrijk uses heraldry to emphasise the firm ties between the local government and the higher authority. The emperor's triumphs were carved in wood in the choir stalls of the Great Church in Dordrecht at the time of the emperor's visit in 1540.[8] During his stay in 1531 the States General presented him with a magnificent series of seven tapestries depicting the battle of Pavia, from sketches by Bernard van Orley.[9] In the vast empire through which the emperor travelled, but where he was inevitably absent from most places, these visual means of propaganda formed a permanent reminder of his glory. The images represented him being helped by the local rulers, who thus strengthened their own position.

During his first two visits to Italy Charles' artistic taste received a powerful impulse from his friendship with Federigo Gonzaga, the marquis of Mantua. Charles made him a duke and appointed his brother Ferrante viceroy of Sicily and governor of Milan. It was Federigo Gonzaga who introduced Titian, the already renowned Venetian painter, to Charles. It was not until his second visit in 1532 that this led to real recognition, when Titian made a copy of the portrait of Charles standing with a greyhound, painted by Ferdinand's court painter, Jacob Seisenegger. Charles found the superior expressiveness of Titian's work so convincing that from 1547, when he commissioned a whole series of portraits of members of his family, he loaded him with commissions and heaped honours upon him. Charles' visits to Mantua brought him face to face with the daring frescoes of Giulo Romano and his school in the newly finished Palazzo Te. Gonzaga's passion for Arab thoroughbreds was evident in a series of paintings in the palace. The deities of antiquity were depicted in frankly erotic poses: Eros and Psyche, and also Charles' favourites, Hercules and Jupiter. Shortly before Charles' visit in 1532 the *Battle of the Titans* was completed, an astonishing panoramic mural in a chamber without any corners. The work could be interpreted as an allegory of the wars between Charles and Francis I: an eagle sat enthroned at the top.

Charles' triumphal journey through Sicily and Italy in 1535–36 provoked competition between succeeding towns with all the previous ones, and between the artists. The entries in Messina, Rome and Florence were reported in print. His victory over the Muslims was the theme of his welcome everywhere. Nine years after the Sack of Rome the entry into Rome was still a delicate matter. The accession of Paul III as pope eased the situation and Charles was able to hold a triumph in the classical manner. With a retinue of veterans of the expedition to Tunis, he rode the length of the Via Sacra, which was specially cleared of some churches and other buildings which had been in the way. Subjects from antiquity and references to Charles' five Habsburg predecessors as Roman king or emperor formed the dramatic theme of the reception. Charles was compared to classical and mythological heroes, giving a Roman aura to his image. In Siena he was depicted mounted on a gilded horse, three provinces at his feet. This was set on a float that was drawn through the town during the procession.

In Florence, where Alexander de Medici was to be married to Charles' daughter Margaret, Giorgio Vasari was responsible for 'magnificent and grandiose decorations to receive the emperor with suitable splendour'. The victory over the Muslims was illustrated in painted scenes, a tableau vivant showed the 'conqueror of Africa'. On the Trinity bridge the Rhine and Danube rivers were depicted in ceramics, Hercules fought the Hydra, Peace reigned. Because of the haste the equestrian statue of Charles was not completed in time, so that the inscription, 'To the most triumphant emperor Charles Augustus', had to serve for the horse alone. Alexander had good reason for this commission for he had the emperor to thank for his restoration to power.

The journey of Charles and Philip through the Low Countries in 1549 provided a good opportunity for all the towns to show their devotion to the dynasty. Here, too, every town vied in its efforts to outdo the others, and all in the new Renaissance style. Ghent was anxious to erase the memory of its subjection nine years earlier and constructed a series of triumphal arches decorated with Charles' emblems, each one depicting a father and son from history or mythology. Philip of Macedonia, count Philip of Alsace and

Charlemagne were dug from the past to make the association even more direct.[10] The metropolis of Antwerp surpassed all the other towns. The town clerk, Graphaeus, himself took charge of the printed report in which he proudly stated that 1726 local artists and craftsmen had worked on the decorations for the triumphal arches and stages. The organisation was in the hands of the painter, Pieter Coecke, who had just published a translation of Vitruvius' classic *Rules of Architecture*. 5,296 people took part in the procession; Graphaeus was obviously extremely precise, a sign of his professionalism. The town presented itself as an obedient maiden, entreating clemency from the new ruler. No fewer than eight historical Philips were exhibited here. Of all the presentations of the foreign trading nations that of the Spaniards aroused the most attention: behind two giant pillars seven great Spanish rulers stood face to face with the seven Virtues in a perspective gallery. A triumphal arch was decorated with Charles' victories and surmounted with the Roman Temple of Janus, to convey the desire for a lasting peace.[11] In Dordrecht the imperial party was similarly welcomed by the States of Holland with decorations, performances and gifts. Commemorative medals were struck. Elsewhere in the north, however, everything was rather more restrained.[12]

In the meantime Charles had been working hard on his self-glorification. On his expedition to Tunis he was accompanied by the painters Jan Cornelisz Vermeyen and Pieter Coecke, and Maarten van Heemskerck who made drawings. Their sketches formed the basis for the series of tapestries, commissioned in 1540 but not woven in Brussels till about 1554, and for the engravings of the Twelve Triumphs of the emperor, which Van Heemskerck published in 1555–56 on Philips' initiative.[13] The emperor's speeches were printed and the government arranged for the distribution of hundreds of pamphlets supporting its viewpoint.

There were a number of chroniclers in service at the court. Pedro Mexia wrote a humanistically coloured eulogy of Charles' reign up to 1530. The emperor took reporters with him on his major campaigns in Tunis and against the Schmalkaldic League, in the hope that their laudatory texts would enhance his eternal glory. His secretary, Johannes Secundus, died in 1536 before completing his epic poem in Latin on the Triumph of Tunis, but his chaplain, Juan Gines de Sepulveda, published *De Bello Africo*, 'The African War', in that same year. Another secretary, Antoine Perrenin, also wrote an account in French that was published in Latin after Charles' death. The most successful was Luis de Avila's narrative extolling the German campaign, which was published in Spanish under the title *Comentario de la guerra de Alemania*. Very soon translations appeared in French, Dutch, Latin and English. He modelled Charles on Julius Caesar, endowing him with fortitude and military talents, and showed him encouraging his troops and delivering speeches, but merciful towards those he conquered. The report by Charles' official historian, Barnabé de Busto, still remains unpublished in the library at the Escorial.[14] During a five-day boat journey down the Rhine from Cologne to Mainz in 1550 Charles began to dictate his memoirs in French to his secretary, William of Male. This dry summary of journeys, events and illnesses was also intended as a sort of self-glorification, which he dedicated to his son.[15]

In 1547–48, at the zenith of his power, Charles was immortalised by Titian and the sculptors Leone and Pompeo Leoni, who also were given a number of commissions by members of his entourage. He had such confidence in these artists that he allowed them much artistic freedom knowing that they would fully express the essence of his own ideas. Related works showing the victory over the Protestants are laden with political propaganda: Titian's *Equestrian Portrait after the Battle of Mühlberg* and Leoni's *The Victory of the Fury*. Titian shows Charles in his richly decorated armour, galloping confidently on a thoroughbred across a peaceful landscape, dark clouds overhead. He holds the holy lance, symbol of his struggle as defender of Christendom, diagonally across the canvas. In Leoni's group, dating from 1551–53 but commissioned in 1549, the emperor is also holding the lance. With it he keeps the fallen and chained heretic in check. He wears the armour of a classical emperor, whose features and athletic figure he has also acquired. Without the armour he has the figure of a naked, ideally built Hercules. The glorification here is far removed from the reality: at the time when this masterpiece was created Charles was in the depths of a political, physical and mental crisis.

The association of the emperor with ancient heroes placed some of the images of him in an almost heathen context. The Latin form of address, *divus* (divine or sacred) acquired a broad rhetorical freedom in relation to the rules of the Church. On one gilded shield Charles was celebrated as a hero receiving a crown of laurels from an angel-like female figure. As captain of the Ship of State he was often represented in a similar manner.[16] In Van Heemskerck's engraving he is enthroned on a pedestal, elevated above all his enemies, including the pope. Unlike Francis I, Charles did not see art as an end in itself, but as a means of political propaganda or religious devotion.

In Titian's *Gloria*, dating from 1553–54, Charles has laid his crown aside, put on a hair shirt and left all worldly glory behind. He implores God for mercy for himself and his family. A striking aspect of the painting is that only the Virgin and a host of angels stand as mediators between them and the Holy Trinity: the allegorical figure for the Church is far below them.

Charles has clearly taken the consequences of his failures after 1551 and detached himself from the earthly glory that was so characteristic of the works commissioned before 1550. This was the painting that Charles had placed on the altar of the monastery church in Yuste so that he could see it from his deathbed. He felt at home among the austere Hieronymite monks of Yuste; the secular church had failed his trust.

Personality and fate

The dynastic calculations of his ancestors and pure chance had consorted to make Charles the heir to an immense number of kingdoms. The double marriage between the houses of Spain and Habsburg in 1496–97 was in no way intended to unite their territories in one person: the alliance was primarily to ward off the French invasion of Italy. Dynastic fate decided otherwise. In the sixteenth century nobody would have thought of questioning the divine will; a prince reigned by the grace of God. The chosen one had an honourable task to accept and fulfil. In the *Instructions* that Charles, with the help of Nicholas de Granvelle, drew up in January 1548 for his son, and which is also considered his political testament, he explained it thus: 'So many and such great kingdoms, states and domains, and so far apart, as God in His goodness has given me, and I shall give to you, if it pleases Him'.[17] The objective must be to avoid war, he suggests, but the evil intentions of jealous neighbours force you to protect your lands.

Philip conscientiously followed his father's instructions in both outline and details.[18] However, in two important respects, he chose a radically different approach, perhaps because of what he had seen happen to his father, for Charles had not mentioned them in his *Instructions*. Charles was an itinerant monarch in the Burgundian, indeed the medieval, tradition. He believed that he had to be in his territories as much as possible, to see things for himself and to make decisions in person. From 1535 the journeys became complicated because he led all the major military expeditions personally, and was thus campaigning for several months almost every year. He was exposed to fatigue, hardship, sickness and danger. In 1547 he was almost hit by a canon ball, an experience that had proved fatal to René of Chalon three years earlier at Saint-Dizier. Charles' was an onerous task, fulfilled increasingly in pain and with great effort, because of his ailments. From 1528 he noted his attacks of gout meticulously in his *Mémoires*. After 1543 he lost count of them somewhere between the tenth and eleventh attack, because they were occurring increasingly often and lasting longer. He prescribed a diet for himself and repeated it in 1547. During the Schmalkaldic War he had to rest his foot in a bandage when mounted on his horse; he was often forced to withdraw or to be moved in a litter. During the siege of Metz in the autumn of 1552 he was kept to his bed in the nearby town of Thionville. In 1554 he led his troops against the French attack on Artois from his litter and was laid low after that, unable to use his limbs.[19]

This existence of campaigns and journeys endangered the very running of government, every aspect of which, and at all times, Charles was so anxious to keep in his own hands. Even in respect of his most trusted governors, his sister Mary and brother Ferdinand, he kept the power of decision-making for himself. This style of government delayed the making of decisions in every corner of his *imperium*. Could he have approached this in a different way? The other great monarchs of his time, Henry VIII, Francis I and Sultan Sulaimān, also led their own armies; they saw it as a matter of personal honour as well as a method of motivation and rapid strategic decision-making. All three of them also had permanent residences housing a permanent apparatus of government. Charles did not have this at the central level, only in the capitals of the various parts of the empire, and not at all in the German Empire. Philip II, however, decided to govern his vast empire from his desk and audience chambers in the Escorial, and to leave the conduct of wars to his generals. He was no longer concerned with the problematic German Empire, on which Charles had spent so much energy. But this had been Charles' own choice, a choice that was different in the first half of his reign from the choice in the second. His (missionary) zeal as leader of Christendom and defender of the Catholic Church explains his enormous personal dedication to the crusades against Muslims and heretics. Early in 1536, and on numerous occasions thereafter, he marched against France in person.

The Holy Roman Empire was the heart of the difference between Charles' *imperium* and that of his son. He had not inherited this empire, although four Habsburgs had sat on its throne, three immediately before him. In his abdication speech in 1555 Charles justified his pursuit of this crown, 'not for his own sake, but for the defence of his lands, in particular the Low Countries'. This rationale lay behind the imperial rights to sovereignty over north and central Italy, which formed important legal grounds for opposing French expansion. The power of France and the Turkish advance constituted the two greatest military challenges to Charles' *imperium*. In such a situation the combination of the French and Roman crowns – there were no other real contenders – would have considerably weakened the whole complex of Habsburg territories. For Flanders and Artois Charles would have been the vassal of Francis I as king of France, while for the rest of the Low Countries and imperial Habsburg domains he would have been the vassal of Francis as Roman king. The cohesion of French and German lands would have been an enormous obstacle to communications between Charles' territories in the Low Countries, Spain and southern Italy. In 1519, to preclude this option was more than just a matter of honour for the Habsburgs; it was an urgent strategic choice.

Charles' election as emperor had the support of the great banking houses of Augsburg and Genoa. Their reasons for the choice must have been based on the expectation of greater protection for their operations in an extended Habsburg empire. It is well known that Charles regularly supported the Fuggers against the powers in the Diet that opposed the monopolists. The exploitation of the mines, especially the copper mines, remained firmly in their hands. Antwerp was their most important outlet, which they served from Slovakia via Cracow, Danzig and the sea route. The unity of political authority within the sphere of their influence, and good relations with Denmark, were therefore clearly very precious to them.[20] The Genoese saw the advantages of political union with Naples and Sicily, their grain suppliers, and with their trading partners in Spain and the Low Countries. In time, the political switch of this trading republic to Charles in 1528 would also be motivated by the possibility of extending its contacts with Milan and south Germany, both now under imperial authority. The loss of its entry to the annual fairs in Lyons was relatively unimportant. In this way all the financial centres of Europe's burgeoning world economy fell under Charles' control, a situation which, in the beginning, seemed to be advantageous to all concerned. The Fuggers, Spinolas, Schetz and other major financiers and merchants received interest on their capital and – more importantly – permits to operate, commercial privileges and protection.

'The primary and most solid basis of your good government is still to tune your existence and property to God's boundless goodness and to subordinate your desires and actions to His will.' In his *Instructions* of 1548 Charles also reminded Philip that his first duty was the defence of the Catholic faith. But, he continued,

> Concerning the present pope, Paul III, you know how he has behaved towards me and how badly he fulfilled his responsibilities in the last war [against the Protestants] . . . Nevertheless, you must behave towards future popes with the humility befitting a good son of the Church, so that they have no just cause to be displeased with you; all this, of course, without surrendering any of the rights, interests, general good and peace of your kingdoms'.[21]

Charles indeed conducted himself with remarkable respect towards successive popes, even when they apparently failed to share his concern for the fate of Christendom. In the middle of the war against the Schmalkaldic League Paul III suddenly withdrew his troops from Germany. Even before that he and his predecessor Clement VII had shown little interest in the expansion of the Reformation. Charles tried to stave off the greater danger of the Turkish attacks on the Empire with the indispensable military support of the Protestants, given in exchange for temporary concessions in religious matters. He consistently stressed that these were emergency measures taken in anticipation of the resolutions that a general council would make on all the religious questions.

The policy was risky, for a number of reasons. First, it made Charles' position in Germany dependent on the pope. Secondly, because the Turkish attacks were primarily directed towards Hungary and Austria, Habsburg dynastic interests were more at stake than those of the empire as a whole, so that all sorts of opposing forces could be played off against the emperor. Thirdly, the emperor created a double reality, and thus legal uncertainty, in the Empire, particularly when he made separate, secret agreements with the Protestants and Catholics, which diverged from the views of the Reformation expressed officially in the Diet. Fourthly, the uncertain situation dragged on for many years because the council did not meet until December 1545. It then quickly made decisions that were unacceptable to the Protestants, and was relocated by the Curia to Bologna, contravening Charles' pledge that it should take place within the Empire. The hopes that Charles had cherished for 20 years, and which he had zealously advocated to the popes and in his treaties with Francis I, were dashed in 1547, just when he managed to get the Protestants under military control. He had counted on taking the wind out of Protestant sails by introducing reforms within the Church which would remove the abuses. The attitude of Clement VII and Paul III, the cardinals and council fathers caused the diplomatic approach to the problem, for which he had striven for so long, to disintegrate. All the religious discussions between theologians, all the political concessions made 'to avoid a greater evil', all the compromises, and thus every hope of a solution that would be acceptable to the Protestants, in short Charles' entire religious policy since 1530, had been in vain.

Whatever reasons the Church may have had – fear of Charles' hegemony or of criticism of the conduct of the clergy – it is obvious that, first through its indecisiveness and then through its lack of concern, it severely weakened the position of the emperor. In September 1544, in the Peace of Crépy, Charles had ceded to Francis all the conquests made that year in exchange for his support for the council, a crusade against the Turks and for abandoning his support of the Protestants. For the sake of peace he had even suggested handing over the duchy of Milan to Francis' youngest son. He had shown clearly how seriously he took his role as protector of the Church and Christianity, and how much he was prepared to sacrifice for it. The grandiose vision dissipated in three years with the deaths of Charles of Orleans and Francis I, the bellicose attitude of the latter's successor, Henry II, and the deadlock over the council.

Had Charles put too much faith in the single option? Did he not appear more Catholic than successive popes, firmer of principle, more idealistic, and perhaps more naive than other rulers? Should he not have realised earlier that his own powerful position in Europe forced his opponents to be pragmatic, even to make common cause with the Turks and Protestants? Should he not have understood that in the uppermost hierarchy of the Church there were many who stood to lose by a council, and were therefore radically opposed to it? Should he not have known that southern Europe was far less bothered by the movement for Reformation and saw little danger in it, perhaps even perceived it as a means of putting pressure on the emperor? Surely he must have realised that the de facto toleration of the Reformation existing in many parts of Germany after Luther's excommunication in 1521, together with the enormous influence of printed propaganda and the powerful attraction of the spoken word, slowly but surely served to increase the numbers of its supporters. The emperor showed little concern for the German problems before 1530, and few of his advisors kept him informed about them. Charles' position was already out of date in 1530 when he opened the first serious negotiations over religious matters in the Diet.

During the discussions, which went on until 1548 under his leadership, Charles was clearly ready to compromise. Even the Diet's decision of 1548, however, was just an Interim, pending the decisions of the council, which by then had been adjourned. Charles' conscience troubled him as soon as the fundamental rights of the Church came under discussion. On the other hand, 31 years after Luther's Theses, the Protestants were unwilling to relinquish what they had achieved. It is amazing that Charles could not see this and, as we see from the advice he gave Philip in 1548 to show towards the pope the 'submissiveness that befits a good son of the Church', that he clung so stubbornly to that illusory trump card, the general council.

Charles was certainly very devout, but he was not especially interested in matters of dogma. He had not a glimmer of understanding for the motives of the reformers, apart from the abuses of the clergy. Does this explain his unwavering adherence to the doctrinal authority of the pope? His decision to concentrate his policies on the patronage of the Church received little support, indeed it aroused determined opposition. This was felt most keenly in the German Empire where the crumbled structures of government made it easier for the Reformation to take root in certain areas than in the Low Countries, which were governed directly in his name. Turkish attacks on the Habsburg lands in particular again put the emperor in the position of having to ask the Diet for help. Of all his crowns, it was that of the Holy Roman Empire – the only one that he had not inherited but had fought to acquire – which brought him the highest prestige but the least power and the most problems. Although he stayed away from Spain after 1543 to deal with the situation in Germany, he was not really able to get it under control. The pact he made with Albrecht Alcibiades of Brandenburg, the Protestant peace-breaker, which enabled him to assemble enough troops against Metz, evidences his lack of power and contributed to his loss of credibility as emperor. Ultimately, it was in the German Empire that Charles' policy radically failed.

Was it even conceivable that a Habsburg could handle German relationships in any other way? Ferdinand proved that there was indeed another path, based on accepting the reality of the Reformation, and he chose to keep his distance from Rome. He did not worry about being crowned by the pope and he enjoyed the respect of the Protestants. Because he did not have a voice in Italy (a disappointment to him), he did not have to concern himself with the delicate situation there, and above all, he did not have to make concessions to the pope. In 1551, when Ferdinand embarked on his own course, free of Charles, he was much more familiar with the situation in Germany where he had his own power base (Charles was dependent on Spain to pay for his sojourns in Germany, or else he had to stay with the Fuggers) and he did not cling so tightly to outmoded principles.

On his mission as a knight of Christ, Charles plunged into an almost unending series of wars after 1535, mobilising ever larger armies. This brought him success in restraining France, the greatest state in western Europe. When peace was finally made in 1559 it was clear that the Habsburgs had defeated French attempts to conquer land in the Low Countries, Italy and Navarre. But the cost had been enormous: vastly increased taxation, an intolerably high national debt, economic upheaval, exorbitant rates of interest, immense material damage and countless human lives. The economic growth, the increase in population and the plundering of the colonies were all used for destructive purposes. The capitalists, whose credit had enabled Charles to be elected emperor in 1519 and still continued to finance him, found themselves on the brink of bankruptcy in 1550, but there was no way back. The only limit to the escalation of the wars seemed to be the mutual exhaustion of the warring parties. To his own subjects, Charles' reign brought not only the proliferation of taxes but also repression of the social movements of peasants and craftsmen, in favour of the aristocracy and urban oligarchies. Religious repression became acute in the 1540s, particularly in the Low Countries.

At times Charles considered giving greater independence to those parts of his empire that were difficult to defend. In his *Instructions* of 1548 he considered transferring the Low Countries to his daughter Mary, who was married to Maximilian, Ferdinand's eldest son. He thought that in this way the region, which was so vulnerable to invasion and foreign influences and so difficult to govern from Spain, could be more closely linked to Germany.[22] Prophetic words, but everything would turn out differently to what he then thought. Much to Charles' displeasure it was Maximilian, not Philip, who would succeed Ferdinand as Roman king, and the dynasty would split into an Austrian and a Spanish branch. Earlier, in 1536 and again in 1544, Charles had offered the Low Countries or the duchy of Milan to the youngest son of Francis I, should he marry Mary or one of Ferdinand's daughters. The impossibility of defending the Low Countries from Spain became apparent during the 80 Years' War. In 1598 Philip opted for the formula of greater independence for the region, with yet another marriage of Habsburg cousins, that of his daughter Isabella to archduke Albert, the youngest son of Maximilian.

The split that took place after Charles' abdication, between the Holy Roman Empire on one hand and Spain, the Italian lands, the Low Countries and the colonies on the other, was the last thing that Charles had envisaged. The fact that it did happen, so much against his own wishes, was a painful reminder of how little feeling he had for the opinions and relationships of power within Germany. Even more fundamentally, it exposed the impossibility of controlling the *imperium* as he had governed it for 35 years.

In 1519 the great international bankers had given their support to the formation of an extensive political unit. After this one experiment reality showed how wrong they had been, even though the only alternative available at the time was probably even less attractive. Charles' *imperium* could not function as a political system: it was too widespread and aroused too much opposition, from inside and out. Charles' own choices contributed to this lack of control: his sense of mission, his obstinacy, his feeling of honour and his royal disdain for the social and economic cost of his policies. The structure was an impossible result of the dynastic game. The person who came to stand at its head lacked the distance and flexibility necessary to take control of the very diverse interests and situations.

This policy produced different results in the different regions. From 1529 Charles' supremacy in Italy brought greater peace there than the land had seen for centuries. On the other hand, if the Habsburgs had restricted themselves to Naples and Sicily then the French would probably have taken control of the north and central regions, with the exception of Venice and the Papal States. In the long term, would this not have resulted in a more stable balance of power in Europe and caused less of a titanic struggle? The massive drain of wealth from Spain to be used for imperial purposes elsewhere in Europe certainly did not help the development of the land. In fact, together with the strengthening of the aristocracy, it produced precisely the opposite effect. In Germany, Charles' religious policy, at first ambiguous and later harsh, was the direct cause of a polarisation that under a less dogmatic emperor – Elector Frederick the Wise had been Pope Leo's candidate – could perhaps have been avoided. All political issues were tied to religious questions during Charles' reign so that all the central institutions of the Empire – Diet, College of Electors, *Reichskammergericht*, imperial taxation, the Imperial Circles – reached a deadlock, and the Empire as such lost its meaning.

Charles' government can probably be seen as least negative in the Low Countries. Although the tax burden, the creaming off of the capital market, economic disruption and religious and political repression were very much felt and led to uprisings, Charles' actions brought about the political unity of the XVII Provinces. The pacification of the larger area brought economic advantages, probably felt most strongly in Holland and the IJssel region. Moreover, there is the question of whether another ruler, with fewer resources than Charles, could have defended the region against French expansion, and how much damage that would have inflicted.

By dint of incredible personal efforts Charles tried to fulfil his mission. More power was centred in his hands for nearly forty years than any other European ruler has held for a similar length of time. In later life he himself said that he had brought his subjects more war than peace, that he had demanded heavy sacrifices of them, that he could not prevent the split of his dynasty and his empire and that he was unable to preserve the unity of the Catholic Church. Had he been catching at shadows for all those years? So much power in the hands of just one person, however well advised, certainly led to aberrations. The single-minded pursuit of the unity of his dynasty through the systematic marriages of nieces and nephews was the most destructive of these. This one person was only a moderately talented man, weighed down by ailments, with an unshakeable vision of his onerous task. He saw his own failures clearly and took the extremely unusual step of abdicating.

Notes:

1. *Hoch Renaissance im Vatikan: Kunst und Kultuur im Rom der Päpste 1503–1534*, exh. cat. (Bonn, 1998), no. 217, *Carolus*, exh. cat. (Ghent, 1999), no. 146.

2. Brandi, *Kaiser Karl V.*, 71.
3. Knecht, *Renaissance Warrior*, 398–477.
4. Ecole Nationale Supérieure des Beaux Arts in Paris, and Koninklijke Musea voor Schone Kunsten in Brussels, respectively.
5. *Maria van Hongarije*, exh. cat.(Utrecht, 's-Hertogenbosch, Zwolle, 1993), no. 196.
6. A. Chastel, 'Les Entrées de Charles Quint en Italie', in G. Jacquot, ed., *Fêtes et cérémonies au temps de Charles Quint* (Paris, 1960), 197–206.
7. Madrid, Palacio Real.
8. B. van den Boogert, 'De triomfen van de keizer', *Maria van Hongarije*, 225–33.
9. Naples, Museo di Capodimonte, 424 x 886 cm; *Napoli*, exh.cat.(Bonn, 1996), no. 19.
10. M. Lageirse, 'La Joyeuse Entrée du Prince Philippe à Gand en 1549', Jacquot, *Fêtes et cérémonies*, 297–306.
11. A. Corbet, 'L'Entrée du Prince Philippe à Anvers en 1549', *ibid.*, 307–10; E. J. Roobaert, 'De seer wonderlijcke schoone triumphelijcke incompst van den hooghmogenden Prince Philips . . . in de stadt van Antwerpen . . . Anno 1549 . . . ', *Bulletin der Koninklijke Musea voor Schone Kunsten*, 9 (1960), 37–73; W. Eisler, 'Celestial Harmonies and Habsburg Rule: Levels of Meaning in a Triumphal Arch for Philip II in Antwerp, 1549', in B. Wisch and S. Munshower, eds, *'All the World's a Stage': Art and Pageantry in the Renaissance and Baroque* (Philadelphia, 1990), 332–56; W. Kuyper, *The Triumphant Entry of Renaissance Architecture into the Netherlands* (Alphen aan den Rijn, 1994); M. A. Meadow, 'Ritual and Civic Identity in Philip II's 1549 Antwerp "Blijde Incompst" ', *Netherlands Yearbook for History of Art*, 49 (1998), 37–67.
12. J. G. Smit, *Vorst en Onderdaan. Studies over Holland en Zeeland in de late middeleeuwen* (Leuven, 1995), 252–8.
13. Madrid, Palacio Real. *Der Kriegszug Kaiser Karls V gegen Tunis: Kartons und Tapisserien*, ed. W. Seipel (Milan and Vienna, 2000).
14. P. Burke, 'Presenting and Re-presenting Charles V', in Soly, *Charles V*, 434–5.
15. Baron de Reiffenberg, *Lettres sur la vie intérieure de l'Empereur Charles Quint de Guillaume de Male* (Brussels, 1843).
16. Madrid, Real Armería, Palacio Real (*c.*1535–40).
17. Fernandez Alvarez, *Corpus documental*, II, 569–611, especially 572–3.
18. Parker, *The Grand Strategy of Philip II*, 77–92.
19. A compilation of the references to gout attacks can be found in J.-P. Soisson, *Charles Quint* (Paris, 2000), 367–70.
20. H. Kellenbenz, 'Das Römisch-Deutsche Reich im Rahmen der wirtschafts- und finanzpolitischen Erwägungen Karls V. im Spannungsfeld imperialer und dynastischer Interessen', in Lutz, *Das römisch-deutsche Reich*, 44–9.
21. Fernandez Alvarez, *Corpus documental*, II, 575–7.
22. *Ibid.*, 592.

Selective bibliography

Biographies

K. Brandi, *Kaiser Karl V. Werden und Schicksal einer Persönlichkeit und eines Weltreiches. Quellen und Erörterungen*, 2 vols (Munich, 1937–41).
F. Chabod, *Carlo V e il suo imperio* (Turin, 1985).
P. Chaunu and M. Escamilla, *Charles Quint* (Paris, 2000).
M. Fernandez Alvarez, *Carlos V: Un hombre para Europa* (Madrid, 1976).
M. Fernandez Alvarez, *Carlos V: El César y el Hombre* (Madrid, 1999).
A. Kohler, *Karl V., 1500–1558. Eine Biographie* (Munich, 1999).
H. Lapeyre, *Charles Quint* (Paris, 1973).
S. de Madariaga, *Charles Quint* (Paris, 1969).
J. Pérez, *Carlos V* (Madrid, 1999).
P. Rassow, *Karl V. De letzte Kaiser des Mittelalters* (Göttingen, 1957).
H. Soly (ed.), *Charles V, 1500–1558* (Antwerp, 1999).
C. Terlinden, *Carolus Quintus. Charles Quint, empereur des deux mondes* (Brussels, 1965).
R. Tyler, *The Emperor Charles the Fifth* (London, 1956).

Source publications

Deutsche Reichstagsakten unter Kaiser Karl V., 7 vols published, edited by A. Kluckhohn, A. Wrede, J. Kühn, W. Steglich and R. Aulinger (Gotha and Göttingen, 1893–1992).
M. Fernandez Alvarez (ed.), *Corpus documental de Carlos V*, 5 vols (Salamanca, 1971–81).
A. J. C. le Glay (ed.), *Correspondance de l'empereur Maximilien Ier et de Marguerite d'Autriche, sa fille, gouvernante des Pays-Bas, de 1507 à 1519*, 2 vols (Paris, 1839).
A. Kohler (ed.), *Quellen zur Geschichte Karls V.* (Darmstadt, 1990).
Die Korrespondenz Ferdinands I. Familienkorrespondenz, 3 vols published, edited by W. Baur, R. Lacroix, H. Wolfram and C. Thomas (Vienna, 1912–84).
K. Lanz (ed.), *Correspondenz des Kaisers Karl V*, 3 vols (Leipzig, 1844–46).
H. Rabe (ed.), *Karl V. Politische Korrespondenz. Brieflisten und Register* (Konstanz, 1999).

Studies

M. Baelde, *De collaterale raden onder Karel V en Filips II (1531–1578)* (Brussels, 1965).
R. Carande, *Carlos V y sus banqueros*, 3 vols (Madrid, 1943–67 and Barcelona, 2000).

C. J. de Carlos Morales, *Carlos V y el crédito de Castilla. El tresorero general Francisco de Vargas y la Hacienda Real entre 1516 y 1524* (Madrid, 2000).

F. Chabod, *Lo stato e la vita religiosa a Milano nell'epoca di Carlo V* (Turin, 1971).

P. Chaunu, *L'Espagne de Charles Quint*, 2 vols (Paris, 1973).

F. Checa Cremades, *Carlos V y la imagen del héroe en el Renascimiento* (Madrid, 1987).

R. Fagel, *De Hispano-Vlaamse wereld. De contacten tussen Spanjaarden en Nederlanders 1496–1555* (Brussels and Nijmegen, 1996).

R. Garcia Carcel, *Las Germanias de Valencia* (Barcelona, 1981).

B. J. Garcia Garcia (ed.), *El Imperio de Carlos V. Procesos de agregación y conflictos* (Madrid, 2000).

R. Garcia Carcel, *Herejia y sociedad en el siglo XVI: Inquisición a Valencia 1530–1609* (Barcelona, 1981).

A. Goosens, *Les inquisitions modernes dans les Pays-Bas méridionaux (1520–1633)*, 2 vols (Brussels, 1997–98).

L. V. G. Gorter-van Royen, *Maria van Hongarije, regentes der Nederlanden* (Hilversum, 1995).

S. Haliczer, *The Comuneros of Castile: The Forging of a Revolution, 1475–1521* (Madison, 1981).

J. M. Headley, *The Emperor and his Chancellor: A Study of the Imperial Chancellery under Gattinara* (Cambridge, 1983).

C. van der Heijden, *Zwarte renaissance: Spanje en de wereld, 1492–1536* (Amsterdam, 1998).

C. J. Hernandez Sanchez, *Castilla y Nápoles en el siglo XVI: El Virrey Pedro de Toledo* (Salamanca, 1994).

H. Kamen, *Spain 1469–1714* (London and New York, 1985).

H. Kamen, *The Spanish Inquisition* (New Haven and London, 1998).

F. Keverling Buisman et al. (eds), *Verdrag en Tractaat van Venlo: Herdenkingsbundel 1543–1993* (Hilversum, 1993).

R. J. Knecht, *Renaissance Warrior and Patron: the Reign of Francis I*, Cambridge, 1994).

H. G. Koenigsberger, *The Habsburgs and Europe, 1516–1660* (London, 1971).

H. G. Koenigsberger, 'The Empire of Charles V in Europe', in G. R. Elton (ed.), *The New Cambridge Modern History, vol. II. The Reformation 1520–1559* (Cambridge, 1990), 339–76.

A. Kohler, *Antihabsburgische Politik in der Epoche Karls V.* (Göttingen, 1982).

A. P. Luttenberger, *Glaubenseinheit und Reichsfriede: Konzeptionen und Wege konfessionsneutraler Reichspolitik, 1530–1552* (Göttingen, 1982).

H. Lutz (ed.), *Das römisch-deutsche Reich im politischen System Karls V.* (Munich, 1982).

H. Lutz, *Christianitas afflicta. Europa, das Reich und die päpstliche Politik im Niedergang der Hegemonie Kaiser Karls V., 1552–1556* (Göttingen, 1964).

H. Lutz, *Das Ringen um deutsche Einheit und kirchliche Erneurung* (Berlin, 1983).

H. Lutz and A. Kohler (eds), *Aus der Arbeit an den Reichstagen unter Kaiser Karl V.* (Göttingen, 1987).

J. Lynch, *Spain 1516–1598: From Nation State to World Empire* (Oxford, 1991).

N. Maddens, *De beden in het graafschap: Vlaanderen tijdens de regering van keizer Karel V, 1515–1550* (Heule, 1978).

J. Martinez Millán (ed.), *Instituciones y elites de poder en la monarquia hispana durante el siglo XVI* (Madrid, 1992).

J. Martinez Millán (ed.), *La Corte de Carlos V*, 5 vols (Madrid, 2000) [Sociedad estatal para las comemoraciones de Felipe II y Carlos V]. vols I and II: *Corte y gobierno*, vol. III: *Los consejos y los Consejeros de Carlos V*, vols IV and V: *Los Servidor de las Casas Reales* [with index and documents].

A. Pacini, *I presupposti politici del 'secolo dei Genovesi': la Riforma del 1528* (Genoa, 1990).

A. Pacini, *La Genova di Andrea Doria nell'impero di Carlo V* (Florence, 1999).

V. J. Parry, 'The Ottoman Empire' in Elton (ed.), *The New Cambridge Modern History, vol. II*, 570–94.

P. P. J. L.van Peteghem, *De Raad van Vlaanderen en staatsvorming onder Karel V (1515-1555)* (Nijmegen, 1990).

H. Rabe, *Reichsbund und Interim: Die Verfassungs- und Religionspolitik Karls V. und der Reichstag von Augsburg 1547/48* (Cologne and Vienna, 1971).

H. Rabe, *Reich und Glaubensspaltung: Deutschland 1500-1600* (Munich, 1989).

H. Rabe (ed.), *Karl V. Politik und politisches System* (Konstanz, 1996).

Recht und Reich im Zeitalter der Reformation: Festschrift für Horst Rabe, ed. C. Roll et al. (Frankfurt, 1996).

M. J. Rodriguez Salgado, *The Changing Face of Empire: Charles V, Philip II and Habsburg Authority 1551-1559* (London, 1988).

M. J. Rodriguez Salgado, 'Habsburg-Valois Wars', in Elton (ed.), *The New Cambridge History*, vol. II, 377–400.

J. J. Scarisbrick, *Henry VIII* (New Haven and London, 1997).

H. Schilling, *Aufbruch und Krise. Deutsche Geschichte von 1517 bis 1648* (Berlin, 1988).

L. Sicking, *Zeemacht en onmacht: Maritieme politiek in de Nederlanden 1488-1558* (Amsterdam, 1998).

A. Spagnoletti, *Principi italiani e Spagna nell'età baroca* (Milan, 1996).

J. D. Tracy, *A Financial Revolution in the Habsburg Netherlands: Renten and Renteniers in the County of Holland, 1515-1565* (Berkeley, 1985).

J. D. Tracy, *Holland under Habsburg Rule, 1506-1566: The Formation of a Body Politic* (Berkeley, 1990).

F. Walser and R. Wohlfeil, *Die spanischen Zentralbehörden und der Staatsrat Karls V.* (Göttingen, 1959).

Exhibition catalogues

Carolus (Ghent, 1999).
Carolus (Toledo, 2000).
Kaiser Karl V (1500-1558):Macht und Ohnmacht Europas (Bonn and Vienna, 2000).
Maria van Hongarije (Utrecht and 's-Hertogenbosch, 1993).

Index

Adolphe, duke of Guelders 52
Adorno, Antoniotto 62
Adrian of Utrecht, pope 16, 22, 44, 109, 110, 118, 130, 162, 163
Alamire, Peter 15
Albert, archduke 6, 182
Albrecht II, Roman king 50
Albrecht, duke of Bavaria 94
Albrecht Alcibiades, margrave of Brandenburg 73, 75, 94, 154, 181
Albrecht of Brandenburg-Ansbach 30
Albrecht, archbishop of Mainz 89, 130
Albret, Henry d' 51, 56
Albret, Jeanne d' 55, 56
Alcuna, Hernando de 16
Alexander Farnese 121
Alexander de Medici 63, 86, 120, 121, 140, 146, 173
Alexander VI, pope 106
Alfonso d'Este, duke of Ferrara 63, 144
Alva, *see* Fadrique
Anna of Austria, daughter of Ferdinand 12, 74, 94, 123, 153
Anna of Hungary 18, 19
Antoine de Lalaing, count of Hoogstraten 55, 101, 128, 130, 132
Avila, Luis de 174

Barbarossa, Kheir-ed-Dhin 41, 69, 72, 139, 151, 152, 155
Beatrice of Portugal 68
Bergen, Antoine of 20
Bergen, *see* Henry of Bergen *and* Glymes, John of
Beukelsz of Leiden, Jan 100, 101
Blomberg, Barbara 121
Boeyens, Adriaan Floriszoon, *see* Adrian
Brandi, Karl 153

Bredemers, Hendrik 15
Bucer, Martin 99
Burgundy, Adolphe of, lord of Beveren 131
Busleyden, Jerome van 17
Busto, Barnabé de 175

Carlos, son of Philip II 121, 123
Carondelet, Jan, archbishop of Palermo 131, 135
Casas, Bartolomé de las 107, 108
Catherine of Aragon 27, 39, 64, 85, 134
Catherine, sister of Charles 14, 47, 123, 124
Centurione, banking family 159
Chalon, Claudia of, sister of Philibert 141
Charles VIII, king of France 38, 43, 65
Charles of Lannoy, viceroy of Naples 28, 57, 59–61, 63, 66, 149
Charles de Bourbon 44, 45, 57, 59, 61, 65–67, 69, 70, 77, 136, 149, 150, 152
Charles the Bold, duke of Burgundy 13, 16, 52, 76, 141
Charles of Egmond, duke of Guelders 52–54
Charles of Orleans, son of Francis I 68, 71, 74, 153, 180
Charles III, duke of Savoy 68, 72, 152
Charles of Croy, prince of Chimay 13, 15
Chièvres, *see* Croy, William
Christian II, king of Denmark 17, 27, 29, 54, 66, 124
Christian III, king of Denmark 54, 55, 91, 108
Christina, daughter of Christian II and Isabella 124

Index

Cifuentes, count 70
Cisneros, cardinal 117
Clement VII, pope 42, 44, 45, 57, 61–64, 84–87, 90, 110,111, 120, 126, 140, 142, 147, 149,150, 171, 179
Cles, Bernhard 86
Clough, Richard 4, 7
Cobos, Francisco de los 131, 132, 135
Cock, Hiëronymus 5
Coecke, Pieter 174
Colonna, Prospero 57
Cortés, Hernando 41, 107
Coxcie, Michiel 3
Croy, Adrian of 55
Croy, Anthony of 131
Croy, Charles of, *see* Charles of Croy
Croy, Philip of 131
Croy, William of, lord of Chièvres 14–16, 39, 130, 132

Dijcke, Johan van den 120
Doria, Andrea 61–64, 69, 71, 132, 136, 145, 155
Doria, Filippino 62, 63
Dorothea, daughter of Christian II and Isabella 54, 124
Ducci, Gaspar 159

Eck, Leonard of, councillor 91
Eleanor, sister of Charles 8, 15, 17, 27, 35, 47, 49, 61, 66, 68, 122, 126, 146
Engelbrecht of Nassau 141
Enriquez Fadrique, admiral 118, 163
Erard de la Marck, bishop of Liège 82, 131,
Erasmus of Rotterdam, Desiderius 17, 19–22, 31, 99, 105
Eric, duke of Brunswick 94

Fadrique Alvarez de Toledo, duke of Alva 75, 96, 131, 151, 154
Farnese, *see*Alexander, Ottavio *and* Pier Luigi
Federigo Gonzaga, marquis (later duke) of Mantua 72, 136, 172
Ferdinand, king of Aragon 7, 9, 13,14, 18, 25, 39, 48, 51, 117, 120, 123
Ferdinand of Habsburg, brother of Charles, Roman king, king of Bohemia and Hungary 6, 8, 10–12, 18, 25, 28, 31, 32, 44, 47–49, 64, 72, 83–87, 90, 92, 95, 96, 98, 99, 108, 111, 123–126, 161, 177, 181, 182
Ferdinand, archbishop of Zaragoza, illegitimate son of Ferdinand of Aragon 117
Ferdinand, son of Charles 122, 124, 127
Fernando, duke of Calabria 120
Ferrante Gonzaga, viceroy of Sicily 55, 72, 73, 97, 104, 136, 151, 172
Floris of Egmont, count of Buren 132
Fonseca, Alonso de 22
Francis I, king of France 21, 27, 35, 38–43, 45, 49–51, 53–62, 64–66, 68, 70–74, 76, 90, 91, 119, 122, 125–127, 139, 146, 149, 152, 153, 170, 175, 177, 179, 180
Frederick II, emperor 49
Frederick III, emperor 49, 82
Frederick the Wise, elector of Saxony 15, 49, 80, 83, 183
Frederick, count palatine 29, 54, 91, 95, 122, 124, 139
Fregoso, Cesare 61
Frundsberg, general 59, 60
Fugger, Jacob, the Rich 51
Fugger, family of bankers 117, 126, 130, 159, 178, 181

Gattinara, Mercurino de 17, 22, 44, 45, 59, 60, 62, 64, 66, 117, 130, 132, 135, 140, 169
Gentile, family of bankers 159
Germaine de Foix 14, 120
Gheynst, Joanna van der 63, 120, 150
Gil, Juan, bishop of Tortosa 106
Glymes, John of, lord of Bergen op Zoom 13, 17, 132
Gonzaga, *see* Federigo *and* Ferrante
Gorrevod, Laurent de, regent 135
Gossaert, Jan 6
Granvelle, cardinal, Antoine Perrenot, lord of 10
Granvelle, *see* Perrenot, Nicholas
Graphaeus 174
Gresham, Sir Thomas 4
Grimaldi, family of bankers 159
Guevara, Antonio de 169
Guicciardini, Francesco 62, 149, 150
Guillard, Louis 52

Hannart, Jean 126, 132
Hans, margrave of Brandenburg-Kstrin 94, 120
Heemskerck, Maarten van 5, 174, 175
Heilly, Anne d' 27
Held, Matthias 90, 132
Henry VIII, king of England and Ireland 15, 17, 21, 27, 32, 36, 38, 39, 42, 44, 52, 57, 58, 61, 64, 65, 68, 72–74, 77, 85, 109, 125, 127, 153, 154, 177
Henry II, king of France 10, 42, 68, 74, 76, 98, 139, 154, 180
Henry III, count of Nassau 52, 69, 70, 128, 141, 152, 171
Henry of Bavaria, bishop of Utrecht 53
Henry of Bergen, bishop of Cambrai 16, 17
Hofmann, Melchior 101
Hogenberg, Nicholas 171
Hoogstraten, see Antoine de Lalaing
Hurtado de Mendoza, Diego 134
Hurtado de Mendoza, Lope 134
Hus, Jan 100

Isabella of Portugal, empress 17, 28, 58, 118, 119, 121–123, 127
Isabella, 'the Catholic', queen of Castile 14, 25, 123
Isabella, queen of Denmark, sister of Charles 15, 17, 27, 29, 54, 123, 124
Isabella, infanta of Aragon, queen of Portugal, aunt of Charles 14, 17, 27, 49
Isabella, archduchess 6, 182
Isabella, natural daughter of Charles 120

Jacques of Luxembourg, count of Gavere 132
Joachim, elector of Brandenburg 83, 91
Joanna the Mad, queen of Castile, mother of Charles 13, 14, 18, 47, 124, 162, 163
Joanna, queen of Portugal, daughter of Charles 119, 121–123
Joanna de Bourbon 141
John III, king of Portugal 14, 15, 123, 172
John of Castile 13, 14

John of Chalon 141
John of Portugal, son of John III 123
John, elector of Saxony 90, 91
John of Weeze, archbishop of Lund 90
John Frederick, elector of Saxony 92–96
Juan, youngest son of Charles 122, 127
Juan, don, natural son of Charles 121
Juana, doña, natural daughter of Charles 121
Julius II, pope 21, 31
Julius III, pope 98, 110, 169

Kampen, Jacob of 102
Kohler, Alfred 153

Lannoy, Charles of see Charles
Lannoy, Philip de, lord of Molenbaix 132
Lautrec, marshal 61–63
Leo X, pope 15, 42, 49, 80, 183
Leoni, Pompeo and Leone 175
Leyva, Antonio de 57, 59, 69
Loaysa, Garcia de, confessor to Charles 121, 131
Louis XI, king of France 141
Louis XII, king of France 17, 38, 52, 65, 76
Louis, king of Hungary 18, 19, 41, 66, 126
Louis, duke of Bavaria 90
Louis, elector of the Palatinate 89
Louis of Male, count of Flanders 134
Louisa of Savoy, mother of Francis I 65, 67, 70, 125
Luther, Martin 42, 80, 83, 100, 165, 170, 180

Maes, Jacob 10
Manrique, Alonso 22
Manuel I, king of Portugal 14, 17, 27, 49, 122
Marche, Olivier de la 16, 169
Marck, Robert de la 52
Margaret of Austria, regent, aunt of Charles 13–15, 17, 27, 28, 63, 67, 80, 123–125, 128, 130, 131, 135, 141, 164, 170, 171
Margaret, duchess of Parma, natural daughter of Charles 63, 120, 121, 125, 140, 173

Index

Margaret of York, duchess of Burgundy 13, 17
Marnix, Jan van 132
Marsilius of Padua 100
Mary of Austria, empress, daughter of Charles 12, 28, 71, 74, 119, 121, 124, 153, 182
Mary, queen of Hungary, regent, sister of Charles 8–10, 12, 14, 16–18, 28, 41, 43, 54, 55, 63, 70, 75, 76, 103, 121–126, 131, 134, 154, 159–161, 170, 177
Mary of Aragon, queen of Portugal, aunt of Charles 27, 49, 118
Mary, duchess of Burgundy 16, 141
Mary 'la Abandonada', daughter of Eleanor 27, 122, 124
Mary Manuela, daughter of John III 123, 127
Mary Tudor, sister of Henry VIII, queen of France 17, 52
Mary Tudor, daughter of Henry VIII, queen of England 6, 8, 17, 58, 61, 119, 123
Mattijsz, Jan 100
Maurice, duke of Saxony 73, 75, 94–98
Maximilian I of Austria, emperor, grandfather of Charles 9, 11, 14, 17, 18, 25, 26, 28, 30, 31, 33, 38, 39, 49–52, 82, 83, 123, 125, 130
Maximilian II of Austria, Roman king, emperor, son of Ferdinand 6, 11, 12, 28, 96, 119, 124, 182
Maximilian of Egmont, stadholder of Friesland, count of Buren 95
Meit, Conrad 170
Melanchthon, Philip 87, 91
Mendoza, Diego de 95
Mexia, Pedro 174
Michelangelo 64
Molinet, Jean 13
Moncada, Ugo de, viceroy of Sicily 63
Montmorency, general 69–71
More, Sir Thomas 20

Naves, Jean 133

Orley, Bernard van 3, 170, 172
Ottavio Farnese, duke of Parma 75, 121
Otto I 11

Parmigianino 171
Paul III, pope 69, 71–73, 90, 92, 94, 95, 97, 110, 111, 121, 151, 171, 173, 179
Pedro de Toledo, viceroy of Naples 28
Peña, Orsolina de la 121
Péril, Robert 171
Perrenin, Antoine 174
Perrenot, Nicholas, lord of Granvelle 91, 111, 131, 132, 135, 176
Pescara, general 57, 59
Philibert of Chalon, viceroy of Naples 28, 62–64, 140–147, 149
Philibert, duke of Savoy 14, 67
Philip II, son of Charles 4, 6–12, 16, 22, 28, 56, 75, 98, 108, 119, 121–124, 129, 131, 133, 159, 170, 173, 177, 178, 182
Philip III, son of Philip II 123
Philip the Good, duke of Burgundy 16, 134
Philip the Handsome, archduke, king of Castile, father of Charles 13–15, 127, 141
Philip, landgrave of Hesse 84, 90, 92–94, 96, 98
Pier Luigi Farnese 72, 92, 97
Plaine, Thomas de, chancellor 135
Plantin, Christophe 3, 6
Praat, Louis of Flanders, lord of 60, 134, 135
Prat, Juan 105

René of Chalon, stadholder 141, 176
Romano, Giulio 172
Rossum, Maarten van 53, 55

Saint-Pol, duke of 63
Santa Cruz, chronicler 149
Sauvage, Jean le 19, 22, 48, 130
Schepper, Cornelis de 134, 135
Schenck von Tautenburg, Georg 53, 102
Schetz, firm of bankers 159, 178
Schore, Louis of 134, 161, 165
Secundus, Johannes 174
Seisenegger, Jacob 172
Selim, sultan 40
Sepulveda, Juan Gines de 174
Sforza, Bianca Maria 14
Sforza, Francesco, duke of Milan 60, 64, 66, 68, 86, 124, 149
Sforza, Ludovico, 'il Moro' 14, 39

Sickingen, Franz von 50
Sigismund Jagiello, king of Poland 17
Simons, Menno 102
Soria, ambassador 62
Spinola, banking family, 159, 178
Steels, Jan 16
Strozzi, Piero 73
Sulaimān the Magnificent, sultan 36, 40, 65, 66, 72, 92, 111, 140, 151, 177

Tadea, natural daughter of Charles 121
Tavera, cardinal, archbishop of Toledo 131
Taxis, family 34
Titian 122, 136, 154, 172, 175
Trivulzio, governor of Milan 62

Ulrich, duke of Württemberg 95

Valdés, Alfonso de 135
Valdés, Alonso 22
Valdés, Fernando de 131, 135
Valdés, Juan 22
Vasari, Giorgio 171, 173
Vasto, general 59

Velasco, commander 118, 163
Vermeyen, Jan Cornelisz 170, 174
Vernois, Pierre de 6
Vettori, Francesco 149
Viglius, Aytta van Zwichem 135
Virués, Alonso de 105, 106
Vital, Laurent 120
Vladislav Jagiello, king of Bohemia 17, 18, 51

Weiditz, Hans 170
Welser, family of bankers 51, 159
Wilde, *see* Sauvage
William IV, duke of Bavaria 15, 90

William of Croy, *see* Croy
William of Jülich-Cleves, duke of Guelders 54–57, 88, 124
William of Male 175
William of Orange 7, 9, 142
Wolsey, cardinal 17, 32, 52
Württemberg, duke of 50
Wycliffe, John 100

Zápolya, Johan 18, 68
Zuñiga, Juan de 131

Printed in the United Kingdom
by Lightning Source UK Ltd.
111238UKS00001B/66